MasterChef
Sensational
Puddings

MasterChef
Sensational
Puddings

DK

Contents

Perfect Pâtisserie

Bake to Impress

Reinvented Classics

Perfect
Pâtisserie

Pear Tatin with Stilton ice cream and walnut brittle

Alex Rushmer ⓜ finalist

Preparation time 40 minutes   **Cooking time** 1 hour 25 minutes   **Serves 4**

Ingredients

For the ice cream
½ vanilla pod, split, seeds scraped out, and reserved with the pod

160ml (5½fl oz) double cream

1.5 litres (2¾ pints) milk

2 egg yolks

30g (1oz) caster sugar

50g (1¾oz) Stilton cheese, chopped

pickled walnuts, chopped

For the Tatin
4 pears, peeled

100g (3½oz) caster sugar

100g (3½oz) unsalted butter, cubed

4 star anise

250g (9oz) ready-made puff pastry

For the brittle
100g (3½oz) caster sugar

25g (scant 1oz) dried walnuts, finely chopped

Method →

Method

1 Place the vanilla pod and seeds in a pan with the cream and milk. Slowly bring to the boil, then remove from the heat and, leave to infuse for 5 minutes. Meanwhile, whisk the egg yolks together with the sugar until pale and creamy. Strain the cream and milk into the egg yolks, whisking all the time. Return to the pan and heat gently, stirring, until the custard is thick enough to coat the back of a spoon. Stir in the cheese, then churn in an ice-cream maker, and freeze.

2 Preheat the oven to 190°C (375°F/Gas 5). Remove the narrowed part of the pears to make neat spheres, then core them. Put four 10cm (4in) individual tart tins or metal ring moulds on a baking tray, Heat the sugar in a dry pan until it is a pale caramel colour, then pour

TECHNIQUE

How to shell nuts

Use a nutcracker. The inner skin may be difficult to peel away, but is fine to eat. Take extra care to keep your fingers out of the way of the nutcracker.

some into each tin. Divide the butter between the tins, then add a star anise and pear to each. Bake in the oven for 20 minutes.

3 Roll out the puff pastry to 5mm (¼in) thick, then cut into four 12cm (5in) rounds. Prick with a fork. Remove the pears from the oven and add the pastry lids, tucking the sides of the pastry down inside the tins. Cook for a further 15–20 minutes until the pastry is golden brown.

4 To make the walnut brittle, heat the sugar with 3 tablespoons water, then boil hard to create the caramel. Add the walnuts to the caramel and turn out onto a silicone mat. Spread thinly and let harden slightly before cutting into strips, or breaking into shards.

5 To serve, turn the tarts out onto 4 plates, then add a spoonful of ice cream. Top the ice cream with a shard of brittle and decorate the plate with some chopped pickled walnuts. Serve immediately.

Sensational puddings

Millefeuille of raspberries and chocolate with honey and lavender ice cream

Steve Groves @ Professionals champion

Preparation time 45 minutes   **Cooking time** 45 minutes   **Serves 4**

Ingredients

250g (9oz) ready-made puff pastry

400g (14oz) raspberries

icing sugar, for dusting

For the ice cream

500ml (16fl oz) double cream

6 heads of lavender

4 egg yolks

175g (6oz) clear honey

For the chocolate mousse

4 egg yolks

200g (7oz) caster sugar

100ml (3½fl oz) whole milk

150g (5½ oz) dark chocolate (70% cocoa), chopped

1 tsp salt

200ml (7fl oz) whipping cream

Method

Method

1 To make the ice cream, bring the cream to the boil. Add 2 heads of lavender, remove from the heat, and allow to infuse for 10 minutes. Strain, then return to near boiling point. Whisk the egg yolks and honey together then pour half of the cream onto them, whisking meanwhile. Return to the pan and heat to 80°C (176°F), then pass through a sieve. Chill and then put into an ice-cream maker and freeze according to the manufacturer's instructions.

2 Preheat the oven to 200°C (400°F/Gas 6). Roll the pastry out to around 3mm (⅛in) thick and cut into 12 rectangles measuring 3 x 6cm (1¼–2½in). Bake for 20–25 minutes between 2 baking sheets, then remove the top baking sheet and return the pastry to the oven if needed to ensure it is golden throughout. Once cooled, trim the edges.

3 To make the chocolate mousse, whisk the egg yolks and sugar together until they are almost white. Bring the milk to the boil and then pour half onto the egg mixture while whisking. Once thoroughly mixed, return to the pan over a low to medium heat and heat to 80°C (176°F). Pour this mixture over the chocolate and stir until all the chocolate is melted and incorporated. Add the salt and allow to cool.

4 Whip the whipping cream to soft peaks and fold gently into the cooled chocolate mix. Put into a piping bag and chill.

5 To serve, arrange rows of raspberries on a layer of mousse on 8 pieces of pastry. Dust the flattest 4 pieces liberally with icing sugar and use a very hot metal skewer to make a crisscross pattern. Stack the layers up with the sugared one on top. Place on the serving plates with a scoop of ice cream garnished with a head of lavender.

Date and chocolate filo sweets with vanilla crème fraîche

Perveen Nekoo Ⓜ quarter-finalist

Preparation time 25 minutes   **Cooking time** 10minutes   **Makes 6**

Ingredients

25g (scant 1oz) dark chocolate (70% cocoa), broken into pieces

6 dried medjool dates, stoned

3 sheets filo pastry

30g (1oz) unsalted butter, melted

500ml (16fl oz) sunflower oil

300g tub crème fraîche

1 vanilla pod, seeds only

30g (1oz) icing sugar, plus extra for dusting

Method

1 Stuff pieces of the chocolate into the stoned dates.

2 Cut the filo pastry into 10cm (4in) squares and brush with the melted butter. Place each date diagonally onto a square of filo pastry and wrap it up, twisting the ends of the pastry to form a sweet wrapper shape.

3 Heat the oil in a small saucepan until it is sizzling. It needs to be hot enough so that the pastry does not go soggy.

Put the "sweets" in the pan and fry for about 1 minute or until they are golden, occasionally turning.

4 Mix the crème fraîche in a bowl with the vanilla seeds and the icing sugar.

5 Transfer 2 filo sweets to each of 3 serving plates and dust with icing sugar. Serve with a tablespoon of the crème fraîche.

Hazelnut and raspberry meringue

Nadia Sawalha ⓜ **Celebrity champion**

Preparation time 20 minutes   **Cooking time** 40 minutes   **Serves 4**

Ingredients

115g (4oz) whole shelled hazelnuts

4 large eggs, whites only

250g (9oz) caster sugar

1 tsp vanilla extract

1 tbsp raspberry vinegar

300ml (10fl oz) double cream

200g (7oz) fresh raspberries

icing sugar, to dust

Method →

Method

1 Preheat the oven to 160°C (325°F/Gas 3). Butter a 20cm (8in) sandwich tin and line with non-stick baking parchment.

2 Halve and dry fry the hazelnuts until lightly toasted, reserving a few.

3 To make the meringue, whisk the egg whites until stiff. Add the sugar 1 tbsp at a time and continue beating until the mixture is very stiff and stands in peaks. Whisk in the vanilla extract and vinegar, then fold in the hazelnuts.

4 Transfer to the sandwich tin. Alternatively, make individual portions by placing dollops of the meringue mix straight on to baking parchment, forming a slight hollow for the filling. Bake in the oven for 20–30 minutes, or the meringue is until lightly browned and holding its shape. Leave to cool in the tin for 10 minutes then transfer to a serving dish.

5 Whip the cream and pile onto the centre of the meringue when it is completely cold. Top with the raspberries. Finely chop the reserved hazelnuts and sprinkle over. Dust with icing sugar just before serving.

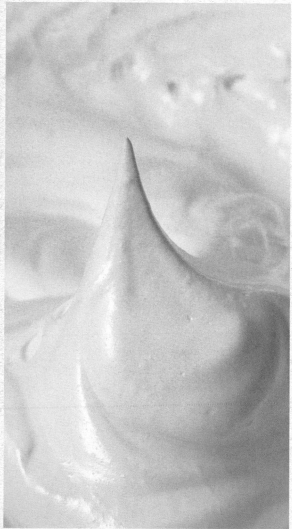

How to make meringue

Whisk the egg whites, perferably with an electric whisk, until they form stiff peaks. Then add the sugar 1 tbsp at a time, until the mixture is very stiff and shiny. The trick to making meringue is to get the consistency of the whisked whites correct. Dip your fingertips in the stiff whites; as you remove them, the whites should hang from your fingers in the hooked shape of a bird's beak.

Pistachio meringues with rose and cardamom panna cotta and cardamom crisps

Kirsty Wark Ⓜ **Celebrity finalist**

Preparation time 30 minutes   **Cooking time** 1 hour 30 minutes   **Serves 4**

Ingredients

For the panna cotta
600ml (1 pint) double cream
150ml (5fl oz) whole milk
100g (3½oz) caster sugar
3 gelatine leaves
a few drops of rosewater
½ tsp ground cardamom
rose petals, to decorate

For the hibiscus syrup
50g (1¾oz) caster sugar
1 tbsp hibiscus cordial
1 tsp liquid glucose

For the meringues
3 egg whites
squeeze of lemon juice
140g (5oz) vanilla sugar

1 tbsp cornflour
75g (2½oz) shelled pistachio nuts, finely chopped
300ml (10fl oz) double cream
1 tbsp icing sugar

For the cardamom crisps
125g (4½oz) unsalted butter
175g (6oz) caster sugar
1 egg
50g (1¾oz) desiccated coconut
175g (6oz) self-raising flour
zest of 1 lemon
¼ tsp crushed cardamom seeds
icing sugar, for dusting

Method

Method

1 To make the panna cotta, put the cream, milk, and sugar in a pan and slowly bring to the boil. Simmer for 5 minutes until reduced by a third. Soak the gelatine in cold water for 5 minutes until soft. Drain and squeeze out excess water. Take the cream off the heat, then stir in the rosewater, cardamom, and gelatine. Pour the mixture into four 100ml (3½fl oz) dariole moulds, then chill for 2 hours.

2 To make the syrup, mix all the ingredients with 1 tbsp water in a pan and bring to the boil. Simmer until syrupy, then leave to cool.

3 For the meringues, preheat the oven to 110°C (225°F/Gas ¼). Whisk the egg whites with the lemon juice to soft peaks, then gradually whisk in the sugar until glossy. Fold in the cornflour and 50g (1¾oz) pistachios, then transfer to a piping bag with a 1cm (½in) round nozzle. Pipe sixteen 5cm (2in) rounds onto a baking sheet lined with silicone paper and place in the oven for 1½ hours. Leave to cool, then whip the cream and icing sugar to soft peaks and use to sandwich the meringues together. Roll them in the remaining chopped pistachios.

4 For the crisps, preheat the oven to 190°C (375°F/Gas 5). Cream the butter and sugar until light and fluffy. Add the egg, beat until smooth, then stir in the remaining ingredients. Shape into 2cm (¾in) balls and place well apart on a non-stick baking tray. Flatten a little with a palette knife. Bake for 10 minutes until lightly golden, then flatten again. Leave to cool and then dust with icing sugar.

5 To serve, arrange a panna cotta, a meringue and a few cardamon crisps of each of 4 plates. Decorate each panna cotta with a rose petal, and drizzle some hibiscus syrup around the plates.

Apple, vanilla, and bay leaf tarte Tatin with Calvados cream

Alex Rushmer ⓜ finalist

Preparation time 15 minutes   **Cooking time** 20–25 minutes   **Serves 4–6**

Ingredients

3 sweet apples, such as Braeburn or Pink Lady

50g (1¾oz) unsalted butter, cubed

50g (1¾oz) caster sugar

2 star anise

2 bay leaves

1 cinnamon stick

1 vanilla pod, split

250g (9oz) ready-made puff pastry

150ml (5fl oz) double cream

1–2 tsp Calvados

Method

1 Preheat the oven to 180°C (350°F/Gas 4). Peel, core, and slice the apples into eighths.

2 Melt the butter in a 20cm (8in) diameter, heavy ovenproof pan. Then add the sugar and continuously stir until it begins to turn golden and caramelizes. Add the star anise, bay leaves, cinnamon, and vanilla pod and stir together. Lay the apple slices in a single layer over the caramel and turn to coat. Cook over low-medium heat for 5 minutes.

3 Roll out the pastry slightly larger than the diameter of the pan and cut out a circle.

Remove the pan from the heat and place the pastry over the apples, tucking it down the sides of the fruit.

4 Cook in the oven for 20–25 minutes, or until the apples are soft and the pastry is nicely browned. Carefully turn out onto a waiting plate and leave to cool. Before serving, remove and discsard the spices.

5 Whip the cream, then gently stir in a generous dribble of Calvados, and serve with a slice of the tarte Tatin.

Chocolate tartlet with sesame-seed snap and crème fraîche

Chris Gates @ finalist

Preparation time 15 minutes   **Cooking time** 20 minutes   **Serves 4**

Ingredients

100g (3½oz) cold butter
50g (1¾oz) icing sugar
175g (6oz) plain flour
2 egg yolks
crème fraîche, to serve

For the filling

225ml (7½fl oz) double cream

1 tbsp caster sugar

1 tsp sea salt

150g (5½oz) dark chocolate (70% cocoa), broken into pieces

3 tbsp whole milk

cocoa powder, to dust

For the sesame seed snap

200g (7oz) caster sugar

25g (scant 1oz) butter

handful of sesame seeds

Method →

Method

1 To make the pastry, put the butter, icing sugar, plain flour, and egg yolks into a food processer and run it until everything comes together into a dough. Wrap in cling film and rest in the fridge for 1 hour.

2 Preheat the oven to 160°C (325°F/Gas 3). Butter four 10cm (4in) individual tart tins.

3 Roll out the pastry to a thickness of about 5mm (¼in) and use to line the tart tins. Prick the pastry and place tins in the freezer for about 15 minutes. Then blind bake (see below) in the oven for 12–15 minutes until the pastry is cooked through and slightly golden. Leave to cool.

4 To make the filling, put the cream, sugar, and salt in a saucepan and bring to the boil. Add

How to blind bake

TECHNIQUE

1 Cut a circle of baking parchment slightly larger than the tart tin or flan ring that you are using. Fold the disc in half several times, then clip the outer edge with scissors.

2 Place the parchment circle on the pricked pastry in the tart tin or flan ring, so that it covers the base and sides, taking the paper above the sides of the tin. Fill with dried beans or baking beans.

the chocolate, remove the pan from the heat and mix until the chocolate has melted. Add the milk and mix well until smooth. Allow to cool slightly and then pour into the cooked tart cases. Leave to set – about 2 hours at room temperature.

5 For the sesame seed snap, in a heavy pan, gently heat the sugar until it forms a golden caramel. Add the butter and sesame seeds and mix. Remove from the heat and pour onto a baking tray lined with baking parchment. Once slightly cooled, you will be able to cut the snap into whatever shape you like.

6 Remove the tartlets from their cases and serve on individual plates topped with a spoonful of crème fraîche and a piece of sesame seed snap.

3 Place in the oven and bake according to your recipe's instructions. For a fully baked case, remove the beans and paper, then return the pastry case to the oven for the required time.

4 Cool on a wire rack. Then remove the pastry case from the tart tin or lift off the flan ring before or after filling, according to the recipe instructions.

Pear and butterscotch frangipane tart

Susie Carter ⓜ quarter-finalist

Preparation time 45 minutes   **Cooking time** 40 minutes   **Serves 4**

Ingredients

50g (1¾oz) caster sugar

clotted cream, to serve

For the butterscotch sauce

50g (1¾oz) unsalted butter

50g (1¾oz) light muscovado sugar

2 tbsp golden syrup

2 tbsp double cream

For the pastry

100g (3½oz) butter

200g (7oz) plain flour

1 egg, beaten

For the tart filling

50g (1¾oz) ground almonds

50g (1¾oz) caster sugar

50g (1¾oz) butter

1 egg

few drops of almond extract

2 pears, with stalks, to serve

Method →

Method

1 To make the butterscotch sauce, put the butter, sugar, and golden syrup into a small saucepan and bring slowly to the boil, stirring. Reduce the heat and simmer for 3 minutes or until thick. Stir in the cream, then remove from the heat and set aside to cool.

2 Make the pastry by rubbing the butter into the flour, then adding enough cold water to bind into a pliable dough. Rest in the fridge for 30 minutes, then roll out on a floured surface and use to line 4 tartlet cases about 10cm (4in) in diameter. Trim the excess with scissors, allowing a little to overhang, and prick all over the base with a fork.

3 Preheat the oven to 180°C (350°F/Gas 4). Line each pastry case with baking parchment and blind bake (see page 26) for 10 minutes. Remove the parchment and beans, brush the pastry with beaten egg and return to the oven for 5–10 minutes or until crisp.

4 Spoon 2 tbsp butterscotch sauce into each pastry case and reserve the rest. To make the frangipane, whisk together all the tart filling ingredients, except the pears, until light and spoon into the pastry cases to come halfway up the sides.

5 Peel the pears and cut in half through the stalk. Carefully remove the core, then slice along the length like a fan, without cutting all the way through at the stalk end. Use half a pear to top each tartlet, snuggling it down into the frangipane. Bake for 20 minutes or until the pear and frangipane are both cooked. Leave to cool a little.

6 Make caramel shards by heating the caster sugar in a small pan, shaking occasionally until it has liquefied and turned light brown. Pour in a thin layer onto a non-stick baking mat and leave to cool for a few minutes. When set, break into shards. Serve the tartlets with a pool of the reserved butterscotch sauce, a quenelle of clotted cream, and a caramel shard.

Fig tarte Tatin with clotted cream and pistachios

Gillian Wylie @ quarter-finalistt

Preparation time 25 minutes   **Cooking time** 25minutes   Serves 4

Ingredients

100g (3½oz) caster sugar

100g (3½oz) unsalted butter

4 ripe figs, cut into segments

375g (13oz) ready-made puff pastry

115ml (3¾fl oz) clotted cream

1 tbsp pistachio nuts, roughly chopped

Method

1 Preheat the oven to 180°C (350°F/Gas 4). To make individual tartes Tatin, you will need a baking tray with portion-sized shallow indents, such as one designed for Yorkshire puddings.

2 Sprinkle the sugar into a non-stick frying pan. Slice the butter, lay it on top of the sugar and slowly let them melt together over medium-low heat until a caramel forms. Resist the urge to stir until the sugar has melted – you need to be patient, as this will take at least 15 minutes.

3 Arrange the figs in a spiral in the base of 4 of the baking tray's indents and put 1 tbsp caramel into each. Roll out some puff pastry on a floured surface and cut out 4 discs the same diameter as the indents in the tray. Place the discs over the figs and tuck in the edges a little.

4 Cook in the hot oven for 20–25 minutes until the pastry is golden and risen. Remove and allow to rest for a few minutes before inverting onto a board – be careful, as the caramel will be hot.

5 To serve, transfer the tartes Tatin onto serving plates, place a quenelle of clotted cream in the centre of each, swirl some extra caramel around the plates, and finish with a sprinkling of chopped pistachio nuts.

Citrus meringue tart with cinnamon cream and passion fruit

Christine Hamilton ⓜ Celebrity finalist

Preparation time 30 minutes   **Cooking time** 1 hour   **Serves 4**

Ingredients

1 egg white

60g (2oz) caster sugar

½ tsp cornflour

For the pastry

60g (2oz) butter

grated zest of 1 lime and ½ tbsp lime juice

85g (3oz) plain flour

30g (1oz) ground almonds

½ tbsp icing sugar

pinch of ground cinnamon

For the filling

1 egg

40g (1¼oz) caster sugar

grated zest and juice of 1 lemon

75ml (2½fl oz) double cream

For the decoration

100ml (3½ fl oz) double cream

pinch of ground cinnamon, plus extra for sprinkling

seeds of 2 passion fruit

grated zest of 1 lime

Method →

Method

1 Preheat the oven to 160°C (325°F/Gas 3) and line a baking tray with greaseproof paper. To make the meringues, whisk the egg white until fairly stiff, then add the caster sugar a little at a time, whisking it in well after each addition. Add the cornflour and whisk until fully incorporated and the mixture is stiff and glossy. Transfer to a piping bag and form 4 meringues, about 6cm (2½in) in diameter, by piping in a swirl onto the lined baking tray. Cook in the oven for 20 minutes, then remove and leave to cool.

2 To make the pastry, melt the butter and add the lime juice and zest, flour, almonds, icing sugar, and cinnamon. Mix together until it forms a dough, then turn it out, divide into 4, and roll out to line four 8cm (3½in) tart tins. Chill for 30 minutes. Prick the base and sides of the dough, line with greaseproof paper and baking beans, and bake blind (see page 26) for 10 minutes. Remove the beans and paper and return to the oven for 5 minutes to crisp up.

3 Meanwhile, whisk together the filling ingredients and pour into the pastry cases. Bake in the oven for about 20–25 minutes. Allow to cool.

4 For the decoration, cinnamon cream can either be served on the side or as a pool of cream under each tart. To make, place cream in a bowl, add a pinch of cinnamon, and either whip until it just starts to thicken for a pool, or until it forms soft peaks to serve on the side.

5 To serve, place a pool or dollop of cream on each plate and sprinkle with a little extra cinnamon. Position the tarts, place a meringue on top, and decorate the plate with the passion fruit and lime zest.

How to prepare lemon zest

Using a peeler, remove strips of zest from a lemon, taking off as little of the bitter pith as possible. Try to select unwaxed lemons for this purpose, and always wash and dry the skin before you begin. If any pith remains, use a sharp knife to slice it off by running your knife along the peel away from you. Then, using a rocking motion with your knife, slice the peel into fine strips.

Assiette of chocolate

Alice Taylor @ contestant

Preparation time 1–2 hours   **Cooking time** 30 minutes–1 hour   **Serves 6**

Bitter chocolate ginger torte

Ingredients

For the torte

½ packet ginger biscuits, finely crushed in a food processor

1 large piece of stem ginger in syrup, finely chopped

45g (1½oz) melted butter

225g (8oz) dark chocolate, 85% cocoa solids, broken into pieces

2½ tbsp liquid glucose

2½ tbsp orange liqueur

300ml (10fl oz) double cream

100g (3½oz) dark chocolate, to garnish

For the orange sauce

120ml (4fl oz) orange juice

2 tsp cornflour

freshly squeezed of 1 orange

1½ tsp caster sugar

2 tbsp orange liqueur

Method

1 Preheat oven to 200°C (400°F/Gas 6). Set 6 cook's rings on a baking tray. Base-wrap each in cling film, making sure it is easy to remove once the rings are filled. For the torte, mix together the biscuit crumbs, ginger, and butter. Sprinkle the mixture evenly over the bases of the rings and press down firmly.

2 Place the chocolate in a heatproof bowl together with the liquid glucose and the orange liqueur. Place the bowl over a pan of barely simmering water, making sure the bottom of the bowl does not touch the water, and leave until the chocolate has melted and become quite smooth. Stir, then take off the heat and leave the mixture to cool for 5 minutes. Don't worry if the chocolate looks a little grainy at this point as it will recover with the addition of the cream.

3 In a separate bowl, whip the cream until very slightly thickened. Fold into the chocolate mixture. When it is smoothly blended, spoon it into the prepared rings. Very gently tap the baking tray on the work surface to even the mixture out, then place in the fridge to set.

4 For the orange sauce, in a small saucepan mix 2 tablespoons of the measured orange juice with the cornflour until smooth. Stir in the remaining juice and the freshly squeezed juice. Slowly bring to the boil, and cook for a minute, stirring all the time, until thickened, then stir in the sugar until dissolved, and the orange liqueur. Pour into a plastic squeezy bottle and chill until serving.

White chocolate mousse

Ingredients

For the mousse

150g (5½oz) white
chocolate, broken into
pieces

4 eggs, whites only

75g (2½oz) caster sugar

150ml (5fl oz) double
cream

For the coulis

200g (7oz) raspberries

mint sprigs, to garnish

Method

1 For the mousse, melt the chocolate in a bowl
set over a pan of simmering water. In another
bowl, whisk the egg whites until they form soft
peaks, then fold in the sugar, 1 tbsp at a time.
In a separate bowl, whip the cream until it also
forms soft peaks. Fold the egg white mixture and
cream together, then add the melted chocolate.
Fold gently until completely combined, then
pipe or spoon the mixture into 6 shot glasses.
Refrigerate immediately.

2 For the coulis, rub the raspberries through a
fine sieve. Set aside until ready to serve.

Milk chocolate choux bun

Ingredients

For the choux buns
60g (2oz) strong white flour
1 tsp caster sugar
50g (1¾oz) salted butter
2 eggs, beaten

For the vanilla cream
200ml (7fl oz) double cream
1 vanilla pod, split and seeds scraped out

For the chocolate sauce
3 tbsp double cream
200g (7oz) milk chocolate, broken into pieces
20g (¾oz) salted butter

Method

1 Preheat oven to 200°C (400°F/Gas 6). For the choux buns, fold a sheet of baking parchment to make a crease and then open it up again. Sift the flour straight on to the parchment sheet and add the sugar.

2 Place 150ml (5fl oz) water and the butter in a pan. Heat gently until the butter has melted. Bring to the boil, remove from the heat, then tip in all the flour and sugar on the parchment sheet and immediately beat vigorously with a wooden spoon until the mixture is smooth and leaves the sides of the pan clean. Place over a low heat for 3–4 minutes, stirring constantly, to dry out a little. Let cool slightly, then beat in the eggs, a little at a time, until you have a smooth glossy paste.

3 Lightly grease a baking tray, then rinse under cold water. (This will help create steam, which helps the pastry rise). Spoon the mixture into a piping bag fitted with a 1cm (½in) plain nozzle and pipe 18 walnut-sized balls, well apart, onto the prepared baking tray.

4 Use a wet palette knife to cut the mixture away from the nozzle each time so you are left with a flat surface on each bun. Alternatively, dip your finger in water and pat each one down to remove the peak. The buns will double in size as they cook, so leave plenty of space between each one.

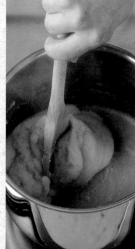

How to make choux pastry

Sift 140g (5oz) strong flour onto a sheet of baking parchment. Add 2 tsp sugar. Bring 240ml (8fl oz) water and 115g (4oz) diced butter to the boil. Remove from the heat and tip in the flour. Beat until smooth, then return pan to a low heat and stir until the dough leaves the sides of the pan. Off the heat, beat in 4 eggs, one at a time, When the dough drops easily off the spoon it is ready.

5 Bake in the oven for 10 minutes, then increase the heat to 220°C (425°F/Gas 7) and bake for a further 15 minutes until the buns are crisp and golden brown. Make a small slit towards the base of each bun with the tip of a sharp knife to let out steam. Cool on a wire rack.

6 To make the vanilla cream, whip the cream with the vanilla seeds until it is fairly stiff, then spoon into a piping bag fitted with a small nozzle. Pipe a little cream into each bun and set them aside until serving.

7 To make the chocolate sauce, melt half the cream and all the milk chocolate in a bowl set over a pan of simmering water, until smooth. Spoon half into a piping bag fitted with a fine writing nozzle and set aside. Stir the remaining cream and the butter into the melted chocolate mixture until it forms a smooth, glossy sauce. Remove the pan from the heat and set aside, keeping warm, until ready to serve.

To serve: To one side of each plate, pipe the chocolate sauce in a flower shape, large enough to hold the torte in the centre. Remove the cling film from the sides of the cooks rings. Run a blow torch round the outsides to loosen the tortes. Invert, crumb-sides up in the centres of the piped flowers and remove the cling film and rings. Fill the 'petals' of the flowers with the reserved orange sauce in the squeezy bottle. Place the white chocolate mousses in the middle of the plates. Spoon some warm raspberry coulis on top of each one. Arrange 3 choux buns next to each glass and spoon some warm chocolate sauce over. Use 2 teaspoons to shape quenelles of vanilla cream and place on on top of each torte and one on top of the buns. Decorate the buns and tortes with a mint sprig and serve straightaway.

Mont Blanc with coffee-poached pear

Tim Kinnaird ⓜ finalist

Preparation time 50 minutes   **Cooking time** 45 minutes   **Serves 4**

Ingredients

250ml (8fl oz) fresh coffee

3 William or Packham pears

400ml (14fl oz) double cream

435g can unsweetened chestnut purée

50g (1¾ oz) icing sugar, or to taste

200g (7oz) blackberries

1–2 tbsp caster sugar

For the meringues

2 egg whites

100g (3½oz) caster sugar

50g (1¾oz) ground almonds

1 tbsp cornflour

Method →

Method

1 For the meringues, preheat the oven to 160°C (325°F/Gas 3) and line 2 baking sheets with non-stick baking parchment. Whisk the egg whites to soft peaks in a clean bowl. Whisk in half the sugar, a spoonful at a time, whisking well between each addition to form a smooth, glossy meringue. Carefully fold in the remaining sugar with the almonds and cornflour.

2 Spread the meringue mixture in a thin layer measuring about 28 x 14cm (11 x 5½in) on one of the baking sheets. Cook for 10 minutes or until beginning to firm. Using a 7cm (2¾in) square cutter, stamp out 8 meringues and place on the second baking sheet. Return to the oven for 10–15 minutes, or until the meringues are dry and crisp.

TECHNIQUE

How to whip cream

1 Remove cream from the refrigerator and wait for it to reach 5°C (40°F). Set it over ice. Whip slowly, at about 2 strokes per second (or the lowest speed on an electric mixer) until it starts to thicken.

2 To create soft peaks, increase the whipping to a moderate speed and for stiff peaks, continue beating the cream. Test by lifting the beaters or whisk to see if the cream retains its shape.

3 Heat the coffee in a saucepan. Peel and core the pears and slice them into thick chip-shaped batons. Poach in the coffee for 6–8 minutes (firm pears may take up to 10 minutes) or until soft, but still retaining their shape. Leave to cool.

4 Meanwhile, whip the double cream to soft peaks and fold in the chestnut purée and icing sugar to taste. Chill until required.

5 Just before serving, push about half of the blackberries through a sieve set over a small pan. Stir in the sugar and dissolve it over a low heat, ensuring the juice doesn't come to the boil or it will become jam-like in consistency. Drain the pears and discard the coffee.

6 To serve, sandwich the meringues with the chestnut filling and place on 4 serving plates. Decorate with a blackberry and arrange a stack of pear batons to one side with more blackberries placed over them. Drizzle the plates with a little sweetened blackberry juice.

Please note: The chestnut filling makes more than you need for the meringue. It will freeze for another time. Simply stir in 1 tsp cornflour to stabilize it and to prevent it from splitting on thawing.

Apple and raspberry filo baskets with a West Country atholl brose

Dick Strawbridge ⓜ **Celebrity finalist**

Preparation time 50 minutes   **Cooking time** 1 hour   **Serves 4**

Ingredients

150g (5½oz) unsalted butter

1 tsp ground cinnamon

4 crisp English apples, such as Golden Delicious, Discovery, or Granny Smith

4 sheets of filo pastry

icing sugar, for dusting

200g (7oz) raspberries

2 tbsp golden caster sugar

1 tsp vanilla extract

4 tbsp medium oatmeal

2 tbsp apple brandy or Calvados

3 tbsp dry cider

2 tbsp clear honey

300ml (10fl oz) double cream

Method

1 Make beurre noisette by melting 100g (3½oz) of the butter in a saucepan over low heat and allow it to separate into butter fat and milk solids. The milk solids will sink to the bottom of the pan and, if left over gentle heat, begin to brown. As the milk solids reach a toasty hazelnut colour, remove the pan from the heat. Stir in the cinnamon.

2 Preheat the oven to 200°C (400°F/Gas 6). Peel and core the apples and toss in the beurre noisette and cinnamon. Place the apples in a muffin tin and cook in the oven for 30–45 minutes until they are soft, turning and basting once. Allow to cool.

Sensational puddings

3 Make the filo baskets by melting the rest of the butter and using it to butter 4 holes of a muffin tin. Unroll the filo pastry and keep covered with a damp tea towel. Cut the filo into 15cm (6in) squares, big enough to line the holes of the muffin tin with a bit of an overlap. Brush the squares with butter and dust with icing sugar. Take one square and overlap with another square placed diagonally on top, so you end up with a star shape. Press this shape gently into the muffin tin. Repeat with the remaining pastry to make 4 baskets. Bake for about 5 minutes until golden. Allow to cool.

4 Simmer the raspberries in a pan with 2 tablespoons water and the golden caster sugar for 5–10 minutes until softened. Add the

TECHNIQUE

How to peel, core and slice apples

1 Remove the core of an apple by pushing a corer straight into the stalk of the apple and through to the bottom. Twist gently and loosen the core, then pull it out with the corer.

2 Using a peeler or small paring knife, gently remove the skin of the apple (and as little of the flesh as possible) by making a circular path around the fruit from top to bottom.

vanilla extract, and allow to cool. Save some raspberries for decoration and liquidize the rest, pass through a sieve and set the coulis aside.

5 Toast the oatmeal in a dry frying pan for 5–10 minutes, stirring frequently until slightly golden. Allow to cool. Stir together the apple brandy or Calvados, cider, and honey in a small jug. Softly whip the cream and fold in the brandy mix, to taste.

6 Place a filo basket on each plate. Insert a cooked apple into each basket topped with a reserved raspberry. Serve with a spoonful of the brandy cream, sprinkle with a little oatmeal, then a drizzle of raspberry coulis with more reserved raspberries.

3 Place the cored apple on its side and hold it steady against a clean cutting board. Using a sharp knife, slice down through the apple. Repeat, making slices of an even thickness.

4 To chop: after slicing, stack the rings, a few at a time. Slice down through the pile, then repeat crossways in the opposite direction, making pieces of about the same size.

Quince croustades with pistachio kulfi, coconut sorbet, and berry coulis

Jackie Kearney Ⓜ contestant

Preparation time 1 hour 15 minutes   **Cooking time** 40 minutes   **Serves 4**

For the croustades

8 sheets of filo pastry

100g (3½oz) unsalted butter, melted

For the quince compote

2 quinces, peeled, cored, and cut into 1cm (½in) cubes

pinch of freshly grated nutmeg

2 cloves

1 cinnamon stick

1 green cardamom pod

3 tbsp caster sugar

3 tbsp port

For the pistachio kulfi

250ml (8fl oz) evaporated milk

pinch of saffron strands, soaked in 2 tbsp hot water

25g (scant 1oz) unsalted, shelled pistachios, plus extra for decorating

25g (scant 1oz) whole peeled almonds

120ml (4fl oz) double cream

For the berry coulis

200g (7oz) blueberries

2 tbsp caster sugar

2 tbsp Kirsch

For the coconut shards

flesh from ½ coconut

For the sorbet

75ml (2½ fl oz) agave syrup

75ml (2½ fl oz) water

juice of 1½ limes

200ml (7fl oz) coconut milk

For the caramel cages

250g (9oz) caster sugar

2 tbsp glucose syrup

Method

1 For the croustades, preheat the oven to 190°C (375°F/Gas 5). Trim the filo pastry sheets slightly, then cut each sheet into four 10cm (4in) squares. Cut each square diagonally in half to form 2 small triangles.

2 Grease the outside of four 10cm (4in) tartlet tins with melted butter and place them upside-down on a baking tray.

3 Drape the triangles of the filo pastry over each mould so that the corners are separate and resemble flower petals, brushing with melted butter between each piece of the pastry. Keep adding them until the "petals" are evenly layered around the moulds (you need 16 triangles per mould).

TECHNIQUE

How to skin pistachios

Place the shelled pistachios in a pan with plenty of cold water to cover them and bring to the boil. When the skins split, place the pistachios between two clean kitchen towels and rub skins off to reveal the pale green nut.

4 Bake for 6–8 minutes until golden brown (don't overcook). Leave to cool, then gently lift off the moulds and turn the croustades the right way up.

5 Alternatively, use 3 filo sheets sandwiched with melted butter. Cut in quarters then press a square into each of the 4 buttered individual tartlet tins so the points stick up. Brush with more butter and bake, as above, until golden. Remove from the tins.

6 For the quince compote, put all the ingredients into a heavy-based saucepan with 100ml (3½ fl oz) water and bring to the boil. Simmer for 15 minutes or until the quinces are soft but still hold their shape. Remove the whole spices from the pan. Set aside the mixture to cool. Alternatively, use diced canned pears heated with the spices, instead of quinces.

7 For the pistachio kulfi, combine the evaporated milk, saffron water, and nuts in a large bowl. In a separate bowl, whisk the cream to soft peaks, then carefully fold into the milk mixture. Transfer to an ice-cream machine and churn until set. Transfer to a plastic container with a lid and store in the freezer. Alternatively, place the mixture in a freezerproof container and freeze until mushy. Whisk until the ice crystals are broken up. Return to the freezer and repeat the process twice. You can use vanilla ice cream, sprinkled with chopped nuts instead if you wish.

8 Meanwhile, line four 100ml (3½fl oz) dariole moulds with cling film. Divide the kulfi mixture between the moulds and transfer to the freezer for at least 1 hour until set.

9 For the berry coulis, put the blueberries in a small pan with the sugar and Kirsch. Bring to the boil and simmer for 2−3 minutes until the sugar has completely dissolved and the fruit begins to break down. Pass the mixture through a sieve into a bowl and set aside until needed.

10 Preheat the oven again, if necessary, to 190°C (375°F/Gas 5). For the coconut shards, thinly slice the coconut using a mandolin, then scatter over a non-stick baking tray. Bake for 8−10 minutes until the shards start to turn golden. Take care not to overcook or they will burn. Cool completely before serving. You can use shop-bought toasted coconut chips instead, if you wish

11 For the coconut sorbet, combine all the ingredients in a large jug, then freeze as for the pistachio kulfi. Alternatively, use can use shop-bought coconut ice cream.

12 For the caramel cages, put the sugar into a heavy-based pan and heat gently. Tilt and rotate the pan to move the sugar as it melts, but do not stir. Once the sugar has melted, add the glucose syrup and continue to cook until the mixture turns a light caramel colour. The temperature should reach 160°C (325°F) on a sugar thermometer.

13 Allow the caramel to cool for a few seconds, and then using 2 forks, scoop out the caramel and drizzle quickly back and forth over the back of a lightly greased ladle. Change directions to create the lattice effect.

14 Remove immediately and set aside to cool. Repeat to make 3 more cages.

15 Use oblong serving plates and place a filo croustade in the centre of each. Fill with the quince compôte. Cover each croustade with a caramel cage. Turn out a dariole mould of kulfi on one side, and decorate with the reserved pistachios and coconut shards. Place a scoop of sorbet on a pool of blueberry coulis on the other side of each croustade.

Bake to
Impress

Gooey chocolate cake with spiced plum coulis

Hannah Miles Ⓜ finalist

Preparation time 45 minutes   **Cooking time** 45 minutes   **Makes 6–8 slices**

Ingredients

250g (9oz) dark chocolate (70% cocoa)

100g (3½oz) salted butter

4 large eggs, separated

175g (6oz) icing sugar

1 tsp cocoa powder

1 tsp icing sugar

4 tbsp crème fraîche

For the coulis

10 ripe red plums, stoned and quartered

50g (1¾oz) caster sugar

1 tbsp amaretto

½ cinnamon stick

For the tuiles

50g (1¾oz) plain flour

10g (¼oz) cocoa powder

60g (2oz) icing sugar

50g (1¾oz) salted butter, melted

2 egg whites

Method →

Method

1 Preheat the oven to 180°C (350°F/Gas 4). Grease a 20cm (8in) springform tin, or 4 individual-sized pudding basins or ramekins, and line the base with baking parchment.

2 Melt the chocolate and butter together in a microwave oven (about 3 minutes on high) or in a bain marie or a pan set over a pan of simmering water. In another bowl, beat the egg yolks with the 175g (6oz) icing sugar until creamy. Fold in the chocolate and butter mixture. Whisk the egg whites (not too stiffly) and fold in. Pour into the tin or basins and bake in the oven for 30 minutes or until the mixture springs back when gently pressed; if making individual cakes they will need less time. Allow to cool slightly, then turn out of the tin or basins.

3 To make the plum coulis, simmer the plums with the caster sugar, amaretto, and cinnamon for about 15 minutes until soft. Purée in a food processor then put through a sieve.

4 For the tuiles, line a baking sheet with greaseproof paper. Place all the ingredients in a bowl and, using a spoon, mix them together. Spoon 8 mounds of the mixture onto the baking sheet and use a palette knife to smooth them into circles about 5cm (2in) in diameter. Place in the oven at 180°C (350°F/Gas 4) for 6–7 minutes. Remove and, while they are still warm, lift them off with a palette knife and drape them over a rolling pin so that they set into a rounded shape. Lift off when cool. Any left uneaten can be stored in an airtight container.

5 To serve, swirl some coulis onto a serving plate or individual plates and sit the cake beside it. Dust with cocoa and icing sugar combined, place a spoonful of crème fraîche on top and set a tuile at an angle.

TECHNIQUE

How to make chocolate tuiles

Mix together 50g (1¾oz) plain flour, 10g (¼oz) cocoa powder, 60g (2oz) icing sugar, 50g (1¾oz) butter and 2 eggs whites in a bowl. Place heaped tablespoons of the mixture onto a baking sheet, lined with greaseproof paper. Smooth into circles about 5cm (2in) in diameter with a palette knife. Bake at 180°C (350°F/Gas 4) for 6–7 minutes. While still warm, drape over a rolling pin so that they set into a rounded shape. Lift off when cool.

Chocolate cake with vanilla whipped cream and raspberry coulis

Nick Pickard @ Celebrity finalist

Preparation time 15 minutes   **Cooking time** 35 minutes   Serves 6–8

Ingredients

For the chocolate cake

4 large eggs

225g (8oz) caster sugar

2 drops of pure vanilla extract

125g (4½oz) unsalted butter, plus extra for greasing

150g (5½oz) dark chocolate (70% cocoa), broken into small pieces

50g (1¾oz) ground almonds

25g (scant 1oz) plain flour, sifted

For the vanilla cream

150ml (5fl oz) whipping cream

150ml (5fl oz) double cream

1 vanilla pod, split and seeds scraped out

50g (1¾oz) icing sugar

For the raspberry coulis

200g (7oz) raspberries

2 tbsp icing sugar

Method →

How to prepare a cake tin

Use a pastry brush to apply a thin, even layer of melted, unsalted butter all over the bottom and sides of the tin, including any corners. Sprinkle a little flour into the tin, then shake and rotate the tin so the flour coats the sides and bottom. Tip away any excess flour. Instead of flouring, you can line the base; place a fitted piece of baking parchment on the greased bottom.

Method

1 Preheat the oven to 160°C (325°F/Gas 3). Grease a 20cm (8in) round loose-bottomed cake tin and line the bottom with baking parchment.

2 Using an electric whisk, whisk together the eggs, caster sugar, and vanilla extract until light and fluffy.

3 Place the butter, chocolate, and 3 tbsp water in a large bowl and heat over simmering water until melted. Stir together until mixed thoroughly and smooth.

4 Using a metal spoon, fold both mixtures together. Stir in the ground almonds and flour, then pour the mixture into the prepared tin. Bake in the preheated oven for 30–35 minutes until firm to the touch. Remove from the oven and leave to cool slightly before turning out onto a wire rack.

5 For the vanilla cream, place the whipping cream, double cream, vanilla seeds, and icing sugar in a bowl and whisk together until soft peaks form. Set aside until needed.

6 For the raspberry coulis, place the raspberries, icing sugar, and 2 tbsp water into a small pan and set over a medium heat for 4–5 minutes until the raspberries have broken down. Remove from the heat and rub through a fine sieve.

7 To serve, cut slices of the cake, place on plates with dots of the raspberry coulis around the edge. Serve the vanilla cream separately or place quenelles on top of the cake.

Orange cake with pomegranate ice cream, and caramelized oranges

Annie Assheton ⓜ contestant

Preparation time 30 minutes   **Cooking time** 1 hour   Serves 8–10

Ingredients

For the cake
60g (2oz) crustless white bread, 2 days old

200g (7oz) caster sugar

100g (3½ oz) ground almonds

1½ tsp baking powder

4 eggs

200ml (7fl oz) sunflower oil

½ tbsp pomegranate molasses

zest of 2 oranges

For the ice cream
30g (1oz) icing sugar

juice of ½ orange

1 tbsp pomegranate molasses

300ml (10fl oz) double cream

For the oranges in syrup
juice of 2 oranges

85g (3oz) caster sugar

1½ tbsp pomegranate molasses

3 whole oranges

juice of ½ pomegranate

For the orange caramel
50g (1¾ oz) caster sugar

juice of ½ orange

To serve
seeds from 1½ fresh pomegranates

Method →

Method

1 Line the base of a 20cm (8in) square cake tin with baking parchment and grease the sides with butter. Make breadcrumbs by whizzing the slightly stale white bread in a food processor.

2 In a large bowl, combine the breadcrumbs with the caster sugar, ground almonds, and baking powder. In another bowl, whisk together the eggs, sunflower oil, and pomegranate molasses, and then stir this mixture into the dry ingredients. Finally, stir in the orange zest. Pour the cake mix into the prepared tin and put into a cold oven. Set the temperature to 180°C (350°F/Gas 4) and leave to cook for 40–50 minutes until firm to the touch.

3 Meanwhile, make the ice cream. Whisk the icing sugar with the orange juice and pomegranate molasses until dissolved. Stir in the double cream and whisk until the mixture is thick and peaking. Shape into quenelles with 2 tbsp and place onto a baking tray lined with baking parchment. Put in the freezer until hardened (about 45 minutes), then cover with cling film.

4 To make the syrup, place the orange juice, caster sugar, and pomegranate molasses into a small pan and heat gently until the sugar has completely dissolved. Simmer for 2–3 minutes until the liquid becomes syrupy.

5 When the cake is cooked, remove from the oven and stand the cake tin on a board. Using a metal skewer, make lots of holes down through the cake. Gradually pour over about half the syrup. Use a pastry brush to spread the syrup evenly. Leave to soak in for 5 minutes, then carefully turn out the cake onto the board. Rest a wire rack on top immediately and, holding the board and rack, invert the cake onto the rack. Leave until slightly warm.

6 Now peel and segment 3 oranges. Cut each segment in half and add to the remaining orange and pomegranate syrup with the pomegranate juice. Simmer for about 2–3 minutes, then remove the orange segments with a slotted spoon and set aside. Continue to simmer the syrup until thickened, but take care not to let it discolour and burn.

7 For the caramel, dissolve the caster sugar into the orange juice. Place over a low heat until completely dissolved, without boiling. Once dissolved, bring to the boil and cook until it becomes a deep caramel colour. Remove from the heat and leave to thicken for 1–2 minutes. Take a tablespoon of caramel and drizzle in pretty curly patterns onto baking parchment. Leave to harden.

To serve: Put the cake on a board and cut off the edges with a bread knife. Then divide the cake into rectangles. Put a piece of cake on each plate, slightly off centre. Spoon a few segments of caramelized orange onto the top of the cake and some syrup round the edge of the plate. Arrange some pomegranate seeds on top of the syrup. Finally, place a quenelle of ice cream next to the plate and top with a shard of orange caramel.

Chocolate and praline gâteau with peanut brittle

Alice Churchill @ Professionals semi-finalist

Preparation time 25–30 minutes   **Cooking time** 50 minutes   **Serves 4**

Ingredients

For the mousse
100g (3½oz) hazelnuts

200ml (7fl oz) milk

1 vanilla pod, split

75g (2½oz) icing sugar

400g (14oz) milk chocolate

1 tsp agar-agar flakes

300ml (10fl oz) double cream

For the sponge
175g (6oz) butter

175g (6oz) caster sugar

3 large eggs

175g (6oz) self-raising flour

For the brittle
400g (14oz) caster sugar

200g (7oz) unsalted roasted peanuts

For the tuile biscuits
2 egg whites

85g (3oz) plain flour

100g (3½oz) caster sugar

For the chocolate ganache
300ml (10fl oz) double cream

300g (10oz) dark chocolate (70% cocoa solids)

To serve
100g (3½oz) good quality white chocolate

100ml (3½fl oz) double cream

Method

1 For the hazelnut and chocolate mousse, first make a hazelnut purée. Tip the hazelnuts into a saucepan with the milk, vanilla pod, and icing sugar. Bring to the boil and simmer for 15 minutes. Discard the vanilla pod. Scoop out the hazelnuts and place them in a blender or food processor. Blend, gradually adding the hot milk, to form a purée.

2 Melt the chocolate in a bowl set over a pan of simmering water. Stir in the agar-agar flakes.

3 Meanwhile, whip the cream in a large bowl until medium peaks form. Fold the hazelnut purée into the cream. Then add the melted chocolate and mix well. Pour into a Swiss roll tin and freeze for about 1 hour to set.

4 For the sponge, preheat the oven to 180°C (350°F/Gas 4) and grease and line a second Swiss roll tin with baking parchment.

5 Cream together the butter and caster sugar until pale and fluffy. Beat in the eggs, one at a time, then fold in the flour. Spoon the mix into the prepared tin and spread out with a spatula. Bake for 20 minutes, or until golden brown. Remove from the oven and set aside.

6 For the peanut brittle, gently heat the sugar in a heavy pan until it liquefies and turns golden. Mix in the peanuts. Pour onto a baking mat and allow to cool. Break the peanut brittle into smaller pieces.

7 To make the tuile biscuits, mix all the ingredients together to form a smooth paste. Spread small circles of the paste very thinly onto a baking mat and bake for 4–6 minutes, or until slightly golden. Remove from the oven and immediately curl over an oiled rolling pin to set in a tuile shape. Set aside and leave to cool.

8 For the ganache, pour the cream into a small pan and bring to the boil. Remove from the heat, break up the chocolate and stir it gently into the cream until smooth. Return to the heat and bring to the boil, then remove from the heat and allow to cool. Keep at room temperature.

9 Melt the white chocolate in a bowl set over a pan of gently simmering water. Remove from the heat and stir in the double cream.

10 To assemble the gâteaux, cut the sponge into 12 rectangles. Repeat with the mouse. Place a layer of mouse onto each serving plate, and top with a layer of sponge. Repeat the layering twice more. Cover with chocolate ganache, reserving some for decoration. Leave the assembled gâteaux in the fridge to chill.

11 To serve, top each gâteau with a tuile biscuit, place pieces of peanut brittle alongside and decorate with the reserved ganache (warmed to help trail on the plate) and the melted white chocolate and cream mixture.

Chocolate and almond torte with amaretto cream, passion fruit, and raspberries

Dhruv Baker @ champion

Preparation time 30 minutes   **Cooking time** 30 minutes   **Makes 8 slices**

Ingredients

150g (5½oz) dark chocolate (70% cocoa solids)

125g (4½oz) unsalted butter

5 eggs, separated

175g (6oz) light soft brown sugar

175g (6oz) ground almonds

100ml (3½fl oz) amaretto, plus 1 tbsp for amaretto cream

100ml (3½fl oz) double cream

2 passion fruit, peeled, cut in half, and flesh scooped out

icing sugar

1 punnet raspberries

Method →

Method

1 Preheat the oven to 150°C (300°F/Gas 2). Line the base of a 23cm (9in) diameter springform baking tin with baking parchment and butter the sides.

2 Melt the chocolate and butter in a large bowl placed over a saucepan of simmering water. Once melted, remove from heat and leave to cool slightly.

3 In a separate bowl, whisk the egg whites until they form peaks.

4 Mix the sugar and almonds into the chocolate mixture, then stir in the egg yolks and the 100ml (3½fl oz) of amaretto.

5 Finally, fold the egg whites into the chocolate mixture using a metal spoon. Pour the mixture into the prepared tin and bake for about 30 minutes or until firm on top and a skewer comes out clean. Remove the torte from the oven and allow to cool for a few minutes.

6 Whip the cream until it forms soft peaks, and pour in the remaining amaretto.

7 Put the passion fruit flesh into a blender or food processor and whisk to a pulp. Push through a sieve and add icing sugar to taste.

8 To serve, place a slice of the torte on each plate. Drizzle over some passion fruit coulis and add a spoonful of the cream and a few raspberries.

Golden syrup chocolate fondants with thick vanilla cream

Andrew Fletcher Ⓜ contestant

Preparation time 15 minutes   **Cooking time** 12–15 minutes   **Serves 4**

Ingredients

100g (3½oz) butter, cubed, plus extra for greasing

cocoa powder, for dusting

100g (3½oz) dark chocolate (70% cocoa solids)

2 large eggs

50g (1¾oz) golden caster sugar

50g (1¾oz) golden syrup

20g (¾ oz) plain flour

1 vanilla pod, split, seeds scraped out and reserved

225ml (7½fl oz) extra thick double cream

Method

1 Preheat the oven to 170ºC (340°F/Gas 3–4). Grease four 150ml (5fl oz) pudding moulds and dust them with cocoa powder.

2 Melt the chocolate and the 100g (3½oz) butter in a bowl over a pan of simmering water.

3 In a separate bowl, whisk together the eggs and sugar until pale. Pour the melted chocolate and butter into the eggs and add the golden syrup, then mix well.

4 Sift the flour and gently fold into the mixture. Divide between the prepared pudding moulds, and place them on a baking sheet.

5 Bake for 12–15 minutes in the hot oven, or until the puddings are set on the outside but still soft and runny inside.

6 Stir the vanilla seeds into the extra thick cream. Turn out the warm puddings and serve with the cream.

Banana soufflé with blueberry coulis

Natalie Brenner @ quarter-finalist

Preparation time 30 minutes   **Cooking time** 25 minutes   **Serves 4**

Ingredients

For the coulis
150g (5½oz) blueberries

50g (1¾oz) sugar

For the soufflés
15g (½oz) unsalted butter

4 tsp sugar

1 large, ripe banana, roughly chopped

1 tbsp clear honey

2 large eggs, whites only

1 tbsp caster sugar

To serve
icing sugar

Method →

Method

1 For the coulis, place the blueberries and sugar in a saucepan with 100ml (3½fl oz) water and bring to the boil. Take off the heat and allow to cool, then blend, using a blender or by transferring to a food processor, and pass through a sieve. Put back on the hob, bring to the boil, and reduce until syrupy. Set aside to cool.

2 Preheat the oven to 200ºC (400°F/Gas 6) and place a baking sheet in the oven to heat up. Evenly grease 4 ramekins with the butter, then coat the inside with a layer of sugar.

3 Place the banana in a food processor, add the honey, and blend until smooth.

4 Place the egg whites in a clean, dry bowl and whisk until the whites form soft peaks. Gradually

TECHNIQUE

How to make a souffle

1 Grease the inside of each soufflé dish and then coat with sugar, biscuit crumbs, or grated cheese. Use sugar or biscuit crumbs for a sweet soufflé, and grated cheese for a savoury soufflé.

2 Whisk egg whites to form stiff peaks: if under-whisked, the soufflé will not rise. Fold into base mixture gently, to retain as much air as possible. Add a pinch of salt before mixing for savoury soufflés.

add the caster sugar, whisking all the time, until stiff peaks are formed.

5 Using a spatula, fold one-third of the egg whites into the banana mixture relatively vigorously, then very gently fold in the remainder. Spoon the soufflé mix into the ramekins, tap on the work surface to expel any air and run a finger around the rim to create a "top hat" effect.

6 Put the soufflés on the preheated baking sheet, and place in the oven and bake them for 10–12 minutes until risen.

7 To serve, put the coulis in a small jug on each plate. Place the soufflés in their ramekins on the plate, and sprinkle icing sugar on them just before serving.

3 Spoon mixture into ramekins. Run a finger around the soufflé mix, along the top edge of each ramekin just inside the rim, to give a professional "top hat" effect and help the soufflés rise up straight.

4 Bake the soufflés immediately, placing them on a thoroughly preheated baking tray. Doing this will heat the base of the ramekins so that the soufflés begin to rise as soon as you put them in the oven.

Rhubarb and strawberry soufflé

Kirsty Wark @ **Celebrity finalist**

Preparation time 15 minutes   **Cooking time** 28 minutes   **Serves 6**

Ingredients

For the rhubarb reduction

500g (1lb 2oz) rhubarb, roughly chopped

200g (7oz) caster sugar

2 tbsp cornflour

2 tbsp framboise or other raspberry liqueur

For the soufflés

6 fresh strawberries, hulled and cut in thirds

3 tbsp strawberry liqueur

25g (scant 1oz) unsalted butter, melted

150g (5½oz) caster sugar

3 egg whites

200ml (3½fl oz) reserved rhubarb reduction

icing sugar, for dusting

Method

1 For the reduction, place the rhubarb in a pan with 100g (3½oz) of the sugar. Bring to the boil, cover, reduce the heat, then simmer for 10 minutes until soft and sticky.

2 Mix the cornflour with the framboise liqueur and stir into the rhubarb until thick. Purée with a hand blender. Transfer to a bowl.

3 Mix 100ml (3½fl oz) water and the remaining sugar in a pan and simmer for 5 minutes until the sugar has completely dissolved. Cook for a further 2–3 minutes until the mixture turns pale gold. Remove from the heat immediately or the mixture will caramelize and become hard. Pour the sugar syrup into the rhubarb and stir well.

4 For the soufflés, combine the strawberries with the strawberry liqueur in a bowl. Leave to macerate for 10 minutes and then drain.

5 Preheat the oven to 180°C (350°F/Gas 4). Butter 4 ramekins using upward strokes, then dust them with 3 tbsp of the sugar, and chill in the fridge until needed.

6 Place the egg whites in a bowl, whisk with an electric whisk until you have soft white peaks, then add the remaining sugar, a little at a time, continuing to whisk until stiff and glossy.

7 Pour 100ml (3½fl oz) of the rhubarb reduction into a large bowl and whisk in a third of the egg whites to loosen. Gently fold in the remaining whites with a metal spoon until just mixed.

8 Half fill the ramekins with the soufflé mixture, then place 3 pieces of soaked strawberries in the middle. Fill with the mixture to the top. Flatten with a palette knife. Run your thumb around the edge of each to make a ridge. Cook in the oven for 10 minutes.

9 Immediately place on serving plates, dust tops with icing sugar, and serve with a little of the remaining rhubarb reduction in tiny jugs on the side.

White chocolate brûlée

Gary Heath @ quarter-finalist

Preparation time 5 minutes   **Cooking time** 25 minutes   **Serves 4**

Ingredients

300ml (10fl oz) double cream

30g (1oz) white chocolate

3 egg yolks

30g (1oz) caster sugar, plus extra for sprinkling

1 tsp vanilla extract

Method

1 Preheat the oven to 180°C (350°F/Gas 4). Put the cream and chocolate in a saucepan and heat gently until the chocolate has melted.

2 In a bowl, use a wooden spoon or electric whisk to beat together the egg yolks, sugar, and the vanilla extract until pale. Then, stirring continuously, add the chocolate cream and sieve into four 6cm (2½in) diameter and about 4cm (1½in) deep ramekins.

3 Place the ramekins in a roasting tin, filled with boiling water to half way up their sides. Bake in the hot oven for 18–20 minutes or until set. Transfer to the fridge and chill for 1 hour.

4 To finish, preheat a grill to medium-hot. Sprinkle 1 tsp of caster sugar on top of each of the brûlées and caramelize under the hot grill for 2–3 minutes. Leave to harden and serve.

Baked lime cheesecake with rum cream

Dennice Russell @ semi-finalist

Preparation time 25 minutes   **Cooking time** 25 minutes   **Serves 4**

Ingredients

8 digestive biscuits, crushed

50g (1¾oz) unsalted butter, melted

300g (10oz) mascarpone cheese

100g (3½oz) ricotta cheese

1 tbsp plain flour

100g (3½oz) golden caster sugar

40g (1½oz) desiccated coconut

grated zest and juice of 3 limes, plus strands of lime zest, to decorate

2 eggs

1 vanilla pod, scraped

For the rum cream

200ml (7fl oz) double cream

1 tbsp icing sugar

4 tbsp dark rum

Method

1 Preheat the oven to 180°C (350°F/Gas 4). Mix the biscuits into the melted butter. Place four 10cm (4in) chef's rings on a baking sheet and press biscuit mix into the base of each.

2 Put the cheeses, flour, sugar, coconut, lime juice and zest, eggs, and the seeds of the vanilla pod into a bowl and whisk until well blended.

3 Pour the mixture onto the biscuit bases in the chef's rings and bake for 20 minutes, until golden. They should be slightly wobbly in the centre when ready. Turn of the oven, and leave cheesecakes in the oven to cool.

4 To make the rum cream, put the cream, icing sugar, and rum into a bowl and whisk to form soft peaks.

5 Put the cooled cheesecakes onto serving plates and top with quenelles of rum cream and strands of lime zest.

TECHNIQUE

How to make a biscuit base

1 Preheat oven to 180°C (350°F/Gas 4). Crush 8–10 digestive biscuits in a plastic bag with a rolling pin, or use a food processor.

2 Mix the biscuit crumbs with 50–60g (1¾–2oz) melted and cooled butter in a large bowl until mixture resembles wet sand. Press into the base of a baking tin.

Marbled chocolate fondant with orange and mint syrup

Adam Young @ Professionals quarter-finalist

Preparation time 35 minutes   **Cooking time** 15minutes   **Serves 4**

Ingredients

75g (2½oz) white chocolate

75g (2½oz) dark chocolate (70% cocoa)

100g (3½oz) unsalted butter, melted

2 egg whites

100g (3½oz) caster sugar, plus 2 tbsp

100g (3½oz) plain flour

grated zest and juice of 2 oranges, plus segments of 1 orange

handful of mint leaves, cut into fine shreds

Method

1 Preheat the oven to 180°C (350°F/Gas 4). Grease four 7cm (2¾in) metal rings and line the sides with baking parchment. Put the rings on a baking sheet, lined with baking parchment.

2 In separate bowls, melt the white and dark chocolates, each with 50g (1¾oz) butter over pans of simmering water. Remove from the heat. Whisk the egg whites and sugar until thick and creamy, then divide into 2 and fold half into each of the chocolates, along with half of the flour.

3 Place each chocolate mixture into a separate piping bag and pipe both together into the metal rings. Put in the fridge to solidify, and then place in the hot oven for 12 minutes until the mixture shrinks away from sides of the rings. Remove from the oven.

4 For the syrup, put the orange juice and 2 tbsp sugar into a saucepan and slowly bring to the boil. Add the zest, mint, and orange segments and remove from the heat. Take each fondant from its ring and put on a plate. Drizzle around the syrup and serve with the orange segments.

Reinvented
Classics

Figgy pudding served with fig sauce and cream

Ruth Goodman @ Celebrity contestant

Preparation time 20 minutes   **Cooking time** 1 hour   **Serves 4**

Ingredients

200g (7oz) ready-to-eat dried figs, roughly chopped

splash of dry sherry

finely grated zest and juice of 1 lemon

50g (1¾oz) butter, plus extra for greasing

50g (1¾oz) self-raising flour

100g (3½oz) fresh breadcrumbs

60g (2oz) light soft brown sugar

2 eggs, lightly beaten

2 tbsp double cream, plus extra to serve

Method →

Method

1 Soak the figs in the sherry and lemon zest and juice for at least 30 minutes.

2 Rub together the butter and self-raising flour. Add to the breadcrumbs with the brown sugar.

3 Add half of the soaked figs along with half the steeping liquid to the breadcrumb mixture. Add the beaten eggs and the 2 tbsp cream. Mix well.

4 Butter 4 dariole moulds. Divide the pudding mixture between the moulds. Place a piece of buttered greaseproof paper over each one, cover with pleated foil, and fasten with string, or twist and fold under the rim of the moulds to secure. Place in a steamer and steam for 1 hour, topping up the steamer with boiling water as necessary.

5 Place the remaining soaked figs along with their steeping liquid into a small blender or food processor. Blend until smooth. Add water to thin to desired consistency – a thick paste or a pouring sauce. Place in a pan and warm gently for 2 minutes.

6 Serve the figgy puddings with the warmed fig paste or sauce and a dash of cream.

Rhubarb and orange cake with flaked almonds

Rachel Thompson @ quarter-finalist

Preparation time 15 minutes **Cooking time** 45 minutes **Makes 8–10 slices**

Ingredients

400g (14oz) English rhubarb, trimmed and cut into 2cm (¾in) pieces

200g (7oz) golden caster sugar

150g (5½oz) unsalted butter, softened

2 eggs, lightly beaten

75g (2½oz) self-raising flour

½ tsp baking powder

100g (3½oz) ground almonds

grated zest and 2 tbsp juice of 1 small orange

25g (scant 1oz) flaked almonds

Method

1 Preheat the oven to 190°C (375°F/Gas 5). Grease and line the base of a 23cm (9in) springform cake tin.

2 Place the rhubarb in a bowl and cover with 50g (2½oz) of the sugar. Leave for 30 minutes while you prepare the rest of the cake.

3 With an electric whisk, beat together the remaining sugar and the butter in a bowl, then whisk in the eggs. Using a metal spoon, gently fold in the flour, baking powder, and ground almonds, then stir in the orange zest and juice.

4 Stir the rhubarb and its sugary juices into the cake mixture and spoon into the prepared tin. Place on a baking tray, sprinkle over the flaked almonds, and bake for 25 minutes. Reduce temperature to 180°C (350°F/Gas 4) and cook for a further 20–25 minutes, or until firm. Allow to cool in the tin for 10 minutes before turning out.

5 Serve warm or cold, with softly whipped cream or custard.

Baked ginger pear crumble

inspired by **Midge Ure** Ⓜ **Celebrity finalist**

Preparation time 20 minutes   **Cooking time** 40 minutes   **Serves 4**

Ingredients

500g (1lb 2oz) ripe pears, peeled, cored, and quartered

100ml (3½fl oz) stem ginger syrup

3–4 pieces of stem ginger, chopped

For the crumble

175g (6oz) plain flour

pinch of salt

125g (4½oz) cold butter, cubed

60g (2oz) porridge oats

125g (4½oz) demerara sugar

extra thick double cream, to serve

Method

1 Preheat the oven to 180°C/350°F/Gas 4.

2 Place the pear quarters in a roasting tin and drizzle the ginger syrup over them, then roast in the oven for about 10–15 minutes. Transfer to an ovenproof baking dish and scatter with the chopped stem ginger.

3 To make the crumble, place the flour, salt, and butter in a food processor and pulse to a crumb consistency. Alternatively, rub the butter into the flour and salt with your fingertips until the mixture resembles breadcrumbs. Tip into a bowl and mix in the oats and sugar, then scatter the mixture lightly over the top of the pears, but do not pack down.

4 Bake in the oven for 30–40 minutes, or until the top is golden and the fruit is bubbling through at the edges. Serve with extra thick double cream.

Trio of British desserts

Tim Anderson @ champion

Preparation time 1 hour   **Cooking time** 1 hour 15 minutes   **Serves 4**

Ingredients

For the custard base

250g (9oz) sugar

8 egg yolks

250ml (8fl oz) milk

250ml (8fl oz) single cream

Method

Beat together the sugar and egg yolks until pale and thick. Simmer the milk and cream together in a saucepan and pour over the egg yolks and sugar. Whisk to combine, then strain into a clean pan. Heat gently, stirring, until the mixture thickens to the point where it coats the back of a spoon evenly. Remove from the heat and transfer immediately to a large bowl.

Cheddar cheesecake with whisky jelly

Ingredients

For the cheesecake base

2 digestive biscuits

2 tsp chopped walnuts

1 tbsp flour

1½ tbsp sugar

1 tbsp oats

40g (1¼oz) butter

For the cheesecake filling

100ml (3½fl oz) milk

30g (1oz) sugar

20g (¾oz) very mature Cheddar cheese, finely grated

20g (¾oz) mascarpone cheese

2 tbsp agar-agar flakes

100ml (3½fl oz) prepared custard base

For the whisky jelly

3 tbsp plus 1 tsp Highland whisky

100ml (3½ fl oz) Lowland whisky

3 tbsp ginger beer

50g (1¾ oz) sugar

1 tbsp agar-agar flakes

To decorate

12 blackcurrants

4 mint leaves

Method →

Method

1 For the base, preheat the oven to 180°C (350°F/ Gas 4). Blitz all the ingredients to a coarse powder in a food processor. Roll out to a thickness of 8mm (⅓in) on a non-stick baking sheet. Bake for 12 minutes until golden. Remove from the oven and leave to cool.

2 Line the sides of four 4cm (1½in) diameter cooking rings with acetate and use to cut discs out of the biscuit base mixture, retaining the disc of the biscuit base inside the ring. Transfer the rings to a baking tray lined with greaseproof paper.

3 For the filling, put the milk and sugar into a small pan and bring to the boil. Add the cheeses and stir to combine. Sprinkle the agar-agar into the pan and boil for 4 minutes until dissolved. Remove from the heat and whisk into the custard base. Pour the mixture on top of the biscuit base in the lined cooking rings to a depth of 5mm (¼in). Transfer to the fridge and chill until set.

4 To make the whisky jelly, put all the ingredients in a saucepan and bring to the boil. Boil for 5–6 minutes until the agar-agar has completely. dissolved. Pour into a small plastic container to a depth of 5mm (¼in). Chill for 20 minutes or until set.

5 Cut out 4cm (1½in) circles of the jelly and leave in the refridgerator until ready to serve.

Sticky toffee crème brûlée

Ingredients

For the crème brûlée

100ml (3½fl oz) double cream

100g (3½oz) muscovado sugar

4 stoned dates

4 stoned prunes

1 vanilla pod, split and seeds scraped out

2 egg yolks

3 tbsp plain flour

100ml (3½fl oz) prepared custard base

caster sugar, for topping

For the sauce

250ml (8fl oz) blackcurrant ale, such as Lindemans Cassis

3 tbsp crème de cassis

100ml (3½fl oz) stout

50g (1¾oz) sugar

3 tbsp double cream

Method

1 Preheat the oven to 180°8C (350°F/Gas 4). Place the cream and sugar in a pan over medium heat and stir continuously until the sugar has completely dissolved. Add the dates, prunes, and vanilla seeds and simmer until the dates have softened.

2 Add the egg yolks and flour to the custard base and whisk until smooth. Pour the date and prune mixture onto the custard and whisk to combine. Transfer to a food processor and blitz until smooth.

3 Divide the mixture between mini ramekins, 50ml (2fl oz) in volume, and place them in a roasting tray. Add hot water to the tray until it comes halfway up the sides of the ramekins, then bake in the oven for 20–25 minutes until set. Leave to cool, then transfer to the fridge to chill.

4 Once completely chilled, sprinkle the top of each crème brûlée with caster sugar and glaze with a blowtorch. Refrigerate until ready to serve.

5 For the sauce, combine all the ingredients in a saucepan, bring to the boil, then simmer until reduced to 100ml (3½fl oz). Keep sauce warm until needed, then transfer to small jugs before serving.

Rhubarb crumble with custard

Ingredients

For the rhubarb compote

2 rhubarb sticks, diced

100g (3½oz) sugar

100ml (3½fl oz) pink champagne

For the custard

250ml (8fl oz) prepared custard base

1 vanilla pod, split and seeds scraped out

For the crumble

50g (1¾oz) plain flour

1 egg

50g (1¾oz) rolled oats

50g (1¾oz) panko breadcrumbs

vegetable oil, for deep frying

icing sugar, for dusting

1 rhubarb stick

Method

1 Put all of the rhubarb compôte ingredients in a saucepan, bring to the boil, then simmer until the rhubarb is very soft. Transfer to a food processor and blitz until smooth. Place in a bowl and chill.

2 Combine the custard base and vanilla seeds in a small bowl, cover with cling film, and chill.

3 To assemble, place the rhubarb compôte and vanilla custard base in a bowl and stir gently to create a rippled effect. Fill 8 hemispheric tablespoon measures, or eight 15ml (½fl oz) hemispheric moulds, with the mixture and transfer to the freezer to set.

4 When frozen solid, dip the back of the spoons or moulds briefly in warm water to loosen the frozen mixture, then turn out onto a chilled baking tray. Brush the flat surface of 1 of the half spheres with a little warm water, then press 2 halves together to make a complete sphere. Return to the freezer and freeze until solid. Repeat the process to make 1 sphere per serving.

5 To make the crumble, whisk the flour, 4 tsp water, and the egg into a thick batter, then set aside. Combine the oats and panko breadcrumbs and blitz in a food processor. Set aside in a separate bowl.

6 Heat the oil for deep frying to 160°C (325°F). Dip each frozen rhubarb sphere in the batter, shake off any excess, then roll in the oat and panko mixture. Fry for 2 minutes until the outside is golden and the inside is completely molten. Drain on a rack set over a roasting tray. When dry, dust with icing sugar.

7 Cut the rhubarb stick into very thin strips and wrap around the base of each rhubarb crumble sphere. Serve immediately with the cheesecakes and crème brûlée.

To serve: Place the cheesecakes on 4 serving plates, loosen the edges, and lift off the rings. Top each with a disc of whisky jelly. Decorate each cheesecake with 3 blackcurrants and a mint leaf. Arrange the brulées, crumble spheres, and jugs of sauce alongside.

How to extract vanilla seeds

1 Vanilla pods can be used whole, but the seeds look especially good in creamy desserts. To extract them, put the vanilla pod on a board and cut along the length of the pod.with the tip of a sharp knife.

2 Using the blunt side of a small knife or a teaspoon, scrape along the inside of the pod to collect the sticky seeds. The empty pod can then be used to flavour syrups and sugars.

Sticky toffee pudding

Wendi Peters @ Celebrity finalist

Preparation time 20 minutes   **Cooking time** 35 minutes   **Serves 4**

Ingredients

85g (3oz) sugared, stoned chopped dates

85g (3oz) light soft brown sugar

45g (1½oz) unsalted butter, softened

1 egg

115g (4oz) plain flour

1 tsp bicarbonate of soda

1 tbsp vanilla extract

For the toffee sauce

150g (5½oz) demerara sugar

85g (3oz) unsalted butter, softened

4 tbsp double cream

Method

1 Preheat the oven to 180°C (350°F/Gas 4). Butter a 16 x 12cm (6½ x 5in) ovenproof dish.

2 Put the dates into a bowl and pour over just enough boiling water to cover them.

3 In a separate bowl, cream together the soft brown sugar and the butter. Beat the egg into the creamed mixture with some of the flour, before adding the rest of the flour.

4 Add the bicarbonate of soda and vanilla extract to the dates and then stir into the creamed mixture until well mixed. Pour into the ovenproof dish and bake in the oven for 30–35 minutes or until well risen and a cake skewer, when inserted, comes out clean.

5 Just before the pudding is cooked, make the toffee sauce. Preheat the grill to hot. Put the demerara sugar, butter, and cream into a saucepan and heat gently. Let simmer for 3 minutes. Remove the pudding from the oven, pour over half the sauce and place under the grill until it bubbles.

6 Serve the pudding while hot with the remaining sauce poured over the top or alongside.

S'more millefeuilles with forest fruit coulis and campfire sorbet

Tim Anderson @ Celebrity finalist

Preparation time 1 hour   **Cooking time** 25 minutes   **Serves 4**

Ingredients

For the sorbet
15g (½oz) butter

1 red bird's eye chilli, finely chopped

1 tsp lapsang souchong tea leaves

250ml (8fl oz) fresh apple juice

100ml (3½ fl oz) clear honey

100ml (3½fl oz) very smoky Highland or Islay whisky

4 sachets strawberry-flavoured popping candy

For the base
125g (4½oz) caster sugar

100g (3½oz) plain flour

85g (3oz) cold unsalted butter, cubed

10 digestive biscuits

50g (1¾oz) hazelnuts

50g (1¾oz) pistachios

For the cream
2 egg whites

150ml (5fl oz) light corn syrup or golden syrup

150ml (5fl oz) icing sugar, sifted

pinch of salt

1 tsp pure vanilla extract

For the ganache
1 tbsp juniper berries

picked leaves from 1 sprig of rosemary

1 small bay leaf

2 tbsp caster sugar

200ml (7fl oz) double cream

1 tbsp gin

400g (14oz) milk chocolate

30g (1oz) unsalted butter, cubed

For the pastry
100g (3½oz) butter, diced

2 egg whites

50g (1¾oz) icing sugar

8 sheets filo pastry

For the forest fruit coulis
100g (3½oz) raspberries

100g (3½oz) blackberries

50g (1½oz) redcurrants

50g (1¾oz) blackcurrants

50g (1¾oz) blueberries

100g (3½oz) icing sugar

juice of 2 lemons

To serve
100ml (3½fl oz) rapeseed oil

10 mint leaves

1 sachet strawberry-flavoured popping candy

50g (1¾oz) icing sugar

freshly grated nutmeg

Method

1 Preheat the oven to 180°C (350°F/Gas 4). Grease and line the base and sides of a 30 x 23cm (12 x 9in) non-stick baking tin with baking parchment.

2 To make the sorbet, melt the butter in a pan over medium heat, then sauté the chilli and tea leaves for 2 minutes until tender. Stir in the apple juice, honey, 2 tbsp water, and whisky. Heat and flambé, until the flames die down. Strain into a jug and leave to cool.

3 Pour the mixture into an ice-cream machine and churn until smooth and set. Transfer to a plastic container with a lid and freeze until needed. Alternatively, pour the mixture in a freezerproof container and freeze until mushy. Whisk until the ice crystals are broken up. Return to the freezer and repeat the process twice.

4 Meanwhile, place all the ingredients for the biscuit base in a food processor and blitz until well combined. Press the mixture evenly and firmly into the lined tin with the back of a spoon.

5 Bake for 10–12 minutes until just set. Allow to cool in the tin for 15 minutes before carefully turning onto a wire rack to cool completely. Cut the cooled biscuit into four 10 x 5cm (4 x 2in) rectangles. Reserve until needed.

6 To prepare the marshmallow cream, whip the egg whites, corn (or golden) syrup, sugar, and salt with an electric whisk on medium speed for 2–3 minutes until well combined. Increase to highest speed for 12–15 minutes until thick and stiff, then fold in the vanilla extract.

7 Fit a piping bag with a 1cm (½ in) round nozzle and spoon in the mixture. Transfer to the fridge to set for at least 20 minutes before using.

8 Meanwhile, make the ganache. Crush the juniper berries, rosemary, bay leaf, and sugar together in a mortar and pestle. Add to a small saucepan along with cream and gin, bring the mixture to the boil, reduce the heat, then simmer for 10 minutes. Remove from the heat and cover with a lid, then leave the mixture to infuse for a further 20 minutes. Strain the mixture into a clean pan, then bring up to a gentle simmer. Whisk in the chocolate and butter until smooth, then remove from the heat.

9 Leave the ganache to cool until the mixture has thickened, and will just hold its shape, then spoon into a piping bag fitted with a 1cm (½in) round nozzle. Transfer to the fridge to firm slightly, to the consistency of whipped cream.

10 Prepare the filo stacks for the millefeuilles. Put the butter, egg whites, and sugar in a small saucepan over medium heat. Stir until the butter has melted and the mixture has thickened. Cut the filo pastry sheets into quarters. Brush each filo layer with a little of the melted butter mixture and arrange into stacks of 8 sheets. Cut into eight 10 x 5cm (4 x 2in) rectangles. Place on a lightly greased baking tray, then bake for 12 minutes until crisp and golden. Transfer the filo stacks to a wire rack to cool completely.

11 Meanwhile, make the coulis by blitzing all the ingredients together in a small food processor. Rub through a fine sieve into a bowl to remove the seeds. Chill before serving.

12 Prepare the decoration. Heat the rapeseed oil in a frying pan. Add the mint leaves and fry for 1 minute until crisp and bright green (take care not to overcook or they will go brown), then drain on kitchen paper and leave to cool.

13 Put the popping candy and icing sugar in a mortar and grind to a fine powder with a pestle.

To serve: Set a biscuit base on each of 4 plates with a tiny amount of the ganache. Pipe the remaining ganache onto the bases in a layer about 1cm (½in) thick. Top each with 1 filo stack, then pipe on the marshmallow cream. Using a blowtorch, toast the top of the marshmallow cream lightly until golden brown. Top with another filo stack. Spoon a small pool of the forest fruit coulis to one side of the millefeuilles. Quickly stir the 4 sachets of popping candy through the sorbet. Scoop 4 quenelles of sorbet, using a dessertspoon, and place in tiny serving dishes. Dust the top of the millefeuilles with the ground icing sugar and popping candy mixture, then decorate the top with a little grated nutmeg and the fried mint leaves. Serve the milllefeuilles straight away with the little dishes of sorbet placed alongside.

Rhubarb and ginger crumble

Lisa Faulkner ⓜ **Celebrity champion**

Preparation time 15 minutes **Cooking time** 45 minutes **Serves 4**

Ingredients

450g (1lb) rhubarb, cut into 2cm (¾in) pieces

2 slices preserved stem ginger, finely diced

2 tbsp ginger syrup, reserved from jar

2 tbsp caster sugar

For the crumble topping

140g (5oz) plain flour

45g (1½oz) oats

85g (3oz) unsalted butter, diced

60g (2oz) golden caster sugar

45g (1½oz) flaked almonds

For the custard

8 egg yolks

75g (2½oz) caster sugar

300ml (10fl oz) whole milk

300ml (10fl oz) double cream

1 vanilla pod, split, seeds scraped out and reserved with the pod

Method

1 Preheat the oven to 180°C (350°F/Gas 4). Put the rhubarb in a 1 litre (1¾ pint) deep pie dish. Add the ginger, syrup, and sugar and mix together.

2 For the crumble, mix the flour and oats in a bowl. Add the butter and rub into the flour mixture until the texture resembles fine breadcrumbs. Add the sugar and almonds and mix well.

3 Spoon half the crumble mixture on top of the rhubarb and pat down. Sprinkle the rest on top and leave sitting loosely.

Place in the preheated oven and bake for about 45 minutes until golden.

4 To make the custard, beat the egg yolks and sugar together in a bowl until pale and thickened. Pour the milk and cream into a large saucepan, and add the vanilla seeds and pod. Bring to simmering point over medium heat, then pour through a fine sieve onto the egg mixture and whisk thoroughly. Place the bowl over a pan of simmering water and stir until the custard thickens and coats the back of a spoon. Serve with the crumble.

American lunchbox

Tim Anderson @ champion

Preparation time 1 hour 45 minutes   **Cooking time** 30minutes   **Serves 4**

Filo "crisps"

Ingredients

3 sheets filo pastry

100g (3½oz) unsalted butter, melted

50g (1¾oz) icing sugar, plus extra for dusting

50g (1¾oz) dry-roasted peanuts

1 tsp ground cinnamon

Method

1 Preheat the oven to 200°C (400°F/Gas 6). For the "crisp packets", brush 1 sheet of filo pastry with butter and dust with icing sugar. Cut the sheet into quarters and fold each piece in half. Fold 4 pieces of foil to fit inside the filo flaps to support the openings and make loose crisp-bag shapes. Place on a baking tray and bake for 5–6 minutes until golden. Cool, then remove the foil.

2 For the filo "crisps", brush the remaining 2 filo sheets with butter and dust with icing sugar. Use a 5cm (2in) biscuit cutter to press out circles of pastry. Roll up 2 or 3 sausage shapes of foil and place on a baking tray. Drape the pastry discs over the foil to form curled crisp shapes. Bake for 4–5 minutes until crisp and golden. Carefully remove from the foil. Cool on a wire rack.

3 Blitz the icing sugar, peanuts, and cinnamon in a food processor until powdered, then sift over the filo "crisps" while still hot.

4 Serve the "crisps" spilling out of the "packets".

Peanut butter and jelly "sandwich"

Ingredients

For the cake
75g (2½oz) unsalted butter

50g (1¾oz) smooth peanut butter

100g (3½oz) caster sugar

5 tbsp crème fraîche

2 eggs

100g (3½oz) self-raising flour

For the banana butter
3 very ripe bananas, peeled and roughly chopped

50g (1¾oz) unsalted butter

100g (3½oz) caster sugar

freshly grated nutmeg, to taste

For the strawberry jelly
120ml (4fl oz) German wheat beer

250g (9oz) strawberries, hulled, and quartered

125g (4½oz) caster sugar

1 tsp agar-agar flakes

Method

1 For the cake, preheat the oven to 180°C (350°F/ Gas 4). Grease and line a 25 x 15cm (10 x 6in) non-stick baking tin.

2 Cream the butter together with the peanut butter, sugar, and crème fraîche until smooth and creamy. Gradually add the eggs and mix until smooth. Fold in the flour, pour into the lined tin, and bake for 20–25 minutes until golden. Transfer to a wire rack and leave to cool completely.

3 Once cool, trim the edges of the cake, then cut into four 10 x 6cm (4 x 2½in) rectangles. Cut each piece diagonally through the middle to make 8 triangles. Set aside until needed.

4 For the banana butter, put all the ingredients in a pan and simmer gently for 10 minutes until the bananas are completely soft. Rub the mixture through a sieve and chill until serving.

5 For the strawberry jelly, put all the ingredients in a pan, bring to the boil, and simmer gently until the strawberries are completely soft. Cool to set.

6 Just before serving, spread 4 triangles of cake with the banana butter, add the strawberry jelly, and top with the remaining triangles of cake to make 4 sandwiches.

"Chocolate milk"

Ingredients

250ml (8fl oz) oatmeal stout (e.g. Samuel Smith's or Mackeson's)

50ml (1¾ fl oz) coconut milk

1½ tsp pure vanilla extract

2–3 tsp brewed espresso

Method

1 Put all the ingredients together in a blender and blitz until well blended. Chill in the fridge until ready to serve, then pour into glasses.

Sensational puddings

Mochi sorbet "apple"

Ingredients

For the sorbet
250ml (8fl oz) apple juice

juice of ½ lime

4 tbsp golden syrup

For the mochi
pinch of saffron

2 tbsp caster sugar

4 tbsp beetroot juice

4 tbsp cranberry juice

1 tbsp golden syrup

185g (6½oz) mochiko (Japanese rice flour)

pinch of salt

plain flour, for dusting

25g (scant 1oz) unsalted butter, for frying

Method

1 For the sorbet, mix together the juices and syrup, then churn in an ice-cream machine until set. Transfer to a plastic container with a lid and place in the freezer until serving. Alternatively, place the mixture in a freezerproof container and freeze until mushy. Whisk until the ice crystals are broken up. Return to the freezer and repeat the process twice.

2 For the mochi, grind the saffron together with the caster sugar in a pestle and mortar until powdered. Put in a pan with the juices, 3 tbsp water, and syrup. Heat gently, stirring, until dissolved.

3 While still warm, whisk in the mochiko and salt until a sticky dough is formed. Wrap in cling film and chill for 1 hour until firm.

4 On a well-floured surface, roll out the mochi to 3mm (⅛in) thick, then cut out four 10cm (4in) circles.

5 Melt the butter in a frying pan and fry the discs for 8 minutes, turning often, until golden brown. Remove from the pan, drain on kitchen paper, and leave to cool completely. Serve underneath the sorbet as a platform.

To serve: Arrange a sandwich, apple, and crisps on each of 4 plates. Serve with the "chocolate milk" placed alongside.

How to make a fruit sorbet

To serve 4, heat 100ml (3½fl oz) water and 50g (1¾oz) sugar gently in a pan until sugar dissolves. Boil to form a syrup. Stir syrup into 500ml (16fl oz) fruit juice in a bowl. Churn in an ice cream maker until set. Alternatively, freeze until mushy. Whisk, then freeze again until frozen. Repeat twice.

Masala tea ice cream and Sauternes-poached pear with a chocolate truffle

Dhruv Baker @ champion

Preparation time 1 hour 20 minutes   **Cooking time** 40 minutes   **Serves 4**

Ingredients

For the masala

6 black peppercorns

5 cloves

5 green cardamom pods

2 cinnamon sticks

1 tsp dried ginger

½ tsp finely grated nutmeg

For the ice cream

250ml (8fl oz) whole milk

1 tsp Ceylon tea leaves

250ml (8fl oz) double cream

4 egg yolks

50g (1¾oz) caster sugar

For the pears

4 Comice pears, peeled and cored but stalks left intact

400ml (14fl oz) Sauternes dessert wine

1 vanilla pod, split

1 star anise

2 cinnamon sticks

For the truffles

35g (1¼oz) dark chocolate (at least 90% cocoa solids)

50g (1¾oz) dark chocolate (75% cocoa solids)

25g (scant 1oz) caster sugar

85ml (3fl oz) double cream

2–3 tbsp brandy

cocoa powder, for dusting

To decorate

1 sheet gold leaf (optional)

Sensational puddings

Method

1 For the masala, put the spices into a dry frying pan and roast over medium heat for 2 minutes, or until they begin to release their aromas. Tip into a pestle and pound with a mortar or, if you have one, grind to a powder in a spice machine. Sift into a bowl and set aside.

2 To make the ice cream, heat the milk with the tea leaves and ½ tsp of the masala mixture in a saucepan. Gradually bring to the boil. Stir in the cream and bring to a simmer for 1 minute. Leave to cool, then chill.

3 Whisk the egg yolks and sugar until pale. Strain the masala tea milk and gradually stir about a third into the egg yolks. Pour in the remainder and transfer to a pan. Stirring continuously, cook over low heat until the custard coats the back of a spoon. Take the pan off the heat and leave until cold. Churn in an ice-cream maker and freeze. Alternativley, pour the cold custard into a freezeproof container and freeze until mushy. Turn out into a cold bowl and beat to break up the ice crystals. Return to the container and freeze again. Repeat the freezing and whisking again once more, then leave in the freezer until ready to serve.

4 For the pears, cut a thin slice from the base of each pear so they sit evenly. Place the wine, vanilla pod, and spices in a pan with 300ml (10fl oz) water and bring to the boil. Add the pears, reduce the heat, and poach gently for 30 minutes, or until very soft. Check after 20 minutes that the pears are not collapsing. Allow to cool, then chill.

5 For the truffles, put all the ingredients, except the cocoa powder, and adding brandy to taste, into a bowl set over a pan of simmering water and allow to melt. Stir gently, then leave until cold enough to mould. Using 2 spoons or your hands, shape truffles, dust with cocoa powder, and set aside.

6 Remove the ice cream from the freezer about 15 minutes before serving. Lift the pears from their cooking liquid. Strain this liquid into a clean pan and reduce until syrupy.

7 To serve, sit 1 pear on each of 4 plates together with a truffle and a quenelle of ice cream. Decorate the pear with a little gold leaf (if using) and dust on some extra cocoa powder.

Apricot and cardamom trifle

Jenny Shanks @ quarter-finalist

Preparation time 45 minutes   **Cooking time** 50 minutes   **Serves 4**

Ingredients

150g (5½oz) caster sugar

juice of ½ lemon

5 apricots, halved and stoned

4 trifle sponges

4 tbsp apricot conserve

100g (3½ oz) amaretti biscuits

60ml (2fl oz) apricot brandy

1 tbsp toasted flaked almonds

150ml (5fl oz) double cream

100ml (3½fl oz) milk

3 cardamom pods, crushed

3 medium egg yolks

150ml (5fl oz) whipping cream

50g (1¾ oz) pomegranate seeds

25g (scant 1oz) unsalted pistachio nuts, chopped

Method →

Method

1 In a medium saucepan, heat 200ml (7fl oz) water with 100g (3½oz) of the caster sugar and the lemon juice. Bring to a simmer, then add the apricots and poach until just tender but still retaining their shape. Remove from the syrup and set aside to cool. Reduce the syrup by about two-thirds and set aside.

2 Split the trifle sponges horizontally and spread over the apricot conserve and sandwich together. Arrange the trifle sponges in the base of a glass trifle bowl. Then break up the amaretti biscuits over the top. Pour 3 tbsp of the apricot brandy and 100ml (3½fl oz) of the reduced poaching liquor over them and scatter with the toasted almonds and then the cooled apricot halves. Cover and chill overnight.

3 To make the custard, pour the double cream and milk into a small saucepan, add the cardamom pods and bring to just below boiling point. Remove from the heat and allow to infuse for 20–30 minutes, then remove the cardamom. Whisk the egg yolks with the remaining caster sugar then gradually pour into the infused cream and milk, whisking as you do so. Over a low heat, gently cook the custard until it is thick, stirring frequently – make sure it does not boil or it will resemble scrambled eggs. Set aside to cool before pouring over the apricots.

4 Finally, whip the whipping cream to soft peaks, gradually adding the remaining apricot brandy at the end, and spoon on top of the custard. Scatter with the pomegranate seeds and pistachio nuts to garnish.

Chocolate and banana brûlée with brioche soldiers

David Coulson @ **Professionals finalist**

Preparation time 15 minutes   **Cooking time** 15 minutes   **Serves 4**

Ingredients

360ml (12fl oz) double cream

120ml (4fl oz) whole milk

3 ripe bananas, mashed

100g (3½oz) dark chocolate, broken into chunks

1 vanilla pod, split

3 tbsp Tia Maria

6 large eggs, yolks only

75g (2½oz) caster sugar, plus extra for the brûlée

2 slices of brioche

Method

1 Place the cream, milk, bananas, chocolate, and vanilla pod in a pan and bring just to the boil. Take off the heat, add the Tia Maria and leave to infuse for at least 30 minutes.

2 In a bowl, whisk together the egg yolks and sugar. Stir in the cream mixture then return to the pan and cook, stirring constantly, until it coats the back of a spoon. Strain through a sieve and pour into 4 ramekins. Leave to set in the fridge for at least 8 hours.

3 When nearly ready to serve, preheat the oven to 180°C (350°F/Gas 4). Cut the brioche into soldier shapes and dust with sugar. Bake for 5 minutes until golden.

4 Remove the ramekins from the fridge. Sprinkle the top of each with a thin, even layer of sugar and apply a blow torch to create the brûlée top, before serving on plates with the brioche soldiers.

Ras malai

Daksha Mistry @ finalist

Preparation time 10 minutes   **Cooking time** 1 hour 30 minutes   **Serves 4**

Ingredients

For the milk sauce
750ml (1¼ pints) whole milk

1 tsp rosewater

175g (6oz) caster sugar

200g can condensed milk

½ tsp cardamom powder

2–3 saffron strands

For the curds
1.2 litres (2 pints) whole milk

4 tbsp lemon juice

For the syrup
225g (8oz) caster sugar

2–3 saffron strands

To serve
3 tbsp toasted flaked almonds

3 tbsp chopped pistachios

Method →

Method

1 To make the milk sauce, gently boil the milk in a heavy pan with the rest of the ingredients for 1 hour, or until reduced by half and thickened slightly. Remove from the heat, leave to cool, and put in the fridge until needed.

2 For the curds, gently bring the milk to the boil and add the lemon juice. Let it boil, but do not stir, until you see curds forming. Then remove it from the heat. Stir gently and pass it through muslin. Gather the muslin together at the top and rinse the curds contained in the muslin under cold water to remove any sourness. Place the curds in their muslin in a colander over a bowl and leave to drain for up to 2 hours. Then once more gather together the muslin at the top and squeeze to press out any excess water.

3 Tip the curds into a bowl and, with a damp hand, form the curds into a dough and knead for 3–4 minutes until they come together into a ball. Pull off a small golf-ball sized piece and knead in the palms of your hands. Flatten it and shape into a disc. Make 12 discs and set aside.

4 To make the syrup, put 500ml (16fl oz) water together with the sugar and saffron into a wide saucepan and bring to the boil.

5 Put 4–5 curd discs into the syrup and cook for 5 minutes until set. Remove with a slotted spoon and drop them into the cooled milk sauce. Repeat to cook the rest of the curd discs. Cover and chill for at least 4 hours.

6 To serve, spoon the pudding into shallow bowls and serve with the toasted almonds and a few pistachios scattered over.

Tangerine soufflé

Helen Cristofoli @ quarter-finalist
Preparation time 20 minutes   **Cooking time** 13minutes   **Serves 4**

Ingredients

1 tbsp tangerine marmalade

2 tbsp fresh tangerine or orange juice

1 tbsp Cointreau

2 large eggs, whites only

2 tbsp caster sugar

4 amaretti biscuits, to serve

Method

1 Preheat the oven to 180ºC (350ºF/Gas 4). Butter 4 individual soufflé or ramekin dishes and dust thoroughly with caster sugar.

2 Put the marmalade in a pan with the tangerine or orange juice and Cointreau. Bring to the boil. Off the heat, stir to break down and melt the marmalade. Transfer to a saucer and leave to cool. Do not allow it to set.

3 Whisk the egg whites in a mixing bowl until stiff. Lightly fold in the caster sugar and the cooled tangerine mixture.

4 Spoon immediately into the prepared soufflé dishes, piling it high like a pyramid, then run a finger round the inside rim of each one.

5 Put the soufflé dishes on a baking tray. Bake in the oven for 8–13 minutes until risen and golden brown on top.

6 Serve immediately on small plates with amaretti biscuits.

Rhubarb crumble tart with syllabub and rhubarb syrup

Dick Strawbridge ⓜ **Celebrity** finalist

Preparation time 45 minutes   **Cooking time** 1 hour   **Serves 4**

Ingredients

225g (8oz) sugar, plus 3 tbsp

450g (1lb) rhubarb, cut into 1cm (½in) pieces

2 pieces of stem ginger, finely sliced

For the nut crust

50g (1¾oz) blanched hazelnuts, toasted

25g (scant 1oz) icing sugar

100g (3½oz) plain flour

50g (1¾oz) butter

½ tsp vanilla extract

1 small egg, beaten

For the crumble topping

100g (3½oz) plain flour

50g (1¾oz) butter

25g (scant 1oz) demerara sugar

finely grated zest of 1 lemon

For the syllabub

300ml (10fl oz) double cream

1–2 tbsp ginger wine or brandy

2 tbsp ginger syrup from the stem ginger jar

Method

1 First make a syrup by dissolving the 225g (8oz) sugar in a saucepan with 300ml (10fl oz) boiling water. Preheat the oven to 180°C (350°F/Gas 4). Add half the rhubarb to the syrup, bring to the boil, then leave until completely cold. Strain the cold rhubarb syrup into a jug and chill. Put remaining rhubarb in an ovenproof dish and sprinkle over 3 tbsp of sugar. Bake in the oven for about 20 minutes or until softened. Allow to cool, then drain and mix with the slices of stem ginger, reserving 8 slices for decoration.

2 For the nut crust, put the nuts and sugar in a food processor and mix briefly to combine. Add the remaining ingredients except the egg and mix on pulse setting. With the machine running, gradually pour in the egg and mix to form a ball. Wrap in cling film and chill for 30 minutes. Divide into 4 equal pieces and press each into the base of a 10cm (4in) tart tins. Chill for 10 minutes.

3 Increase the oven heat to 190°C (375°G/Gas 5). Bake the tart cases for about 8–10 minutes or until pale golden. Meanwhile, make the crumble. Put all the ingredients in a food processor and mix briefly to form crumbs. Spread out on a baking sheet and bake for 8–10 minutes,or until pale golden. Stir the crumble halfway through cooking.

4 Divide the baked rhubarb between the tart cases and top with the crumble. Return to the oven and bake for 10 minutes or until heated through.

5 For the syllabub, put the cream, wine, and ginger syrup into a bowl and whisk to form soft peaks. Chill for 10 minutes.

6 Serve the tarts warm with the syllabub, decorated with the reserved slices of ginger. Place a cup of pink rhubarb syrup alongside.

Spiced plum crumble

Stacie Stewart @ semi-finalist

Preparation time 25 minutes   **Cooking time** 50minutes   **Serves 4**

Ingredients

50g (1¾oz) plain flour

50g (1¾oz) demerara sugar

75g (2½oz) butter, softened

50g (1¾oz) ground almonds

50g (1¾oz) small oats

5–6 dark plums, halved and stoned

1 vanilla pod

1½ tbsp caster sugar

1 star anise

generous grating of nutmeg

1 cinnamon stick

3 tbsp red wine

2 tbsp golden syrup

250g tub mascarpone cream

Method

1 Preheat the oven to 190°C (375°F/Gas 5). For the crumble topping, rub the flour, demerara sugar, 50g (1¾oz) of the butter, and almonds together until the mixture resembles breadcrumbs, then mix in the oats.

2 Fry the plums in a saucepan in the remaining butter until soft. Halve the vanilla pod and reserve the seeds. Add the caster sugar, 1½ tbsp of water, spices, vanilla pod, and half the seeds, and stir. Add the wine and syrup, and reduce until the plums are slightly soft.

3 Drain the plums, discarding the cinnamon stick and star anise, and reduce the sauce until syrupy. Put the plums in an ovenproof dish, spread the crumble evenly on top, and bake for 30–35 minutes, or until the crumble is crisp and golden. Serve with the mascarpone cream, mixed with the rest of the vanilla seeds.

Warm treacle tart with pecan brittle and vanilla ice cream

Nick Pickard @ **Celebrity finalist**

Preparation time 30 minutes   **Cooking time** 1 hour   **Serves 8**

Ingredients

For the pastry
225g (8oz) plain flour

pinch of salt

25g (scant 1oz) caster sugar

115g (4oz) very cold unsalted butter, diced

For the ice cream
500ml (16fl oz) double cream

2 vanilla pods, spit and seeds scraped out

3 egg yolks

75g (2½oz) caster sugar

For the filling
350g (12oz) golden syrup

1 heaped tbsp black treacle

finely grated zest and juice of 1 lemon

4 eggs, beaten

25g (scant 1oz) fresh breadcrumbs

For the brittle
100g (3½oz) caster sugar

25g (scant 1oz) pecan nuts, roughly chopped

Method

1 Preheat the oven to 180°C (350°F/Gas 4). To make the pastry, place the ingredients in a food processor. Blitz until resembling breadcrumbs. With the food processor running, slowly add 150ml (5fl oz) water until the mixture forms a ball. Knead gently until smooth. Wrap in cling film, and rest in the fridge for 30 minutes.

2 Roll out the pastry thinly and use to line a 23cm (9in) tart tin, set on a baking tray, leaving the edges folded over the sides of the tin. Rest again in the fridge for 30 minutes. Line with baking parchment and fill with baking beans. Trim the edges. Bake for 12 minutes. Remove the beans and parchment. Bake a further for 5 minutes to dry out. Set aside in tin.

3 For the ice cream, bring the cream with the split vanilla pod and seeds to the boil, then set aside for 2 minutes. Remove the pod. Whisk the eggs and sugar until thick and pale. Add the cream, whisking all the time. Let it cool. Pour into an ice-cream machine and churn until set. Transfer to a plastic container with a lid and store in the freezer until serving. Alternatively, pour the mixture in a freezerproof container and

How to line a tart tin with pastry

TECHNIQUE

1 Use the rolling pin to gather up the pastry by rolling the pastry halfway over it. Then carefully lift the rest of the pastry circle away from the work surface.

2 Dust off any surplus flour, and gently unroll the pastry circle across the tart tin, making sure that there is plenty of excess pastry to cover the sides of the tin.

freeze until mushy. Whisk until the ice crystals are broken up. Return to the freezer and repeat the process twice.

4 For the tart filling, mix the syrup, treacle, and lemon juice and zest. Whisk in the eggs and breadcrumbs. Pour into the pastry case. Bake for 35–40 minutes until set. Set aside, keep warm.

5 For the brittle, slowly heat the sugar in a small frying pan until golden brown. Add the nuts, mix in, and pour onto a baking tray lined with baking parchment. Leave until hard. Roughly crush.

6 With a warm knife, cut slices of the warm tart and serve on plates with a ball of ice cream with some brittle sprinkled on top.

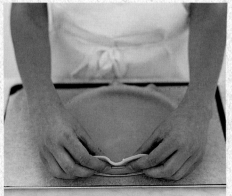 

3 Carefully smooth the pastry from the centre of the circle then, using your thumbs and forefingers, gently press the pastry into the inside edge of the tin and and up the sides.

4 Now use your rolling pin to trim away the excess pastry and give a clean edge, by pressing the rolling pin over the top of the tart ring to cut away the pastry hanging over the top.

Index

Acknowledgments

Shine TV and Endemol Shine Group would like to thank:
Frances Adams, David Ambler, Alice Bernardi, Martin Buckett, Claire Burton, Bev Comboy, Kerisa Edwards, Jessica Hannan, Ozen Kazim, Angela Loftus, Lou Plank, Lyndsey Posner, Franc Roddam, John Torode, and Gregg Wallace.

MasterChef alumni whose recipes and quotes are reproduced in this book:
Tim Anderson, Annie Assheton, Dhruv Baker, Natalie Brenner, Susie Carter, Alice Churchill, David Coulson, Helen Cristofoli, Lisa Faulkner, Andrew Fletcher, Chris Gates, Ruth Goodman, Steve Groves, Christine Hamiliton, Gary Heath, Jackie Kearney, Tim Kinnaird, Hannah Miles, Daksha Mistry, Perveen Nekoo, Wendi Peters, Nick PIckard, Alex Rushmer, Dennice Russell, Nadia Sawalha, Jenny Shanks, Stacie Stewart, Dick Strawbridge, Alice Taylor, Rachel Thompson, Midge Ure, Kirsty Wark, Gillian Wylie, and Adam Young.

Dorling Kindersley would like to thank:
Libby Brown and Amy Slack for editorial assistance, Philippa Nash for design assistance, and Vanessa Bird for indexing.

Senior Editor Cécile Landau
Senior Art Editor Alison Shackleton
Managing Editor Stephanie Farrow
Managing Art Editor Christine Keilty
Jacket Designer Steven Marsden
Producer, Pre-Production Robert Dunn
Producer Stephanie McConnell
Special Sales Creative Project Manager
Alison Donovan
Art Director Maxine Pedliham
Publisher Mary-Clare Jerram

First published in Great Britain in 2018 by
Dorling Kindersley Limited, 80 Strand, London, WC2R 0RL
A Penguin Random House Company

Material previous published in:
The MasterChef Cookbook (2010), MasterChef At Home (2011),
MasterChef Kitchen Bible (2011),
and MasterChef Everyday (2012)

10 9 8 7 6 5 4 3 2 1
001—309620—Feb/2018

A CIP catalogue record for this book is available
from the British Library.
ISBN 978-0-2413-3337-2

Copyright © 2018 Dorling Kindersley Limited
MasterChef recipes and images copyright © 2018
Shine TV Limited

MasterChef is based on a format by Franc Roddam and is
produced by Shine TV in association with Ziji Productions
Limited for the BBC.

MasterChef
www.masterchef.com

Printed and bound in China

A WORLD OF IDEAS:
SEE ALL THERE IS TO KNOW
www.dk.com

By Loyalty Bound

By Loyalty Bound

Elizabeth Ashworth

PEN & SWORD
FICTION

First published in Great Britain in 2013 by
CLAYMORE PRESS
An imprint of
Pen & Sword Books Ltd
47 Church Street
Barnsley
South Yorkshire
S70 2AS

ISBN 9781781593707

A CIP catalogue record for this book is
available from the British Library

Printed and bound in England
by CPI Group (UK) Ltd, Croydon, CRO 4YY

Pen & Sword Books Ltd incorporates the Imprints of Claymore Press, Pen & Sword Aviation,
Pen & Sword Family History, Pen & Sword Maritime, Pen & Sword Military, Wharncliffe
Local History, Pen & Sword Select, Pen & Sword Military Classics, Leo Cooper, Remember
When, Seaforth Publishing and Frontline Publishing

For a complete list of Pen & Sword titles please contact
PEN & SWORD BOOKS LIMITED
47 Church Street, Barnsley, South Yorkshire, S70 2AS, England
E-mail: enquiries@pen-and-sword.co.uk
Website: www.pen-and-sword.co.uk

Acknowledgements

I would like to thank the members of the history board at C19 for all the knowledge they shared with me during my research for this novel. I also want to thank Damaris who suggested the book's title. It was inspired and very appropriate.

PART ONE
1470 ~ 1472

Chapter One
March 1470

Anne Harrington paused, mid-stitch, at the sound of hooves on the stone bridge that crossed the river. Laying her work aside she hurried to the narrow window that overlooked the approach to Hornby Castle. She shielded her eyes against the March sun, which hung low in the sky, and watched as the group of horsemen came nearer.

"Who is it?" asked her sister, Izzie, coming to stand beside her, her breath unsteady against Anne's cheek.

"I can't see. Surely Uncle James would have told us if someone was expected?"

No one came to Hornby uninvited, except the Stanleys, and Anne and her sister lived in constant fear of the abduction and forced marriage that would follow any breach of the fortifications. Their uncle had kept them safe so far, but Anne feared that it was only a matter of time before Lord Stanley forced them to go with him.

She felt her heartbeat quicken as she watched. The men and horses were clearer now, yet the emblem on the unfurled banner that was snapping in the sharp wind was still indistinguishable to her.

"Who has the badge of a white boar?" asked Izzie.

"A white boar? I don't know. But at least it isn't the eagle's claw that you see," said Anne, though she didn't find much reassurance in her own words. Any stranger was a potential enemy in this remote northern stronghold. She watched as the riders reached the gatehouse and guards stepped forward, sun reflecting off drawn swords and polished armour. Then a figure ran up the slope towards the gate of the inner bailey and disappeared from view. Moments later there was a shout of consent.

"They're raising the portcullis!" said Anne as the creaking and groaning of the mechanism drifted upwards and a flock of rooks flew up in alarm from the woodland. "Uncle James must know who it is. Do you think we should go down?"

"Of course," said Izzie. "How else will we discover who has come?"

"They must be Yorkists," said Anne as she followed her sister down the dark winding stairs. Then she hesitated as they reached the floor below. "Wait!" she called. She grabbed at the trailing sleeve of her sister's gown as Izzie lifted the latch on the heavy door that opened onto the steps down to the bailey.

"Let's watch from here – until we are sure it's safe," she said, pulling her sister to where they could peep down through a slit in the castle wall, through a gap designed for firing arrows but which equally fitted the purpose of observing people below.

As they peered down, pushing against each other to try to get a better view, Anne saw guards pull back the huge beam of wood that held the doors closed and, as they swung open, she saw Uncle James hurry down the wooden steps from the hall, pulling his best fur lined coat straight as he greeted the visitors.

"Welcome to Hornby, Your Grace!" he said, his voice carrying as it echoed off the surrounding walls.

"Who is it?" asked Izzie again.

"Shush!" scolded Anne. "I'm trying to hear, and to see if you'd move out of the way!"

She elbowed her sister again to watch the man her uncle was greeting. He dismounted agilely from his huge grey stallion and patted its steaming, muscular neck. He was dark haired and looked young, not much older than herself she thought, and not particularly tall, though his shoulders looked broad enough underneath his armour. And as she studied him he glanced up in her direction, as if he was aware of being watched, and she drew back with a sharp intake of breath.

Her movement allowed Izzie to take her place and Anne's view was blocked by her sister's head, Izzie's thick brown braids bouncing against her shoulders in excitement.

"I don't recognise him," she said.

"Come away," said Anne, pulling at her sister's arm again, embarrassed that they had been caught spying. "We will soon discover who he is."

"Well Uncle James is treating him with too much respect for him to be a Stanley. Do you think he has come from the king?"

"Perhaps," said Anne. The voices faded to a murmur as the men went inside, leaving only the gentle clip-clop of the horses being led away to the stables. "Now that the rebellion has been put down and Warwick revealed as a traitor the king may have changed his mind about our inheritance."

"You sound as if you would be pleased if we were robbed of what is rightfully ours!" replied Izzie and Anne saw the blaze of defiance in her eyes. She knew that her younger sister was finding it hard to accept what was virtually imprisonment by their uncle and that at thirteen years old she was on the brink of both womanhood and a rebellion of her own. "This castle and its estates are rightly ours," she said, waving an arm around to indicate the nearby villages of Hornby and Melling. "Why should we be forced to give them up?"

Anne sighed. "You know well enough that the control of our wealth and even of ourselves belongs not to us but to our guardian. If we no longer owned these lands then Lord Stanley would have no interest in us and would leave us in peace."

"Stanley," spat Izzie as if the name was a sour plum. "He can't force us to marry. A woman cannot be married without giving her consent."

"I doubt we would have that choice if he ever broke through these walls," said Anne, running her slender fingers over the dark stone that was all that protected them from being carried from their home. "If the king changes his mind and gives the castle to Uncle James at least it will remain in the family.

Stanley wouldn't want our guardianship if he had nothing to gain from it, and then we would be free to accept a husband of our uncle's choosing. Our ownership of Hornby brings us nothing but trouble and grief."

"But it is rightfully ours!"

"You are so naive!" burst out Anne, tired of the way in which this argument always led them in circles. She often thought that Izzie would never grow up and see the truth – that women were always at the mercy of greedy men and that wealthy women were the most attractive.

"And you're so feeble!" answered Izzie as she pulled open the door that led down to the bailey.

"Where are you going?" asked Anne as her sister lifted her skirts.

"To find out who our visitor is. Coming?"

"No," said Anne, although immediately she'd refused she regretted it. She was eager to know who the dark haired man was and it was only her squabble with her sister that meant she would now have to wait until suppertime to find out.

She climbed back to the chamber in the octagonal tower where she and Izzie spent much of their time and the castle settled back into its brooding defiance, locked down and barricaded against all comers. It was what she had become used to. She had no reliable memories of the time before the deaths of her father and grandfather, just half-remembered glimpses of days of laughter and sunshine and happiness when she had felt safe. She had only been five years old when her life had changed irrevocably and for the last ten years had lived here under the care of her uncle as the arguments raged around her about the Harrington inheritance.

She watched the cold east wind toss the branches of the trees that would soon be bursting into leaf. She would be fifteen soon and lately she had found herself thinking more and more about what her future held. Although Lord Stanley had already tried and failed to take possession of the castle, she knew that he would not give up. She would either be forced into a marriage she did not desire or she would remain locked in this tower for the rest of her life. Neither was a prospect she relished. She listened to the rooks quarrelling over their nest sites and she felt a gnawing desire to know what it would be like to be married to a man. And as she considered it she found herself thinking about their visitor. She remembered the way he had glanced up at her. There had been something about his face that made her stomach flutter as it sometimes did when she heard the guards running up the stone steps to the battlements in response to the alarm call. Yet this was a different kind of fear – a fear that was not entirely unpleasant.

As the bell in the chapel chimed the hour Anne walked down to supper. She could hear a buzz of excited conversation coming from the hall and when she went in she saw that careful preparations had been made. Extra braziers were well alight and the room was uncharacteristically warm, if a little smoky. The best table linen and cups had been laid out with precision and there were delicious aromas rising from the kitchen. Uncle James had plundered the stores for the best of what Hornby had to offer and Anne was curious to know who it was that deserved such a lavish welcome.

Their guest was in conversation with her uncle and, as she approached them, both men stopped speaking and looked at her.

"Your Grace," said her uncle, "this is my niece, the lady Anne."

Anne made a slight reverence, finding it difficult to wrench her gaze away from the blue eyes that openly assessed her. "Anne, this is Richard, Duke of Gloucester."

"Lady Anne," he said in a voice that was deeper than she expected. He gave a formal bow though his eyes held hers and didn't falter until she looked away – a blush burning her face. When she glanced back his expression was a mixture of amusement and something else that she couldn't quite define. There was an aura about him that was almost tangible.

"Shall we eat?" asked Uncle James, indicating that his guest should precede him to the top table and that Anne should sit beside him. She closed her eyes and clasped her hands in prayer as the grace was said and then, as the musicians began to play, the servants brought myriad dishes to the table – salted mutton and venison pasties, tarts filled with dried fruit and nuts. The supply of food and drink seemed endless and Anne wondered how her uncle had managed it.

After ensuring that her trencher was filled from the dishes of her choice, the duke turned his attention to his own food. He sliced his meat with a sharp, jewelled knife drawn from the sheath on his belt and ate eagerly.

"Forgive my lack of attention to you, my lady," he said after a few minutes. "I fear my hunger has overcome my good manners."

"There is nothing to forgive, Your Grace. I am pleased to see a guest who is so appreciative of my uncle's hospitality. You must have had a long ride?"

"Long and difficult."

"And you are on your way to join the king, at York?" He frowned slightly at her words. "Forgive me. I did not mean to pry..."

"As you said, there is nothing to forgive," he replied. "No. I will not be joining the king at York. I mean to remain here."

"At Hornby?" she asked.

"You sound surprised."

"I must confess I am. We do not often receive visitors – well not of the welcome sort," she added.

"I'm pleased you count me as welcome. As for the unwelcome I presume you speak of Lord Stanley," he said, nodding permission to a servant to pour more wine into his cup. Anne watched him as he raised it to his lips and sipped. She was unsure what he knew of the dispute between her uncles and the Stanleys, but she could offer no other explanation for his coming.

He turned his vivid blue eyes on her again. There was a haughtiness about them that she had not noticed before. "Lord Stanley and I do not agree on many things," he said, "one of them being your inheritance." He hesitated as he replaced the cup with care on the bleached white cloth before continuing. "If my views cause you any offence, my lady, I can only apologise."

"You cause me no offence," she assured him.

"But you may not be aware that I have raised this matter with the king. I support the claim of your uncles to the Harrington inheritance. It seems to me only fair that the loyalty of your father and grandfather should not result in the loss of the family's lands to Stanley. If that makes you dislike me then I am sorry."

"I have no thought of disliking you!" she assured him, troubled that his earlier friendliness had been replaced by this cold tone.

"I would expect you to dislike a man who thinks your land and wealth should be taken from you."

Anne shook her head slightly. "The inheritance makes me a prize to be awarded to a guardian of the king's choosing. It is a fortune that does me no favours," she said. "And I am not sure that my father would have wanted me and my sister to be left so vulnerable. I doubt it was his intention that Hornby should have passed to two children so young. He would have realised what trouble it would bring."

As she spoke she realised that she was quoting words that her uncles, James and Robert, had repeated to her since she was old enough to comprehend them.

The duke nodded as she spoke. "I think you are right," he said, "and that you are wise to see the reason in it. Had things been different at Wakefield and your father had died before your grandfather then Hornby would have passed to your uncle without question. It seems to me a disservice to your family that the king chooses to award your guardianship to Lord Stanley. The man is an opportunist who only wants Hornby to add to his power across Lancashire, which is already too widespread. Your welfare is not his concern, Lady Anne, and he will only seek to use you. I will do my utmost to make my brother see reason and to ensure that justice is done and that you are kept from Stanley's control."

"Thank you, Your Grace," she said as his face softened and he raised his cup to drink. "You are very kind," she added as her imagination conjured images of St George, that gallant and brave knight who rode and fought the fearsome dragon to rescue the maiden who was held captive.

Anne did not remember much about her father, but she did remember the day, not long after her fifth birthday, when muddied and exhausted riders had arrived at Hornby Castle with their faces white from terror and exhaustion. She remembered how the men had crowded into the hall and spoken with hushed voices and how her mother had fallen to her knees and broken the silence by wailing and crying and calling on the name of the Lord God to save them all from the wickedness of such evil men.

It wasn't until Anne was much older that the full tragedy and horror of that day had been revealed to her. Her grandfather, Sir Thomas Harrington, and her father, John, had both died at Wakefield fighting an army of rebel Lancastrians who were incensed at parliament's decision to name the Duke of York as the heir to the throne. Led by the Duke of Somerset they supported the exiled queen Margaret of Anjou and were determined that the throne would pass to her son, Prince Edward.

"It isn't as if the boy is Henry's son anyway," Anne's mother had commented as she told the story to her daughters. "You tell me how a man who can neither move nor speak can father a child?"

Anne remembered how she had squirmed at her mother's words when her younger sister had asked why such a man couldn't be a father. Their mother had ignored the question and gone on with the story. "I wouldn't be surprised to see that the prince carries the features of Somerset," she had told them, and although Anne hadn't understood what her mother meant at the time she now knew that it was common gossip that the former queen and the Duke of Somerset were lovers.

Her mother remained bitter about what happened that day at Wakefield. "The Lancastrians broke the Christmas truce," she said. "But the Duke of York was impetuous. He should never have left Sandal Castle to fight with so few men, even if their supplies were dangerously low. He should have waited until he had an army strong enough to defeat them. Then your father and your grandfather would still be with us." She always began to cry at this point as she told the story. "They cut the head from your grandfather's body and stuck it up on a spike on Micklegate Bar," she wept. "At least your father was spared that indignity."

Anne was in the tower next morning when the door creaked open and her sister came in and sat down by the fire. Izzie picked up her embroidery, stared at it for a moment, then put it down again before beginning to speak. "The soldiers are taking up positions on the outer wall and I have heard that the Stanley army is not far away."

"Stanley is never far away," remarked Anne. "But we are safe enough if we remain in the castle." She caught the expression of guilt on Izzie's face. "You haven't been out to the village, have you?" she asked her sister. She knew that Izzie didn't always take her own safety seriously and was in the habit of putting on an old cloak and slipping past the guards, especially on a market day when many people passed to and fro.

Her sister's face coloured a little. "It's so dull in here," she complained. "Surely no harm can come to me in Hornby?"

"Izzie! This is no game. We are not confined here as a punishment, but to keep us safe."

"But it is boring!" she said. "I am going out of my mind with nothing to do but this... needlework!" She picked up her embroidery and threw it angrily onto the fire. Anne watched in astonishment as the flames first singed the edges and then took hold, consuming the painstaking stitching that her sister had taken the long winter months to complete. And as she watched it burn Izzie's expression changed to one of regret and Anne had to restrain her as she reached towards the hearth to try to save what small fragments were left.

"Let it burn," she said as the tears flowed down her sister's cheeks. "You cannot save it now."

"What will happen to us?" she sobbed. "The Duke of Gloucester has come to rob us of our inheritance."

"Hush, hush," comforted Anne with her arms around her sister. She wished that their mother was there to help and advise them. They rarely saw her since her new husband, Sir Edmund Sutton, had taken her away to his family home at Dudley. And although their mother had pleaded with Uncle James to allow her daughters to go with her, he was adamant that Anne and Elizabeth could never be safe except at Hornby.

"The Duke of Gloucester had a stand-off with some of Stanley's men yesterday," Izzie said, wiping her cheeks on a scrap of linen as she became calmer. "There was some fighting at a crossing point on the Ribble. The Stanleys are planning a siege," she said. "They are bringing up a siege machine and a huge battering ram and there is rumour of a cannon too."

Anne went to the window and stared down the valley to the south. For the moment it looked peaceful enough under the clear skies.

"Who has told you all this?" she asked as she noticed women and children making their way across the castle bailey towards the keep, their arms filled with bundles.

"It is the talk of the village. People have been told to take shelter."

Anne crossed the room quickly. "I must speak to Uncle James," she said, "and discover what is happening."

Outside the door she almost bumped into two guards who were climbing up the twisting steps to the battlements, carrying a crate of arrows between them.

"Sorry, m'lady," they muttered as she stepped back to allow them to pass.

She hurried down to where her Aunt Joan, with baby William on her hip, was ushering the crowd of women and children towards the kitchens and the cellars beneath the hall.

"Is it true?" she asked. "Are the Stanleys coming?"

"So we've been told," she said. "Go back to your chamber – and stay away from the windows."

"Let me help. Tell me what to do," she asked.

"Anne!" The sound of her uncle's voice rang across the courtyard. "Go back to your chamber!"

"Let me help. Let me do something," she pleaded.

"Go back to your chamber. I need to know that you're safe," he said. "Where is your sister?"

"She's in the tower, but –"

"Then join her," he interrupted.

"But –"

"I think you should do as your uncle tells you." Anne turned at the authoritative voice. The Duke of Gloucester's face was serious and stern. "Come," he said, taking her elbow in his hand, "I will escort you."

If it had been anyone else Anne would have shaken them off, but she allowed herself to be led across to the stairs. The duke followed her up and, as she paused at the top and glanced into the hall where women and children were milling in what looked like complete chaos, she felt his hand enclose her upper arm. "I believe your chamber is in the tower," he said.

She was about to protest that she could go wherever she liked inside the castle, but his eyes quelled her outburst without a word being spoken.

"Is it true that the Stanleys have a cannon?" she asked him as they reached her door.

"Yes," he replied. "I have seen it."

"They won't succeed, will they?" She turned to him for reassurance and was suddenly aware that he was standing very close to her. She watched a moment of hesitation cloud his face.

"I promise I will do everything I can to keep you safe. Come," he said, his upper arm brushing against hers as he reached to open the door for her, "go into your chamber."

Anne went inside and was surprised when he followed her and stood quietly before the hearth.

"What have you been burning?" he asked after a moment, peering at the ashes that still held the aroma of the blackened fabric.

"My sister, Elizabeth, was discontent with her sewing and threw it on the fire," said Anne.

"It was poor sewing anyway," said Izzie from where she was peering out at the scene below.

"Come away from the window," the duke told her and Anne was surprised to see her sister obey him. "The slit may look too narrow for an archer's aim, but a stone from a siege engine can cause much damage and you must stay back from the outer wall if a bombardment begins. In fact I will speak to your uncle about moving you from here. You would be safer in the hall."

Anne was sorry when the door thudded shut behind him and his footfalls faded down the stairs.

"What a very unpleasant person he is," remarked Izzie.

Anne looked at her sister in surprise. "Do you think so?" she said.

"Oh don't tell me you like him," groaned Izzie. "He's insufferable. Who does he think he is, coming here and taking charge of everything? Perhaps he will change his mind about the inheritance now that he has seen you making eyes at him. Perhaps he will ask the king to award him your guardianship instead of Lord Stanley so that he can take you to wife and gain himself another castle into the bargain."

"I very much doubt it. I think the Duke of Gloucester will be seeking a richer heiress than me."

"You wouldn't turn him down though, would you?" persisted Izzie.

"It will not happen, so it is of no matter," replied Anne, annoyed that her sister could read her emotions so well. "We have more immediate concerns. I fear our uncles cannot hold out for ever, even with the support of the Duke of Gloucester."

"I don't want to be taken from here," said Izzie, her mood suddenly changing and her chin trembling as she struggled to control her tears. "I don't want to be married," she said and Anne's heart was wrenched as she saw the frightened little girl inside the hard shell that her sister presented to the world. "I... I feel afraid," she confessed.

Anne put her arms around her sister and rubbed her back as their warm faces pressed together. The familiar scent of the herbs that Izzie used to rinse her hair filled Anne's nostrils as she searched for some words of comfort, but her own fear was too great.

"It will be all right," she said at last, trying to convince herself. But as Izzie pulled away from her there was an unspoken understanding between them that they were vulnerable and there was nothing that they could do. Their fate was to watch and wait and be taken with no more compunction than a chest of silver as the victor's prize.

James Harrington glanced up as the young duke came into the hall. He had been upstairs with Anne and Elizabeth for quite some time and despite being in the throes of locking down Hornby, James had had time to consider the way his niece had looked at the duke as he'd led her away – and the way that the king's young brother had looked at Anne. He saw the obvious attraction that each had for the other and he wondered if it was something to be encouraged.

It had always been assumed that the duke would marry Warwick's younger daughter. But now that Warwick had rebelled there would be no such match and the Duke of Gloucester would be forced to look elsewhere for a bride. A week ago James would not have dared to think that the king's brother would want any form of alliance with the Harrington family, but his unexpected arrival at their gate and his determination to help them defend the castle against Lord Stanley had changed that. Could it be possible, wondered James, for his niece to become a member of the royal family and so link the Harringtons to the Plantagenet dynasty? The problem with that idea, he acknowledged to himself as he nodded in response to a question from one of his men-at-arms, was that Anne was no prize without Hornby.

In the tower chamber, Anne ignored the duke's advice and crossed to the window. The great wooden doors that secured the curtain wall were shut tight, the portcullis lowered and the drawbridge raised. Everyone was watching for an army from the south who would set up camp outside the castle and wait; wait until those inside were left to choose between starvation and surrender. Would her Uncle James concede? Would he allow the castle and his nieces and the inheritance he believed should be his fall into the hands of his enemy? Anne shivered as she realised that he might have no choice. And for herself? Which would she prefer, she asked herself. A slow death from lack of food or the prospect of marriage to an unknown son of the Stanleys?

A flash of sunlight reflecting on metal caught her attention. She thought she saw a movement near the riverbank.

"Men," said Izzie, standing beside her. "They are hidden in the long grass and behind the trees."

"So it will soon begin."

"God damn them!" burst out her sister, then crossed herself in penitence for the oath. But as she turned away Anne saw that Izzie's fear had been replaced once more by a gleam of excitement in her eyes, and she worried that the time would come when she would be unable to protect her.

Balderstone Hall, where Isabella de Balderstone lived with her widowed mother, stood in the fertile valley of the River Ribble. Its dark stone walls were surrounded by trees and in another month it would be almost hidden to the casual observer. As Robert Harrington approached he heard the dogs begin to bark; first one hesitant voice and then a gradual cacophony of sound that brought servants out from the barn and stable block to see who was coming. But Robert sought only one figure and he smiled when he saw Isabella come out of the dairy with a brown cloak pulled around her shoulders as protection against the flakes of snow that were falling from an overcast sky. He forgot his own weariness as she came forward to greet him. Her fair, curly hair was escaping in damp tendrils from beneath her plain linen cap and her smoky grey eyes were filled with both welcome and concern. He took her in his arms and pressed his icy lips to the warmth of her cheek. Each time he saw her he thanked God for his fortune in gaining the permission of her mother to take her as his bride. Her wealth was not spectacular and the estates were shared between her and an older sister, but they would be a welcome addition to his own and for a third son of a family such as the Harringtons she was a good match.

"I did not expect to see you so soon," she told him as they walked towards the manor house.

"But I sent word that you should expect me. Don't tell me that the idle lad never arrived. I paid him well."

"The message came," she reassured him as she helped him take off his coat and gestured for the servant to bring more logs to the hearth. "But I thought that you would have ridden straight to Hornby."

"Why so?" he asked as she spread his coat to dry.

"Then you don't know?"

"I had a missive from the king asking me to rally my men yet again and meet him at York." He stopped to listen as he saw that she had urgent news.

"Lord Stanley has taken an army and weapons to lay siege to Hornby Castle."

"Are you sure? Yes, of course," he added as she began to nod. "You would not have told me otherwise."

He winced at a pain in his leg. The sharp edge of a sword had ripped open his flesh at Lose-Cote Field when he had been a moment too slow to turn his horse. And worse, the wound had been inflicted by a man he had thought of as a friend – a man he had known well during his years at Middleham Castle when they had both served the Earl of Warwick, before he turned traitor. "It seems that Stanley grasps the opportunity to take Hornby whilst he believes we are pre-occupied elsewhere." Robert paused and looked towards the part-shuttered window where he could see the snow beginning to settle on the higher ground. "I hope that my brother has remained at Hornby and not gone to York," he said. "If the castle is left with only a meagre garrison then it may not hold out." He turned back to her with a worried face. "I need to go," he said, reaching for the cloak she had set to dry.

"You cannot go in this," she protested. "You need to eat and rest – and so does your horse. It would be madness to leave in this weather."

Robert saw that she was right. The snowstorm was thickening and flakes like goose down were already blotting out the trees that skirted the moat. His journey would have to wait until at least the morrow.

Anne wakened in the night and thought that she could hear thunder rumbling around the castle walls, but as she sat up and struck a flint to re-light her candle she realised that the sound was of heavy footsteps on the stairs and urgent voices.

"It's the Stanleys," said Izzie with a mixture of fear and anticipation quivering in her voice.

A moment later there was a perfunctory knock on the door and it was pushed open. Uncle James came in carrying a horn lantern.

"Get dressed quickly," he said. "You must go downstairs."

Moments later they were in the hall where Aunt Joan was sitting wide-eyed by a lit brazier with baby William on her lap, and the nurse was soothing their little cousin Peggy who was crying in fear at the huge shadows that flickered across the tapestries on the walls.

"Whatever happens, stay here!" instructed Uncle James as the Duke of Gloucester came in, dressed and armoured. "They mean to take the castle for their own use so they have no reason to either destroy it or burn it to the ground. You are quite safe so long as you stay in the hall," he told them.

The servants brought blankets and mattresses stuffed with flock and, once the children had been lulled to sleep, Anne lay down near the remnants of the log fire in the hearth. In spite of the earlier pandemonium the castle had now fallen eerily silent, as if it and everyone in it were holding their collective breaths, waiting for the first Stanley strike. But the silence remained unbroken and as the night went on Anne drifted into a restless sleep and did not rouse fully until the whispering of the servants bringing breakfast awoke her. She felt a heavy arm lying across her body and saw that her sleeping sister had rolled closer to her for comfort. Izzie looked fragile and pale in the morning light and Anne could see the streaks of tears on her cheeks and heard her mumbling troubled thoughts as she gently moved her arm. Aunt Joan was still sitting in the chair with baby William in her arms and looked as if she had been awake all night; beside her the nurse and Peggy slept on the same mattress.

The servants had brought bread and small beer and were setting it out on a trestle table at the side of the hall. Anne bent to lift the sleeping baby from her aunt's arms so that his mother could go and eat. The breakfast was meagre, she noticed. An order had been given for the strict rationing of food and she wondered how long the supplies they had would last.

She knew that during the winter many of the barrels of salted meat and fish and sacks of grain had been used up and that the absence of her uncles and their men to fight with the king against Warwick's rebellion meant there had been little chance for the cellars to be properly re-stocked. The Stanleys could bring continuous supplies from their land to the south. Once Hornby's food had gone they would be beaten.

Anne rocked the restless baby against her shoulder and wondered if it would be better to give up now. The end seemed inevitable and this siege could only extend the agony, not only for them but for the children. She kissed the soft head of her small nephew as she cradled him. All this might be his one day if her uncle could reclaim it, and as the baby hiccupped and sighed in her arms she resolved that she would do all she could to keep this land for its rightful owners. Her own possession of it was not as important to her as the Harrington name.

Anne heard someone running up the outer steps from the bailey and the Duke of Gloucester strode into the hall. He must have been awake all night yet his eyes and face were as bright and alert as a man who had just wakened from a long rest. His thin, stern face turned to a smile at the sight of her rocking the baby in her arms.

"Did you manage to sleep?" he asked.

"A little, though I think my aunt has been awake all night. It seems quiet," she added.

"They are biding their time. They think themselves in the stronger position." He frowned as he glanced around the hall, his eyes shrewdly estimating the number of loaves on the platters. "Your uncle seems unsure about the level of supplies. I would not have eaten so heartily if I had known your stocks were low. I am on my way to discover the amount of grain and flour that is stored to see how long we can hold out."

"So they are in a stronger position?" she asked.

"No," he reassured her. "We are well protected and have ample ammunition. We can make their life uncomfortable, especially if there is more bad weather. Pray for more snow, Lady Anne," he advised as he went to the door that led down to the cellars.

The baby in her arms shifted and began to cry and the nurse took him to be fed and have his swaddling changed. Anne took a cup of ale and her apportioned piece of bread and went to sit on a bench by the fire that had been re-kindled with an extra log. She wondered how many logs were left. There was plentiful woodland but it was all outside the castle walls, good only to supply the Stanleys with wood for the fires they would burn to try to undermine the foundations.

"Oh..." moaned Izzie as she woke and sat up on her narrow mattress. "I thought it was all a bad dream," she said, rubbing at her reddened eyes.

"Here, have something to eat," said Anne, passing what remained of her own meal to her sister. "It's not that bad. The duke thinks that they will withdraw before long, especially if the weather worsens."

"I presume you're talking about Gloucester," said Izzie as she broke off a piece of bread. "Your confidence in his ability to predict the future amazes me. Anyone would think that you were in love with him."

Annoyed by her sister's taunting, Anne snatched up her cloak and, leaving Izzie eating the food, followed the Duke of Gloucester down to the stores. Izzie's words had stung her. She wasn't in love with him, but there was something about the duke that excited her, and it wasn't just because he was the king's brother and had shown them such favour.

Outside the sky was grey, like metal, and the dull cold make her body ache. As she passed the open door of the kitchen she could see that it was filled with women and children cowering in every corner. She was approaching the low doorway to the grain store when she saw the duke come out.

"What are you doing out here?" There was a mixture of concern and anger in his voice. "Go inside!"

Anne faced him, ready to challenge his belief that she should do everything he told her, but before she could answer him his strong hand closed around her arm and he pushed her back towards the keep. Without giving her a moment to protest he urged her past the kitchen, up the steps and into the small solar at the back of the hall.

"I did not want to embarrass you by reprimanding you in front of the servants, Lady Anne, but you must understand that you are not to go out of the castle... for any reason!" His steely eyes glinted with suppressed anger and the retort she was about to make failed on her tongue. "Do you understand?" She watched him silently, aware that it was not fear he provoked in her with his manner but a desire she had never known the like of; a desire that he would close the short space between them, take hold of her again and use his body to subdue the cravings that she was at a loss to comprehend. "Do you understand?" he repeated.

"Yes, Your Grace," she managed to reply, her lips fumbling as she spoke.

"I have enough to do without rescuing you from your own stupidity," he told her and, hurt at his words, Anne swallowed back her unbidden tears. He obviously thought that she was just a silly and wilful little girl. Izzie was probably right about him after all, she told herself. But as he brushed past her, he momentarily laid a hand on her shoulder and his touch burned into her body long after he was gone.

James Harrington glanced up as he felt something soft and wet fall onto his ungloved hand. Snow. The Duke of Gloucester had seen it too, he thought, as he saw the young man glance upwards as he came along the wall-walk.

"If we implement rationing we can last two, even three weeks," said the duke as he reached him and turned to stare down. Below the castle walls James could see more tents than he cared to count pitched just beyond the range of his archers, though if Stanley had hoped for some spring sunshine to launch his attack then it seemed he was going to be thwarted and that God was on the side of the Harringtons after all.

"It will be cold and wet for them if this snow moves in," said the duke as he looked up at the heavy skies to the west. "But Stanley is a determined man and will not easily give up."

"Now that Anne is of an age to be married his attempts to take the castle can only increase," replied James. "If he takes possession of her and Elizabeth and marries them into his family then my lands will be lost."

"It is unjust," said the duke, "but my brother sees it from a different perspective. He believes that rewarding Stanley will keep him loyal."

"And he gives no reward to those who are already loyal," said James, bitterly.

"If I did not agree with you I would not be here," replied the duke, "but do not expect me to express disloyalty to my brother. I believe he has misjudged this matter and that if you can keep possession of Hornby for now he will change his mind."

"I am more grateful for your support than I can say, Your Grace. You do the Harringtons a great honour by your presence here."

"Your father and brother gave their lives for my father. I would like to see that debt of honour repaid."

James met the duke's eyes and saw his sincerity. He was so much like his father that it was almost like seeing the same person, he thought, unlike the king whose height and fair features betrayed his ancestry to the Nevilles of Raby. He took a breath, determined to bring the conversation back to his niece Anne and wondering if he dared to suggest that the duke's family debt to the Harringtons might stretch as far as his considering a marriage. But the opportunity was lost as a resounding thud made them both look to where a scaling ladder was now positioned against the outer wall. The archers were firing at the men attempting to climb and James smiled in satisfaction as he heard one fall to the ground with an agonised cry, an arrow protruding from his right shoulder.

"It seems that Stanley is not frightened by the snow after all," said the duke, "though it can only make the rungs more slippery. The man is a fool."

But a dangerous fool, thought James, and a persistent one too.

Inside Hornby Castle the days fell into a routine. At daylight the women would wake to the sounds of men on the battlements hurling abuse and arrows at the Stanley army below as they emerged from their tents. The insults were most likely returned and, although she couldn't make out the words, Anne was in no doubt that they were equally coarse and demeaning and called into question the manhood of the Harrington retainers.

Breakfast in the hall consisted of what was left of the previous day's bread and a small cup of ale, leaving Anne with a constant thirst that she found harder to bear than the hunger. The brewing of ale had also been rationed to preserve the grain stores. At dinner time they were allowed a little salted fish or bacon with a small portion of potage; on other days it was sops and potage and this grew weaker and more watery as time passed. Suppers were frugal affairs too and Anne found she often lay down to sleep feeling hungry.

The days became long and monotonous trapped in the fetid atmosphere of the unaired hall, and apart from playing with baby William to allow her aunt to get some sleep, singing to little Peggy and arguing with her sister, there was little to do; although Anne spent much of her time thinking about the duke and yearning to catch a glimpse of him.

Occasionally a thud would reverberate through the castle as a rock or boulder was hurled from the trebuchet that had been built and often her head would pound along with the rhythmic battering of the ram on the outer gate. Throughout the day there would be shouting as arrows were rained down on men who emerged from the tunnel they were mining under the curtain wall, though Uncle James reassured her that little progress was being made and that the walls were thick and strong.

Then, one morning, Anne was woken at first light by the sound of laughing from nearby. She sat up in alarm, clutching her cloak to her chest and trying to steady the rate of her pounding heart. She strained to try to make sense of what she could hear. Were Stanley's men inside the castle, she wondered. She stared at the door and expected them to storm through it at any moment to take her and Izzie captive.

She clambered to her feet as the latch clicked and the door was pushed open. She stood straight and proud, braiding her hair, which had become loosened as she slept, resolved to face the consequences of defeat with dignity. But it was Uncle James who came in with a delighted grin sweeping the exhaustion from his face, and her fear turned to hope.

"They've gone!" he announced in wonderment. "They must have begun to withdraw during the night. There are just a few stragglers left striking camp." He took his wife in his arms as she ran to meet him and lifted her up and spun her round. "We won!" he laughed and kissed her on the lips in full view of everyone. "You're safe," he said to Anne.

"What's happened?" asked Izzie, from where she sat on her flock mattress, rubbing the sleep from her eyes.

"The Stanleys have gone. We saw them off!"

Robert Harrington woke with a jolt to the familiar sound of an army on the move. For a moment he thought he was on campaign. Then he recalled that, as he had approached Hornby the previous night, and was relishing the thought of a tub of hot water and a hearty meal, he had seen that the castle was surrounded by Stanley's army and he had been forced to take cover in the forest.

He rubbed his painfully cold limbs to life. He had ridden ill-equipped for camping and had slept, wrapped in a horse blanket, on the damp forest floor. He eased himself up to a crouching position and grasped clumsily for the sword that was sheathed beside him. The steady tramp of booted feet and the occasional snicker of an excited horse came closer and he realised that the army was moving south. Why he was not sure. It could mean that Stanley had got hold of his young nieces, Anne and Elizabeth, but it seemed unlikely given the way that his brother kept them closely guarded, and would have guarded them closer still with the enemy outside the walls.

Shivering, he rose to his feet and picked up his make-shift bed. His horse was tugging at the reins that tied it to a nearby tree. It too had heard the other horses and was keen to join them.

"Shush," soothed Robert, running his hand down the animal's bony nose and over its soft muzzle, hoping that it would not give him away. He hoped that if he kept his hand pressed down, preventing the horse tossing back its head, it was less likely to give off a revealing whinny. And, with luck, the Stanley army would have no interest in pursuing some felon even if they did catch sight of him lurking in the trees as they passed.

When Robert was sure that the last of the foot soldiers had gone he led his horse towards the road. It was churned to mud with the melting snow and the multitude of feet and, together with the distant sounds of the men, a steaming pile of horse dung gave testament to how recently they had passed. Robert turned his own mount north, gathered the reins and having pushed his foot to the stirrup pulled his aching body into the saddle. He would be home soon and with luck there would be breakfast waiting.

James Harrington stood alone in the hall with the Duke of Gloucester. His earlier euphoria at the sight of the Stanley army disappearing southwards had been replaced by unease and the duke had echoed his own thoughts. Something more than their resistance had caused the withdrawal and another uprising was not beyond possibility.

"I'll ride to York," said the duke. "If I need you I will send word."

"You know my loyalty to you is without question," James told him. "Your support here has been more than I am worthy of. If you need me to fight alongside you then I will come."

The duke's sharp blue eyes met his for a moment. James knew that he acknowledged the unspoken meaning that it was to him, rather than the king, that the Harringtons were loyal now that Warwick was no longer their lord.

"I've sent Ratcliffe to the stables to see our horses are prepared. We'll leave as soon as they are ready."

"But you will take breakfast first," said James as a servant carried in some bread and set it on the trestle.

"A quick meal only," said the duke. "I would like to reach York by nightfall. And that means we will have to ride at speed."

Anne was in her bedchamber. She hadn't been back there since the night the siege had begun. The bed was still unmade and her chamber robe lay on the floor where she had left it in her haste to dress. She picked it up and folded it before pulling the sheets and covers straight. Then she crossed to the window and opened the shutters to let in some slanted sunshine. In a moment, she thought, she would call for a servant to bring her some warm water so that she could wash and change her underlinen, but in the meantime she felt compelled to look out, to be sure that the siege really was over.

She could see men leading donkey-carts laden with fresh supplies up to the castle. For the moment the outer gate stood wide open to the market place and as far as she could see there was no sign of the Stanley army.

"They've left a mess," commented Izzie, coming up behind her.

"Have they?" asked Anne, wishing that she had her sister's acute eyesight. But then, she reflected, she didn't really want to see rubbish on the banks of the Wenning.

"There'll be hot water soon," said Izzie. "I can't wait to get out of this gown. I feel like I've spent a lifetime in it." As she spoke Anne heard the sound of wood being chopped for fires. It was reassuring and calmingly familiar, and she looked forward to mutton for supper and fresh baked bread. Life would return to normal, for a while at least. But deep down, she knew that sooner or later the

Stanleys would return.

James beckoned his brother forward and Robert came towards them with a frown, as if he was seeking an explanation for why the Duke of Gloucester was eating breakfast in Hornby Castle whilst wearing his armour. Robert made a distracted bow to the duke and glanced from him to his brother with wary brown eyes. He looked cold and wet and very tired, thought James, wondering where his brother had been sheltering during the Stanley siege.

"Your Grace," said Robert.

"Do you bring news?" asked the duke eagerly.

James watched as his brother reached into his pouch for a damp letter. "The king is gathering an army again. There is talk of Warwick returning with the backing of the French queen."

The Duke of Gloucester slammed his fist down on the table, making the board leap from its supports. The cups and platters quivered. "I knew there was more to the Stanley withdrawal than a distaste for inclement weather. When did you receive word from the king?"

"A few days past," admitted Robert.

"My brother could not have brought news any sooner," pointed out James.

The duke nodded, though it was obvious that his thoughts had already moved on.

"I must leave," he said.

Stripped of the wet clothing that had clung coldly to his body, Robert stepped into the tub of water. It was hot. Too hot, and he stood for a moment as feeling flooded back into his lower legs turning them from white to a vivid red. Then he eased himself down, cursing as the hot water touched his nether regions. The servant stepped forward with a bucket of cold, but Robert waved him away. It would cool quickly enough and for now the pain was almost pleasurable as he allowed the fragrant liquid to wash over him and the steam to unclog his blocked nose. He leaned his head back on the hard edge of the tub and stared at the thick oak beams that straddled the roof of his bedchamber. It would have been pleasant to sleep, but his mind was still too busy pondering on the events of the morning.

When he'd climbed the outer steps in search of his brother he had never expected to find him with the Duke of Gloucester. He'd known the young duke since his days at Middleham when he was being educated under the tutelage of the Warwicks. As a squire there, Robert had been given responsibility for overseeing young Diccon's training in the tiltyard and he'd found the boy a talented horseman though more interested in hunting with hawks than refining his skills in the joust. He also remembered how the boy was often to be found in a quiet corner reading a book or playing chess with anyone who would indulge him. The earl had been apt to mutter worried comments about such sedentary pastimes, but what Diccon had learned from them had not been wasted. He was a tactician and his assurances that he would intercede on their behalf about the inheritance gave Robert hope. He knew the king was fond of his youngest brother and if anyone could persuade him to change his mind then Diccon could.

He shifted in the tub and began to ease the bandage from his leg to inspect his wound. He winced as the cloth stuck to the dried blood, but underneath the cut looked clean and there was no sign of any yellowish seepage. He was gently splashing some water over it when a cold draught at his back alerted him to the opening of the door and a moment later his brother came round the screen. He had changed his clothes and his face was freshly shaven. He carried a flagon and two cups, which he placed on the floor before fetching a stool, sitting down and pouring wine.

"Here," he said as he handed him a cup. "I managed to keep this back."

"I would have preferred my betrothed to perform such duties," remarked Robert as he took it and drank the rich red burgundy that sent heat radiating from his chest outwards to his limbs.

"I will not offer to wash your back then," replied James, "but I would like to hear your opinion on a matter concerning Anne whilst the women are not around."

"Indeed? I thought it would have been sieges and rebellions that troubled your thoughts, not our niece."

"It is all intertwined," said James as he twisted the cup in his hand. "I have been set to thinking these past few days."

"On what?" asked Robert, intrigued by his brother's serious expression and at a loss to guess what he was about to say.

"Gloucester seems interested in Anne," his brother told him. "After all, they are of much the same age and she is not unattractive."

"And what of her?"

"She sought out his company at every opportunity. I believe she likes him."

"But a marriage is out of the question. He is as much as promised..." Robert fell silent as he realised the implication. There would be no match now between Diccon and Warwick's daughter. "But whilst Stanley is her guardian we have no say in the matter of a husband for her. Or are you guilty of letting your thoughts run ahead of you and thinking that we need to make a match for her when the castle is returned to us?"

"I hope that the young duke can persuade the king to return the castle. But he may argue more forcefully if he has some reward. I will not discourage a friendship between him and Anne."

Robert looked up from where a swirl of fresh blood from his leg was clouding the water and stared at his brother.

"How far are you prepared to encourage it?" he asked.

His brother stood up and drained his cup in a hasty gulp. "Would it worry you if Stanley were to receive spoiled goods?" he asked with a raised eyebrow.

Chapter Two
March 1470,~ April 1470

Anne picked at the food on her trencher without interest as her uncles discussed Hornby yet again. It was almost a week now since the Duke of Gloucester had left. There had been no word from him and the dull ache in her throat and behind her eyes had not lessened.

Beside her Izzie groaned as Uncle James began to retell the tale of how he had tried to prove his loyalty to the Yorkists by taking King Henry prisoner. It was a story they had heard many times before, about how, after the battle at Towton and the defeat of the Lancastrian army, Henry had run off and spent months hiding in the houses of northern nobles who were still loyal to him.

"He was just sitting down to dinner with the Dean of Windsor when we burst in," related her uncle. "We took him to the castle at Clitheroe and locked him up overnight before taking him to London." He paused with a gloomy look. "Yes, I was rewarded, but not with what I desired and now it seems that even keeping Henry in the Tower has not secured Edward on the throne."

"Henry is only a pawn," said Robert. "It always was his queen who made the moves. And it doesn't surprise me that she will not give up striving to secure the throne for her son."

"And is the old king really mad?" asked Anne.

"Mad enough," remarked James, pouring more wine from their replenished cellars. "But maybe not as mad as Warwick. Whoever would have believed that he would turn against Edward and ally himself with his old enemy Margaret of Anjou?"

"Warwick wants to show Edward that he can't rule without his support," said Robert. "He always was a man to exploit weakness for his own gain."

"Perhaps he would like to be king himself," suggested James.

"If not a king then a man who makes kings. If he could be rid of Edward he might put Clarence on the throne."

"That would indeed be a tragedy. I've met Clarence and I am of the opinion that he's a mile short of midsummer."

"What do you mean?" asked Anne.

"Your uncle means that Clarence is the idiot of the family; easily led by promises of grandeur."

"What will happen?" asked Anne.

"Rumour has it that Warwick and Clarence have met with Margaret of Anjou at the court of the French king Louis."

"Sworn enemies joining forces?" laughed James. "Nothing will come of it. He'll be home soon enough with his tail between his legs like a whipped dog."

"I don't know," said Robert seriously. "Warwick will do whatever it takes to get his own way, and he and Edward never did agree about which side to support in the French war. I think that there may be more battles to come," he said and, although the hall had grown warm from the generous fire, a cold shiver ran through Anne as she listened to their words.

"We may be called away to fight for the king," Uncle James told her. "If the Duke of Gloucester sends for us we cannot refuse him."

"What if Lord Stanley comes?" she asked.

"He will ride to fight for the king as well. You will not be in any danger from him."

Robert dropped the latch on his bedchamber door, but rather than lying down to sleep he stood and stared at the clear night sky. A coloured iris surrounded the full moon. The night would bring a frost that would turn the water in the rutted roads to ice. He shivered and hoped that no messenger would come from York just yet. Cold days spent in the saddle and even colder nights under the flimsy cover of a tent held no appeal for him, and a campaign against Warwick also meant that his marriage to Isabella would have to be postponed. Damn the man, he thought, as he got into the deathly cold bed. He was tired of waiting to have his betrothed's warm body to heat his sheets. His whole life seemed to consist of waiting: waiting for the king to give them Hornby, waiting for peace, waiting to be wed.

As he lay awake, not daring to move his feet from the one spot that was warmed, he considered what James had said about Anne. His niece had certainly seemed more distracted than was her nature this past week, though what was the cause he could only guess. Women's minds were never easy to understand and Anne had changed from the little girl who was happy with a plate of sweetmeats or a new doll to play with into a moody creature who often displeased her aunt with her desire to be left alone in her bedchamber; and Elizabeth was even worse. Heaven preserve the man who took her to wife, he thought, as he risked turning over to ease the pressure on his sore leg.

When his father and brother had died at Wakefield he and James had ridden through the night to reach Hornby Castle to secure it and their young nieces against any other claim. James had been confident that even if Hornby did pass to Anne he would be given the guardianship of his niece and would retain the castle until she came of age, when he would choose a suitable and compliant husband for her who would not cause him trouble. Yet despite their continued support of King Edward he still insisted that the guardianship should be Stanley's. But what if James was right and Anne was enamoured of the Duke of Gloucester? Could it be used to their advantage, he wondered. Despite his brother's ambitions, Robert could see no hope of Anne becoming a duchess, even with Hornby Castle as her dowry. But as a bribe to keep the duke petitioning the king on their behalf she could be used. It was a shame, he mused, as he thought of Anne with her thick, dark hair and green eyes. She was a pretty girl and would have made some man a desirable wife. But if that man was to be a Stanley then Robert agreed with his brother that there was no reason for her to be claimed as a virgin bride.

Anne sat up in the bed, huddled under her cloak for warmth. The pain in her abdomen was striking through her in intensifying waves and she pulled her knees up to her chest to try to get some relief from it. By the low light of the flickering night candle she could see the flask that held the rest of the herbal brew that the aptly named Mistress Payne, the village wise woman, had brought for her. Hoping not to wake Izzie, who slept silently beside her, Anne eased her bare feet to the scratchy rushes that covered the floor. With one hand clutched to the place where the pain threatened to rip her apart, she felt her way to the coffer and poured a little of the foul smelling liquid into the cup and sipped at it, pulling a disgusted face at the darkness.

"Tis part of becoming a woman," Mistress Payne had told her. "There is nothing to be afraid of. Tis nature's way of clearing a woman's unused seed. Once you are married and carry a child it will cease."

The first time Anne had found blood on her bedsheets she was at a loss to explain it. She'd thought that she must have somehow injured herself as she slept and her sister's frantic cries had done little to calm her. But the servant who had come to take the sheets for laundering had explained that it was coming from her womb and that it happened to all women who were not bearing a child. She'd found Anne some linen cloths to catch the blood and taken the soiled bedlinen away without further comment. At first Anne had thought the pain was something she had to endure, until her aunt found her curled and weeping on the bed and having discovered the cause of her agony had sent for Mistress Payne.

Anne had felt able to ask the wise woman all the questions that she had not dared to ask her aunt and later she had shared her new knowledge with Izzie, who had been horrified and declared that it was a pretty poor trick for God to visit on women – and Anne had been shocked and told her to pray for forgiveness for her blasphemy.

Anne had also asked Mistress Payne about how babies came to grow inside a woman's womb and the wise woman had explained how the mixing of a man's and a woman's seed was achieved. At first Anne had been astounded by what she was told. She thought about the two children of her aunt and Uncle James and found it hard to believe that such an act as the one described had taken place between them. But Mistress Payne had laughed at her doubt and told her that it was an act to be enjoyed, though at the time Anne could not comprehend how lying down whilst a man pushed his private member inside her could possibly give her any pleasure. But when the Duke of Gloucester had grasped her arm and taken her to her uncle's solar she had felt something clench inside her, near the place that pained her now, and it had brought a feeling that she craved to experience again. She looked at the bed as the pain began to ease and she imagined herself lying down on the mattress for the duke. It was a thought that both frightened and excited her.

James read the message, written by a secretary and signed by the Duke of Gloucester with his seal attached. It seemed that the threat from France was credible and that Warwick and Margaret of Anjou were gathering troops for an invasion force to remove Edward from the throne. The king, said the duke, was worried, especially as he had already been forced to put down a rebellion in Yorkshire led by Sir John Conyers and John, Lord Scrope of Bolton. The duke wrote to ask James to encourage the local men who were still loyal to the Harringtons to turn out for the king. Of the inheritance he said nothing, though a footnote, added in his own hand, said that he would come to Hornby soon and James hoped that he would bring better news; perhaps news that he didn't dare set on paper until it was more certain.

He told the messenger with the boar badge pinned to his hat to go down to the kitchen and ask for food and drink. "The steward will find you a pallet for tonight. There's no point in your riding back to York if your lord is to attend on us here," he told him and as the man left he began to consider why Richard of Gloucester had decided to return to Hornby when he was supposed to be gathering troops to meet with the king's forces to the south.

The attraction had to be Anne he decided, and he clicked his fingers at a servant who had just come into the hall with a basket of logs for the hearth.

"Find the lady Anne and tell her I desire a word with her in my solar," he said.

James busied himself with his secretary, dictating a letter to be sent around to the villages and hamlets reminding men that although their lord was for the moment Thomas Stanley, they owed their ultimate fealty to the king and that they must leave their homes and rally once again, with horse and harness, to fight for him. When he saw his niece at the door he beckoned her to come inside and pointed to the stool near the fire. He remained silent until the scribe had finished his work and gathered his pens and ink to go to his desk in the hall to make the copies ready for the messengers. Then James turned to Anne who was looking up at him expectantly. Of his two nieces she had always been the more biddable and he hoped that she would not make a fuss about what he intended to ask of her. Now that Warwick had fled, the Harringtons were in need of a new lord and who better than the king's youngest brother, Gloucester. Once Warwick and Clarence were defeated, the young duke would be next in line to the throne after Edward and he was becoming increasingly influential. His intervention on their behalf concerning the castle and the lands had been gratifying and James had decided that the time was right to offer the duke something to keep his favour; a gift that would also serve to spite Lord Stanley.

Anne studied her uncle's face as he moved his chair a little before sitting down and brushing some unseen mark from his sleeve. He smiled uneasily at her and she felt her heart quicken as she hoped that he was not about to impart some bad news. She had seen the messenger and knew that he had come from York.

"I have had word from the Duke of Gloucester," he said at last.

"Does he send word about the inheritance, Uncle?" she asked.

"No. But I hope that he will have something to say on the matter when he comes."

"The duke is to return to Hornby?" Anne heard the rising pitch of anticipation in her voice and wasn't sure what to make of her uncle's smile. She waited to see what else he had to say. She was sure that it wasn't just to share this news that he had sent for her.

Anne recalled the other times that she had been summoned into the solar. As far as she could remember they had all been occasions when she had been brought before her uncle to receive some punishment for a misdemeanour: giggling with Izzie during mass, doing badly at her lessons, or the time when she had allowed her aunt's merlin to escape from its perch in the hall and it had flown out of the open door never to be found. But today it was her uncle who seemed to be the penitent as he shifted restlessly on his chair before he spoke again. "You are pleased that the duke favours us with his presence?" he asked.

"I... I... Yes, it pleases me," she stammered, feeling her cheeks burn hotly as her uncle smiled at her again.

"It would please me if you would show the duke some friendship," said her uncle. "I have seen that he is drawn to you, as you are to him... and I am minded to offer encouragement to an association."

Anne stared at her uncle. Was he trying to arrange a marriage between her and Richard of Gloucester? But how could that be achieved when her guardianship belonged to Lord Stanley?

"Do not hope for marriage," he continued as if he could hear her thoughts. "Your legal guardian would never agree and without Hornby you would be no heiress. But there are other ways of gaining the favour of influential men."

He looked away from her and went to stand by the window, which opened onto the inner courtyard. "Get on with your work you lazy wenches!" he suddenly bellowed at some servants below. Anne jumped. They had, no doubt, only paused to gossip for a moment as they went about their tasks and her uncle's reaction betrayed his own discomfort. "You know that I have a son, John," he continued, still watching the scene below. "His mother still lives. I provide her with a yearly pension and a town house in Lancaster. She was never my wife."

Anne continued to stare at her uncle's back. He was wearing a dark brown coat, lined with fur and his hair, where a few threads of silver shone amongst the brown, curled neatly inwards as it touched the collar. He didn't turn and she was unsure if she was expected to reply, and if so what response would be appropriate. She had known John a little when he'd lived at Hornby during his days as a squire. She remembered being taken down to the tiltyard to watch him cutting the heads of cabbages in two with a series of precise sweeps of his sword as he rode past them at speed on his horse. She had thought him handsome and brave, but had not known him well enough to miss him when he left Hornby to work as a secretary to the Earl of Warwick. Where he was now she had no idea and she wondered for a moment if her uncle knew.

James turned back to face her with his arms folded across his chest. "There is a gift that a wife may save for her husband on their wedding night," he said with an expression of acute embarrassment sketched across his face. "If the choice of your husband were in my power I would expect you to guard that gift." He paused. "Do you understand what I'm speaking of, Anne?" he asked.

"I think so," she told him, hesitantly. "I think you mean that a woman should accept no seed but her husband's. Mistress Payne has spoken to me about such things," she added to reassure him that she had some knowledge.

He nodded, looking relieved that she understood him. "If your wardship was mine then I would expect to send you to a husband as a virgin," he said. "But you are Lord Stanley's ward and he is my enemy. It would not displease me if the gift was bestowed on another."

Anne nodded slowly. Her uncle spoke in riddles. She was still unsure, but he seemed to be suggesting that she should lie with the Duke of Gloucester as if they were man and wife.

"But surely such a thing would be a sin?" she whispered, wondering how she could face Father Adam, the Harrington's chaplain, with such a confession.

Her uncle sighed and unfolded his arms to scratch his nose. "There are sins, and then there are sins," he remarked enigmatically. "The bible tells us that it is a sin not to honour our father and mother. But your father is not here and as I am your nearest kin I expect you to do my bidding. What I'm asking is that you abide by my guidance and show loyalty to your family. We can all benefit from this, Anne.

"Do you understand what it is I ask of you?" he said when she didn't reply, but sat and twisted her sleeve between her fingers.

Anne looked up. His brown eyes looked worried, even a touch desperate. "You want me to become the mistress of the Duke of Gloucester," she said. The words tasted strange yet appealing on her tongue. "I would prefer marriage."

"There is a chance that marriage may follow," he told her in a reassuring voice. "The duke is a good man who always strives to do the right thing, as he has shown in his support of us here at Hornby. But if the king will not change his mind about the inheritance then a marriage can only be arranged for you by your guardian and Stanley will never agree to your marrying Gloucester. But if the duke has... has known your body," he explained, looking away from her again, "he may feel he has an obligation towards you... and your family."

Anne nodded. What her uncle was suggesting was something she had never considered. She was vaguely aware that such agreements were made, but had never thought that she might become part of such an arrangement. Her only fear had been that she would be taken by the Stanleys and forced into a marriage not of her choosing with someone whom she did not like or who was cruel to her. This alternative both startled and tempted her. She liked the duke and thought that he would be kind. Besides, she knew that a refusal would anger her uncle.

"Will you agree, Anne?"

"Yes," she said after a moment, knowing that she had no choice.

It was almost a week later, as the evening sun disappeared below the battlements leaving a desperate chill in the air that Robert moved forward to take hold of the bridle of the Duke of Gloucester's horse. He was rewarded by a companionable grin.

"Time was you would have given me a tongue lashing for bringing home a horse in such a state," he remarked as he ran a hand over his mount's sweat-stained neck and patted it, the sound echoing around the inner bailey. "We rode hard to arrive before nightfall. I would not have liked to have met with any of Stanley's villains in the dark whilst we were so few."

Few indeed, thought Robert. The duke rode with only two companions. They carried no banner nor wore any tunic that would give them away and although they wore armour it was closely covered by their cloaks and their heads were bare.

"The rest of my men are riding to meet the king's forces, but I thought I would not be missed for a day or two."

Robert watched the duke's gaze search the upper windows and knew that he was seeking Anne. James had related some of the conversation that he'd had with their niece and although he had assured him of her willingness, Robert still felt uneasy. Anne was only young and it would have been impossible for her to gainsay her uncle, whom she had been brought up to respect and obey. He knew that James was immovable once he had formed an opinion or idea. It served him well in battle and gave him the determination not to back down over Hornby, but he was using Anne as a pawn, a piece that was worth sacrificing, and Robert couldn't help feeling sorry for the girl.

As he followed the duke and his men up the steps James came out to greet them. Anne was with him and he knew that his brother had gone to seek her to make sure that she was there to greet the visitors. She looked flushed and was glancing at the duke from below her thick lashes as if she didn't dare look at him directly. James on the other hand looked pleased and greeted the duke warmly as if he was expecting good news.

James gestured to Anne to pour some wine and Robert saw her hands shaking, making the red liquid surge across the cup like waves breaking on the sea shore. He saw Diccon smile at her as he took his drink and colour rose to Anne's cheeks as she looked down at the floor. Like a sacrificial lamb, thought Robert, as he watched. He hoped the outcome would be worth the sacrifice for all of them, but especially for Anne. Though the alternative was not any better. Perhaps it was just the proximity of what was planned that plagued his conscience. If she had been taken and wed to a Stanley would he have felt so much disquiet about her fate, he wondered.

James guided his guest forward to a seat near the fire, sending servants scurrying for warm water and towels, whilst the duke's men delved into their bags for clean, dry hose. Cloaks were set to dry, steam rising to the rafters as the smell of the damp wool fought with the aromas of the dishes being carried in for a late supper. Robert could sense that his brother was overeager to hear the news about the king's decision on Hornby and he watched as James pressed his fingers to his lips for a third time as if in an attempt to stem the flow of his questions.

At last they were clean and dry and seated at table. "Do you bring word from the king?" asked James.

The duke hesitated and Robert knew him well enough to expect bad news. "He will not relent," he said. "He is adamant that the letter of the law be upheld and that the land belongs to your nieces." He paused and Robert watched as he looked at Anne. Beside her James' expression was guarded, but he knew that his brother was both angry and disappointed.

"I won't give it up," he muttered. "But I am grateful for your interventions on our behalf, Your Grace," he added, remembering his manners.

The duke shrugged awkwardly. "You have possession for the time being," he said, "of both the castle and your nieces. But I have also come to ask you to join with me in support of the king against Warwick. I know that you have no lord now and I would like to offer you both places within my own household." He brought out a small parcel wrapped in grey silk, which he carefully unfolded to reveal two badges. They were fashioned in silver gilt and depicted a boar with fierce tusks and a small curly tail: his chosen emblem. "I would be honoured if you would accept this," he said as he held one out towards James.

"Your Grace, it is you who do me the honour. You show me great favour."

Robert watched as his brother knelt to the duke who pinned the badge to his doublet.

"You will find me loyal and worthy, and I will repay the favour that I owe to you," said James. He looked at Anne and Richard's gaze followed. Nothing was said and Robert wasn't certain that the meaning was fully understood, but as he knelt to receive his own badge he acknowledged that the Harringtons did indeed owe a debt of gratitude to the Duke of Gloucester.

Later that evening Anne followed her uncle up the twisting stone stairs to the guest bedchamber. The horn lantern that he carried swung as he mounted the steps and strange shadows leapt out at her from the bare walls. She understood now why little Peggy had cried in fright. She was barely succeeding in keeping her own tears under control.

After they had finished eating, her uncle had told her to ready herself and that he would come for her before the bell chimed Compline. She had gone to her own chamber and by the light of a candle had splashed her face with stale water from the basin on the coffer, had used the latrine and then knelt at the small prie dieu and picked up her rosary beads.

She was still at prayer when her uncle had come for her. He had come into the chamber unbidden and had frowned as she'd looked up at him.

"Come," he'd said, though not unkindly. "It is time for you to do your duty to your family."

Now she stood meekly behind him as he knocked at the dark oaken door and she heard the duke's voice as he told one of his companions to see who was there. The eyes of the man who opened the door widened in surprise. He turned in some confusion and for a moment there was an awkward silence.

"Go and find beds in the hall," said the duke to his men and Anne pressed herself against the hardness of the wall as they passed her with their eyes politely averted. Then she felt her uncle grasp her arm and urge her over the threshold into the bedchamber.

"Your Grace," said her uncle and before Anne realised that he had released her and stepped back, the door thudded shut and she was alone with the duke. She heard her breath judder in her chest as she tried to steady the wild pounding of her heart. He was undressed for bed and wearing a chamber robe that belonged to her uncle. It was overlarge for him and the blue cloth trailed down onto the floor around him like a puddle. As he walked towards her she saw that his feet were bare. They were small with even toes and well-trimmed nails that looked almost girlish. They stopped a little distance from her and the material of the robe sank and covered them again.

"Your uncle assures me that you have willingly agreed to come to me. But I would like to hear it from your own lips," he said quietly.

Anne continued to look at the folds of the robe, strewn over the red and green threads of the tapestry that covered the bedchamber floor. It was the most opulent chamber in the castle, reserved for visits from royalty and she had rarely been here before. She heard the crackling of the fire as a log sighed and settled in the hearth and she knew that there was a fine bed, with thick mattresses and rich red hangings, although she didn't dare look at it. Neither dared she look at the duke. She hadn't been able to meet his intense blue eyes all evening knowing what her uncle had planned.

"Anne?" She darted him a look and saw that he was watching her carefully. "I do not expect you to do anything against your will," he told her, and the kindness in his voice, so at odds with her uncle's insistence that she must fulfil this as her obligation, only served to destroy her self-control and she suddenly sobbed as she felt the hot tears race down her cheeks.

His warm hands pressed against her upper arms as he gently rubbed them up and down to comfort her. His touch sent fire through her body but she pressed her palms against his chest to prevent him coming nearer. The robe had fallen open and she could feel his hard, taut muscles beneath his thin linen nightshirt. For a terrifying moment she thought that he was going to overpower her and pull her against him, but he dropped his hands and stepped back, pulled the chamber robe closed and turned away from her to the fire.

"Go to your own bed," he told her.

"But... my uncle..."

"Then sleep here. I will use one of the pallets. Your uncle need not know." His voice was tight and dismissive.

"I will not take your bed..."

"Just do it!" he shouted at her without looking around. "Pull the hangings closed and try to let me forget that you are within such close proximity."

Anne hurried to the bed and did as she was bidden. She sat curled like a cat inside the curtained enclave and listened as he poured wine and walked about the chamber extinguishing all but one of the candles. She wished that he would say something, but all she heard was the creak of the wooden frame of the small bed that had been provided for a servant as he lay down. She could hear his breathing, but it was not the deep regular breathing of someone who slept and she sat and listened for what seemed like many hours, thanking the holy virgin for answering her prayers, until she must have fallen asleep herself.

She woke in confusion when she found herself lying on the unfamiliar bed. Then guilt and foreboding flooded through her as she remembered what had happened. If her uncle discovered that she had not fulfilled her promise he would be very angry and she was fearful. She sat up and strained to listen, wondering if the duke still slept beyond the curtains and if there was time to make amends. It seemed barely dawn and she thought that she would have wakened before if he had stirred. She reached out cautiously and twitched at the hangings. By the first light that was probing the edges of the shuttered window she could see a shape on the pallet in the corner of the chamber. Trembling with anticipation she slid from the bed and tiptoed across the floor and stood beside him, watching the rise and fall of his chest as he slept. His blue eyes, that were usually so serious yet could light with amusement in a moment, were closed and long dark lashes swept his cheeks. His strong nose and prominent chin lay against the rough pillow and his small, but strong hands that had touched her so gently, were curled around the blanket.

He stirred as she watched him and then opened his eyes. "Anne?" he murmured. His voice was puzzled and sleepy.

"I'm sorry," she said, not knowing for what she was apologising; whether it was for watching him sleep or for not fulfilling her obligation. He reached out a hand and she knelt beside the low bed and stretched hers towards it. They made an almost perfect pair in size, though his were darker, rougher, calloused with the handling of swords and bows and she could feel the roughness of his skin as he intertwined his fingers with hers.

"There is nothing to forgive. I would not want you to come to my bed unwillingly."

He reached up and pushed a strand of her uncovered hair behind her ear then slid his hand around the back of her neck to pull her towards him. She closed her eyes as he drew her down until his soft lips touched hers. "Go now," he said firmly as he took his hands away from her. "Go to your own chamber before my desire for you overwhelms me."

She hesitated for a moment then stood up and walked slowly to the door. She paused for one last look at him as he sat on the edge of the bed watching her before she opened it and slipped through, regretting that she had been so reluctant and fearful that he had sent her away.

Robert watched his niece as she ate breakfast. He thought that James had been too eager to sacrifice her virginity. The duke had already decided to take them both into his household and sought no reward other than their loyalty to him and the king. He would see them fed and armed and horsed whilst they were in his employment and if they were indeed to lose Hornby and its lands it would be some recompense. He fingered the white boar badge with its sharp tusks. It would please him to serve Richard, Duke of Gloucester.

"I have the promise of almost fifty men from Hornby and Melling," James was saying. "They refused to turn out for Stanley saying that they did not recognise him as their lord whilst I still held the castle, but they will ride under my banner and will be ready to leave by the morrow."

"I'm pleased to hear it," said the duke. "It matters not to which lord each man owes his allegiance as long as he is willing to support the king. We must put aside our differences and fight together for this just cause; even if that means you must fight alongside the Stanleys," he warned them. "There will be time to pursue your quarrel when we have dealt with Warwick."

"Yes, my lord," agreed Robert and watched his brother's non-committal nod. He knew that James would do the right thing despite his hatred of Stanley. If they lost the support of the duke then keeping Hornby would be impossible. And for himself, the sooner this latest threat was dealt with the sooner his marriage could go ahead. The thoughts of Anne and the duke had made him long to take Isabella to his own bed and he hoped that she would stay faithful to him now that it seemed as if their marriage would be put off at least until the autumn.

Anne was avoiding Izzie so that she wouldn't have to explain why she had been absent from their bed. And she was also avoiding her uncle as she feared that he might question her and she would be revealed as a fraud.

She had lurked in the kitchen with its roaring fires where a deer was being turned on a spit by a bored boy wearing only his braies. But the heat had made her feel that she would melt and she had gone out into the bailey and listened to the banter of the grooms as they brushed the horses. Now she was shivering in the dairy, watching a fresh batch of cheese being stirred and skimmed.

Soon he would be gone, she thought. He would go to war, and men were killed when they fought. What if he died and she never had another chance to be with him?

She found him by the river, at the bottom of the Steep. He was staring moodily at the fast flowing water as it skirted the castle. He looked up, sensing her approach and half-smiled at her.

"When do you leave?" she asked him.

"Tomorrow at first light," he said as he tossed a smooth pebble in the palm of his hand.

"Will Lord Stanley fight for the king?"

"I would hope so," he said as he threw the stone. It bounced twice on the surface of the water before disappearing.

"But he will come again, won't he?" she asked. "When this rebellion is put down he will come again. He will not be satisfied until he has taken possession of Hornby, and of me."

The duke looked at her for a long moment. "Yes," he agreed. "He will come again, and although I made a promise to you that I would try to keep you from his control I fear it is a promise I may find difficult to keep. I'm sorry."

"I did not mean to seem so reluctant last night," she said, her eyes on the place where the stone had submerged. "I was willing... I am willing." She was afraid that he would say no, and perhaps even more afraid that he would say yes. After a moment of silence she looked at him and he held her gaze.

"Are you certain?" he asked.

"Yes. I am certain."

She followed him up the grassy slope towards the castle. Their arms touched as he opened the outer door for her and as the servants glanced up from their chores Anne was sure that every one of them could see what they intended to do. He preceded her up the winding stone steps and she followed, her skirts clasped in her hands. He pushed open the door and stood aside for her to go in, leaving the ultimate decision to her. Without hesitation she stepped inside and turned to watch as he closed and barred the door behind them.

"I will be gentle," he promised her. "You do not need to be afraid of me."

With a strong arm around her waist he pulled her body against his. Hesitantly, she rested her hands on his shoulders then allowed her inquisitive fingers to touch his hair. It felt soft and silky. He was warm and hard and her senses filled with the taste and masculine smell of him as he kissed her. Then his thighs began to press against hers forcing her to step backwards until she felt the hard frame of the bed against the backs of her legs. The red hangings had been tied back and the covers neatly straightened. The fur coverlet was smooth beneath her palms as he pushed her down until she was lying on its sumptuousness. She stroked the fur and then reached up to touch his cheek, which felt rough by comparison.

"Do you know what to expect?" he asked.

"Yes," she told him. "I think so." As he looked down at her she saw tenderness and she knew that she could trust him. "And I would rather learn about this mystery with you than some son of the Stanleys," she added.

Chapter Three
May 1470

Anne and Izzie were allowed to watch from the small chamber above the guardhouse as the army gathered in the market place. There was a palpable sense of excitement and even though men said that they did not want another battle there was a joviality that reminded Anne of a feast day, except that today they were drunk on anticipation rather than cheap ale. The horses, attuned to the atmosphere, chomped at their bits and pawed the ground as their riders lined up. Then finally, with a shout of command from the Duke of Gloucester, they moved off, the morning sun reflecting from their well-polished armour and the interlocking black and white stripes of the Harrington banner.

As they went Anne bit at her bottom lip. She was determined not to cry in front of her sister. She had cut short Izzie's curious questions and, as they normally shared everything, the exclusion was making her angry. But this was something that Anne could not speak of. The things that Richard had done to her had been strange and unexpected and whenever she thought of them she found herself flushing with embarrassment. Yet when they had been together such things had seemed natural and she had enjoyed them and was bereft that he was leaving and that she might never have the chance to experience them with him again.

Izzie pushed past her without a word and went down the steps. Anne followed, but by the time she reached the bottom Izzie was nowhere to be seen. Hoping that her sister would not sulk for too long Anne walked back up the incline to the keep.

The castle was quiet and cool when she went inside. Not wanting to talk to anyone but to be alone with her thoughts Anne climbed up to the bedchamber, which had been Richard's. She closed the door and sat down on the edge of the huge bed. The linen had been stripped from the mattresses and taken away to be laundered, but the soft fur coverlet remained and she lay down on it, trying to recreate his physical presence in her imagination.

Gradually she became aware of her name being called over and over again by one of her aunt's women. "Lady Anne! Lady Anne!"

She jumped up guiltily and pulled the dark brown fur straight before lifting the latch on the door and slipping out. As she descended the twisting stairs the urgency of the calls increased and other voices were added. Anne began to hurry, even though the steps were narrow and she was afraid of falling. She was beset by thoughts of her uncles and Richard having come to some harm.

"There you are!" exclaimed her aunt as she entered the hall. She waved a letter in her hand and clutched Anne's arm so tightly that she could feel her sharp fingernails through the fabric of her gown. "Your sister has been taken by the Stanleys and they are threatening to attack us if we don't release you as well."

Anne stared at her aunt's anguished face. How could the Stanleys have taken her sister? Wasn't Izzie in the castle? And hadn't the Stanley army ridden to support the king? Her thoughts whirled in confusion. But what if Lord Stanley hadn't ridden to support the king after all? What if he had decided to take the opportunity to snatch her sister and herself from an under-guarded Hornby? Fear pulsed through Anne. Her uncle had left only a small force to guard the castle in his absence as he had judged any threat to be negligible – and the men left behind were those bent with old age or injured in battle like Cedric, her uncle's steward, who had just come in through the open doorway. His one good hand grasped a youth whom she recognised and as he pushed the boy forward the curtain of blond hair fell back from his face and Anne saw that his cheek was red and swollen.

Cedric briefly shook his head. "The lady Elizabeth is not in the castle. We have searched everywhere. But this boy says he witnessed what happened. Tell Lady Harrington what you saw!" he instructed the boy, giving him a dig between the shoulder blades.

"Please, my lady, this man came," said the boy, overawed to be the centre of so much attention. "He were a big man on a big 'orse. He had a beard. We were only talkin', m'lady!" he said without looking up. "We were just talkin' and he came up. He got off th'orse and he took hold of Lady Elizabeth. She screamed, and he put 'is hand over her mouth and he dragged her off backwards. I tried to pull her away from 'im but he hit me and knocked me to the ground." The boy glanced up then with wide eyes and Anne remembered that she had seen him in the bailey working at the blacksmith's forge. She also recalled seeing her sister standing watching him on more than one occasion.

"You must take men to find the lady Elizabeth and bring her back," Aunt Joan told Cedric.

"I cannot leave the castle, my lady," he reasoned. "My lord instructed me to stay within the walls and guard you. There may be dozens of men, or more, surrounding the castle. And if we venture outside the gates and are killed then Hornby will be completely undefended. Besides, we are no longer fighting men," he added, raising the stump of his right arm.

"I heard them say they were bringing a cannon," ventured the boy into the stunned silence.

"A cannon!" Her aunt looked to where the nurse was playing with William and Peggy. "They will kill us. They will kill us all!" she burst out in anguish. "They will kill my babies!" She turned back to Anne. "You must go with them," she told her. "It is the only thing that will save us."

Panic struck Anne like a physical blow and she began to gasp for breath as her heart raced.

"My lady. Is that wise?" asked Cedric.

"What choice is there?" demanded Aunt Joan, her voice rising with hysteria. "They will not harm the girl. And when the king returns the castle to us, they will let her and Elizabeth go. But if I defy them and they attack us we cannot defend ourselves. No," she continued as if convincing herself as she spoke. "Anne must go with them as they demand."

Both baby William and Peggy, sensing their mother's anguish, had begun to cry and their wails filled the hall to its high wooden beams as the nurse tried to comfort first one and then the other. Anne said nothing. The prospect of being handed over to the Stanleys terrified her, yet she couldn't bear the thought of her sister being taken away by them alone. She felt helpless, as she had done so many times in the past when she knew that nothing she could say would make any difference. Her aunt was adamant. "Go and pack some belongings," she told her. "I am sure it will not be for long."

Anne continued to stare at her without saying a word, but all she could see in her mind's eye was Izzie – afraid and weeping for her to come. And after what seemed an eternity she roused herself enough to give her aunt a curtsey.

"Yes, my lady," she managed to whisper in a voice that seemed to come from someone else and, feeling as if she was walking in a dream, she went up to the bedchamber. She touched the cold stone of the wall as she climbed, wondering if this was just another of the nightmares that plagued her. But the wall felt rough and solid and she realised that the dream had become reality. The thing she feared above all others had come about.

Rather than waiting for a servant to help her Anne began to gather some clothing, packing no more than she was able to carry. She hoped that her aunt was right and that she would not be gone for long. She was sure that as soon as her uncles received word of what had happened they would come to find her. They had an army and they were not afraid to fight. She crossed to Izzie's coffer and found some of her linen and her comb. She packed them with her own things and after pulling her cloak around her shoulders she took a last look around the bedchamber before going to face her future.

Her aunt kissed her briefly on the cheek and told her not to worry and to be brave and then instructed Cedric to escort her to the gate. The steward took her pack in his good hand and walked beside her in silence down to the gatehouse. The huge iron bolt squeaked as it was drawn back on the small door and with a sympathetic nod Cedric handed the pack to her and waited for her to step through.

Fighting the impulse to run back to the safety of the castle, Anne took a trembling breath and stepped outside. She was prepared for armed men to seize her as they would a prisoner, but as she looked warily around she saw only a tall, broad man with a neatly trimmed beard and a dark coat waiting beside the market cross. He was holding the reins of two horses: one was a huge, fearsome looking animal, black with a wide white blaze down its nose; the other was a smaller, more docile looking, bay mare.

"Lady Anne," he said bowing his head slightly then turning to beckon forward a servant who ran to take the pack from her arms. "I am Sir William Stanley. I am here to escort you into the care of your legal guardian – my brother, Lord Thomas Stanley. Can you ride?" he asked as she stared from him to the horses and back again. She shook her head. There had never been the need to ride a horse before. She had never left the castle.

"Do not be alarmed," said Sir William. "The mare is very friendly and I will lead her along. Come. I will assist you if you will permit me."

Anne had not thought that her captors would be either kind or considerate. The village boy had said that Sir William had slapped him and taken Izzie by force. She had seen the boy's bruised face. Yet the man standing here seemed well-mannered and respectful.

"Lady Anne?" She saw that Sir William had cupped his hands to make a step to lift her up onto the horse.

"I... I am not accustomed to riding," she said as she met his dark brown eyes.

"You will be quite safe," he said. "I promise that no harm will come to you, or your sister Elizabeth. Your guardian has entrusted me with your well-being."

"Where is my sister?" ventured Anne.

"She is safe and she is well. You will be with her in Lancaster by nightfall... if we leave now," he added in encouragement.

Anne placed her foot on the folded palms of his hands and felt herself thrown upwards as if she had no weight at all. She grabbed for the saddle to steady herself as her tender parts landed heavily on the hard leather and she let out a slight cry of shock and pain. Sir William helped her find the stirrups then handed her the reins, though he kept a leading rein in his own hand. Anne clung onto the pommel of the saddle. It looked a long way to the ground and she was afraid that she was going to fall.

"Don't worry," said Sir William, patting the horse's neck, "we will go slowly."

The mare moved beneath her and Anne held on tightly as Sir William led it away from Hornby, down the valley of the River Wenning towards Lancaster. Even though her eyesight was not as acute as Izzie's she could see no besieging army, no battering ram or cannon and as she glanced at the man who led her along she wondered if her aunt had been tricked. Sir William, who had been whistling a tune, turned to smile at her as if he was satisfied that he had her in his possession. Anne looked down at the dark springy mane of her horse and her stomach knotted in a panic that made her want to cry. She turned to look back at Hornby Castle, clinging to the shoulder of the hill. It looked small and as the road dropped it disappeared from view. The countryside around her was unfamiliar and she felt lost.

The river valley widened as they headed south and the land to the west became flat.

"The sea," said Sir William and pointed to a shimmer of grey that stretched to the horizon. "And ahead of us is Lancaster. We will be there soon."

Anne watched as a different castle rose into view on a hill in front of them. It was much larger and more imposing than Hornby. "There's been a fortress here since Roman times," Sir William told her. He had been pointing out various landmarks all through their journey in an attempt to engage her in conversation, but she had found it impossible to reply and a brief nod was all she could manage now as she stared at the huge stone keep.

She had heard her uncles speak of Lancaster, but hadn't realised how large it was compared to Hornby. As they approached she saw that there were more and more houses, some surrounded by gardens where a few goats and cattle grazed and crops grew in neat rows. Then the buildings became crowded together. They reached the walls and passed under a gateway into the centre of the town where the houses jostled for space with shops and forges, inns and cook houses. There was noise and dirt and a foul smell pervading everywhere from the rotting food and excrement piled up waiting to be buried. People moved reluctantly out of their way as the horses almost trod on their ill-shod feet. They stared insolently at Anne and she risked letting go of the saddle with one hand to pull up the hood of her cloak as protection against their inquisitive eyes.

At last they turned into the courtyard of a building with a picture of a sunrise painted on a board above its door. Trampled straw covered the ground and there were horses and dogs and people all around. Sir William Stanley got down from his horse and after handing the reins to his servant raised his arms to clasp her by the waist.

"Lady Anne. May I assist you?"

She stared around in bewilderment. Surely this wasn't where she was to be held? She thought that she would have preferred the dungeon in the castle to this. A man, obviously drunk, staggered by and her horse flinched from his loud and tuneless singing, forcing her to cling to Sir William as he lifted her from the saddle. For a moment the male scent of him and his warm hands on her body reminded her of Richard and she had to push the thought forcefully from her mind. She recoiled from his touch and struggled for a moment to steady herself, having become accustomed to the swaying of the horse. She felt his large hand grasp her elbow.

"Careful, my lady!"

Beyond an open door she could see an ill-lit and crowded room filled with men sitting on benches around wooden tables drinking ale, talking and laughing loudly. Some of the women were dressed in gowns that showed the rise of their breasts as they leaned over to pour ale from large flagons and at least one of them had her hair uncovered and snaking over her shoulder for everyone to see.

"Where is my sister?" asked Anne, speaking for the first time since they had left Hornby. She felt sickened that Izzie might have been left alone in such a place as this.

"She is inside, in a private upper chamber, waiting for you." Anne glanced up at the shuttered windows of the wooden building and shuddered. "It is quite respectable," said Sir William in an amused tone.

Anne's legs were stiff and she stumbled as she tried to walk, but Sir William supported her and steered her towards a steep flight of wooden steps. At the top a man dressed in the blood red of William Stanley's livery with its hart's head emblem was lounging against the wall by a stout door. He jerked upright when he saw his lord approaching.

"Open the door," Sir William instructed him and the man bent to turn the large iron key that protruded from the lock. It squeaked as it opened and Sir William reached past her to give a perfunctory knock before twisting the handle and pushing the door. As it swung back Anne saw her sister sitting on a small stool in front of a blazing fire.

"Nan!" Izzie ran into her arms and Anne clung to her fiercely and kissed her wet cheeks.

"Are you well?" asked Anne, after a moment, taking her sister's face between her palms and studying her closely for any bruises or other signs of mistreatment.

"Nan, I'm sorry," she wept. "I am so sorry."

"I will have some supper sent up," said Sir William from the doorway and Anne heard the door being locked.

"Have you been treated well? Has he hurt you?" she asked, turning her attention back to her sister.

"I... I'm all right," she said. "I was just so scared. I didn't know what would happen to me. I'm so glad you're here. It's all my fault," she added before beginning to sob. "I'm sorry. I'm so sorry, Nan. I know I shouldn't have gone to the village."

"Hush, hush," Anne comforted her, taking Izzie in her arms again, stroking her hair and murmuring empty reassurances.

All through the long and tiring ride from Hornby to Lancaster her anger had increased with every mile as she had thought about the recriminations she would shout at her sister when she found her. But now she realised that no words would make any difference. Izzie was well aware that her disobedience had caused their greatest fear to come to pass. Little had she thought when she had watched Richard and her uncles ride away that by nightfall she would be held captive in an inn at Lancaster.

After a while she heard voices outside the door and the key scraped again. Sir William stood to one side as two of the women from downstairs brought in dishes of potage, bread and ale.

"Eat," said Sir William from the doorway, "then get some sleep. We must leave early in the morning. We have a long journey."

"Where are we going?" asked Anne in alarm.

"To a place of safety," he told her. "There is no need to trouble yourself, Lady Anne. I will take care of you now."

He left the room with a brief 'goodnight' and Anne turned without appetite to the food and then to inspect the bed to see if the linen was clean and if there were any signs of fleas or bugs.

Chapter Four
September 1470 ~ October 1470

Robert Harrington applied more oil to the blade and rubbed it vigorously with a rag. The past few days had been humid, with the constant threat of a thunderstorm rumbling in the heavy air and a hanging drizzle that left everything shrouded in dampness. The spot of rust he had seen on the Duke of Gloucester's sword had alarmed him. He had lectured Diccon often enough in the past about the need to take good care of his weaponry and he was keen not to be caught out neglecting his duties to his new lord.

He glanced up as the tent flap was pushed back and the duke came in with a grim face. He met Robert's eyes for a moment before going to the small trestle and pouring wine into a horn beaker from the flagon that stood there. Robert continued to work, though with half his attention on Diccon. He knew him well enough to sense when he was upset but also knew that it was better to wait until he was ready to talk rather than to question him.

"Montagu has declared for his brother," he said after watching him for a moment. Robert stopped what he was doing and looked up. The implication was clear to him. If Montagu had decided to support Warwick, the king's forces would not be strong enough to have any chance of winning a battle. And despite his brother's confidence that the Stanley army would move to the king's aid there was still no sign of them, and every day more lords seemed to desert their sovereign.

The duke reached to pour another cup of wine, then changed his mind and put the flagon down. His actions were calm but Robert could see that he was only just in control of his temper. If it had been the king then Edward would have thrown the cup and probably the wine as well, and the sound of raised voices from the direction of the king's tent confirmed that his displeasure was being expressed in a predictably vociferous manner.

Robert slowly rubbed the sword again and twisted it to the light to check that the rust had been removed.

"I doubt I shall have need of that," remarked the duke. "My Lord Hastings has advised the king to flee."

"Flee, my lord?" asked Robert in surprise. He had thought that they would have to withdraw north and raise more men, but a decision to leave the country and allow Warwick and Clarence to take control was not what he had expected.

"We are to go to Lynn and take a boat for Holland. From there we will go to Burgundy and ask our sister's husband for assistance." He sat down on the edge of his camp bed and for a moment rested his face in his hands. "This will be the second time I have had to leave England," he said.

Robert didn't reply. He was unsure what to say and it no longer seemed appropriate to put an arm around Diccon's shoulders to comfort him as he had done in the past when he had found him despondent – though back at Middleham his problems had mostly centred on an inability to accept defeat in the tiltyard or being beaten at chess by Anne Neville.

"Will you pack?" he said. "We are to leave at once."

"The threat is so great?" asked Robert as he returned the sword to its scabbard with a grating sound. The duke nodded.

"Will you accompany me?"

"Of course, my lord. I am yours to command," Robert reassured him, his fingers reaching to touch the white boar badge. "My brother and I..."

"James must remain," the duke interrupted, standing up and recovering his composure. "I want him to return to Hornby and guard it until the king confirms his holding. I am sure he will on his return. Have no fear. We will not be gone for long," he said. "Warwick need not think that this is the end. Nor my brother Clarence. The king will raise money and men. We will return to defeat them."

As James Harrington urged his horse northwards he was relieved to see that Hornby Castle looked unscathed on the horizon. He glanced up at the overcast sky as a westerly breeze rustled the trees and he hoped that his brother had safely made landfall in the Low Countries. He had bade Robert farewell with a forced jollity that he hoped had not betrayed his anxiety at the outcome of Warwick's determination to take power. It worried him that the king had been forced into exile. To regain power was often more difficult than to hold it from within a country and he had been praying fervently that the Duke of Burgundy would hear Edward's pleas and equip him with the forces he needed to return and reclaim this throne.

As he clattered into the inner courtyard of the castle he saw Joan waiting to greet him with the children and their nurse. Their sombre faces told him that all was not well. He looked for his nieces and when he saw neither Anne nor Elizabeth his disquiet grew.

"My lord." His wife curtseyed as he dismounted the horse and threw the reins to a waiting groom. Her eyes remained fixed on some spot on the ground and behind her Cedric was fingering his collar with his one hand as his other arm hung limply at his side. He too had downcast eyes and a protracted silence hung in the air.

"What troubles you?" he asked, addressing them both.

"My lord, we were attacked by the Stanleys not long after you left," said Joan. "They took the lady Elizabeth and the lady Anne." The slight sob in his wife's voice betrayed her fear that he would blame her for the news. She cowered in front of him although he had never raised a hand in anger towards her.

He looked at his steward. "How could that happen?" he demanded. "Where are they now? Do you have them safe?"

The slight shake of the steward's head told him that the news was worse than he had first imagined. He looked back at Joan. Her trembling fingers touched her lips as she stared at him beseechingly. "What else could I do?" she pleaded when she had finished her explanations. "I thought it important to safeguard the castle.

They were threatening to attack us with a cannon."

"So you simply allowed them both to be taken?" he raged.

"They would have destroyed the castle and killed us all!" protested his wife, tears dripping from her chin. She wiped them away with the back of her hand. "Please do not be angry with me, my lord. You are frightening the children."

His daughter was clinging to her nurse's skirts and sobbing and the baby set up a wail that rebounded from the stone walls. "Take them inside," said James irritably. "I'll speak to you later."

"My lord." She curtseyed again and ushered the children and their nurse up the outer steps.

"See to the horses!" he bellowed at the grooms before turning to his men-at-arms. "You may go to your homes. I thank you for your loyalty to me and to the king."

The men who had ridden in with him moved away in an awkward silence, saving their comments until they were out of his hearing.

The grooms took the horses and James looked again at Cedric. He had known the man all his life. He had fought hard for the Harringtons and had almost died of his injuries. It had only been the skill of his father's surgeon that had saved his life and rather than leaving him to eke out the rest of his life in penury his father had rewarded him with the stewardship of the castle. Cedric was a good and competent man and he knew that he would not have relinquished his duty to Anne and Elizabeth without good reason.

"We could not have prevailed against them if they had attacked us," said Cedric. "It seemed the only thing to do."

James nodded. "Yes," he said after a moment. "Sometimes our strength has to be in knowing when it is better not to fight. The king has fled," he told him. "What will happen to Hornby now I do not know. But at least we hold the castle for the time being."

Sudden tiredness drained him and he found it difficult to climb the steps. He called his squire to help him unarm. His wife had busied herself organising water for washing and food and drink and when he saw her watching him warily he was sorry that he had been so angry with her. He supposed that it was his own fault for not leaving more men to guard Hornby. Damn the Stanleys. They had better treat those girls well, he thought, as he filled his cupped hands with warm water from the basin and plunged his aching face into it.

Anne woke and, as sleep was unwilling to release her from its grasp, she struggled to remember where she was. After ten years of sleeping in the same bed she found it strange not to be at Hornby Castle. She stared around at the stone walls and the high narrow windows, and as her senses gradually composed themselves she remembered that this was Skipton Castle in Craven.

They had been here for several weeks now but every new morning was like the first. When they had ridden out of Lancaster on the road south she had thought that they were being taken to Lathom House in West Lancashire, but after crossing the bridge over the River Ribble at Preston Sir William and his men had turned their horses northwards again, up the valley through Clitheroe and

Gisburn. Beyond the village and its market place with the stocks and pillory, the grey castle had loomed over them.

As they'd crossed the bridge over the moat, Anne had stared up at the two formidable round towers that flanked the gatehouse. There would be little chance of rescue from here, she'd realised as they were taken inside.

"Are we to be your prisoners?" she asked Sir William as she stood in the inner courtyard, secluded from attack by a long stone tunnel, a stout portcullis and a pair of studded and securely barred doors.

"Of course not, my lady!" He had looked shocked and a little hurt at her suggestion. "You will be my guests. It is my duty to take care of you now," he added, and Anne had been struck by panic as she realised that it was possible she had been promised to him as a wife. On the journey Sir William had told her that he was a single man, a widower since his wife had died four years before, and that he was anxious to marry again. She could hardly bear it when he looked at her and the thought of him touching her was repulsive; he was old, probably more than twice her age, and the fleeting vision she'd allowed herself of him lying on top of her in a marriage bed made her stomach lurch with horror.

Now, Anne looked down at her sister who was still sleeping and felt angry with her all over again. It was Izzie's stubbornness that had brought them to this. If she had obeyed their uncle and not gone to Hornby village they would still be safe. Anne shivered as she waited for a servant to come and re-kindle the fire; as September progressed the sun grew weaker and didn't seem to warm the chamber at all. After a while she got up and began to dress herself. She tiptoed across the room and pulled on the heavy door. It squeaked and groaned a little on its hinges and Izzie turned and muttered in the bed but didn't wake. Anne squeezed through the narrow gap and went down the stone steps.

The hall was empty and she walked to the small ante-chamber beyond, where the steps came up from the courtyard. There was a small herb garden below and a kitchen girl was knelt gathering some fresh leaves and placing them carefully in a basket. Anne was about to go down to where a patch of early morning sun had crested the castle walls when she heard booted footsteps ring across the hall behind her. She turned and saw Sir William following her. He took the weight of the door from her grasp and stood over her, so close that she could smell his odour and feel his breath on her face as he smiled down at her.

"You are up early," he commented as he studied her. His intense gaze made her feel uncomfortable. She was still afraid of him. "It is a shame that you have spent your life shut away," he said, as he touched her cheek gently with warm fingers. "You are pretty enough to grace any court."

"We were not prisoners at Hornby," she said, stepping away from him.

"Of course not. And neither are you a prisoner here."

"Then how long must we stay?" asked Anne, as she watched his eyes linger over her.

"I cannot say." He paused as they both heard the sound of a horn from the lookout tower. "News, I think!" he said. "And brought by the light of the full moon. Let's hope that it is good."

He passed her, his body brushing against her breasts, and signalled for the messenger to be brought in through the stone passageway. The mud splattered rider went down on one knee and handed a message to Sir William who unfolded the parchment and scanned it quickly.

Anne, having followed him half-way down the steps, watched as his expression turned from anticipation to apprehension. He looked up at her, speechless for a moment.

"What is it?" she asked. "What has happened?"

"The king has fled," he replied in an astonished voice.

"Fled?" she repeated as she stared back at him.

Sir William looked back at the message to re-read it. "Warwick and Clarence landed in Devon and many lords turned in their favour. The king was deserted. He has gone... gone by boat from the east coast... some say to Holland. The queen has sought sanctuary in Westminster Abbey."

"What will happen now?" asked Anne as he continued to stare at the words as if he could scarcely comprehend their meaning. Where was Richard, she wondered. Please God, keep him safe, she prayed silently over and over again, hoping that her thoughts would protect him.

"We can only wait and see," said Sir William, turning to dismiss the messenger and his panting, sweating horse. "I wonder if Warwick will put Clarence on the throne or if he will bring old Henry out of the Tower."

An air of anticipation hung over the castle as they waited for more news and on the third day another messenger arrived wearing the livery of Lord Thomas Stanley.

"You are to go to London, to your guardian," said Sir William to Anne and Izzie at supper that evening. "I have received word from my brother. We are summoned to court to see the rightful king restored to his throne."

Anne's first thought was one of dismay at the prospect of the lengthy journey. "How far is it?" she asked.

"Do not distress yourself on that account, my lady," replied Sir William. "I know that you are fearful on horseback so I will arrange a litter for yourself and your sister. We will travel slowly and take plenty of rest along the way." Then he paused with a cup part way to his lips and stared at her. "You will need new clothes for the coronation," he remarked as his gaze travelled up and down her body, "a gown more fitting to your status."

Anne squirmed under his gaze. She was glad that she had Izzie to share a bed with for the present, but the future held unknown terrors that were beyond her control. If she was given in marriage to this man then she would have to submit to his attentions and demands like a good wife, meekly and without protest, and the prospect terrified her.

She and Izzie huddled together in the open carriage that Sir William provided, holding hands tightly as they rocked and jerked along the muddy, puddle strewn roads. Even with cushions to sit on, the journey made Anne ache as much as riding a horse and she felt constantly sick. Izzie spoke in whispers of outlaws and robbers and, although Anne kept telling her not to worry, she did

51

not succeed in reassuring herself. She was tired and anxious and did not know for how many days they would have to travel, or what awaited them when they arrived.

At last they saw the walls of the city in the distance with myriad towers and spires rising above their height. Anne had never seen so many people in one place and the buildings were so crowded together in labyrinthine streets that there was hardly room to pass between them in places and Sir William, on horseback, rode ahead to clear a way through the stalls, which spilled out from the shops into the lanes. As Anne looked upwards she thought the houses leaned so precariously that they would tumble into the street below and it was only the narrowness of the gaps that kept them upright. Everywhere there was noise: people shouting, hammers clanging, dogs barking. Then the huddled, lime-washed homes and shops of the traders gave way to the houses of the wealthy as they approached the river to the south. She saw that they were coming to the edge of the city wall where it reached down to the riverside and on the shoreline there was a huge palace with round towers at each of its corners.

"That is Baynard's Castle," said Sir William as he drew his horse level with the litter to point out the sights. "And if you look to the other side you will see the tower of St Paul's church." Anne craned her neck at the high wooden steeple that seemed to reach up to the heavens and then at the houses and warehouses that clung to the shore of the river. "There is St Benet's church. And this is St Paul's Wharf. My brother's home, Stanley House, is nearby."

Izzie leaned across her to get a better look at the broad archway and wooden gates that were opened to admit them into a square court surrounded on three sides by buildings rising four storeys high and topped with pointed, shingled roofs.

A dark figure, silhouetted in the light from the lamps inside, came down the wooden stairs from the first floor and greeted her. "I am pleased to see you at last Mistress Harrington. I am Lord Thomas Stanley, your guardian."

Anne stared at the thin-faced man with the light brown beard. He looked younger than she had imagined, though his eyes were narrow and his unsmiling face had a mean foxy look. He was dressed sombrely in black, with a small cap on his head. She made a brief curtsey and he stood aside to indicate that she should enter.

He took them through the lower hall, past the kitchens and buttery to a solar where Anne could make out the river in the fading twilight. Here a woman of around middle age stood waiting to greet them.

"You are welcome," she said. "I am Lady Stanley. I hope your journey was not too difficult."

"It was bearable, my lady," replied Anne, studying the small and slender woman in her expensive satin dress that barely skimmed the floor; a blue and gold necklace glowed above the low cut bodice, and the jewels of the rings on her fingers danced in the candlelight. She felt shabby beside her in her soiled cloak and shoes and old gown.

"Come and sit close to the fire. You look cold," she said and beckoned them forwards as servants hurried in with flagons of wine and trays of honeyed cakes to refresh them.

"Sir William," she said as he bent to kiss her hand lightly. "Thank you for bringing Lord Stanley's wards safely to us."

"It has been a pleasure," he said, his eyes meeting Anne's before she turned away to sip a little wine to settle her stomach.

"You are welcome in my house," Lord Stanley told them. "You are fortunate that the misplaced loyalty of your uncles has made your rescue possible. From now on you will be treated properly and you will attend court and the coronation of the king."

"How is old Henry?" asked Sir William with faint derision in his voice.

"He is still resting in his rooms at the Tower. The day after tomorrow the Earl of Warwick will conduct him to St Paul's for his readeption. Then we will have a true Lancastrian king once more; a holy and saintly man, not one who lives a debauched and immoral life – and for that we should thank God."

"Come," said Lady Stanley in a gentle voice. "We will leave the men to their talk of kings and politics. You look in need of rest."

The men politely nodded their heads before Lady Stanley led Anne and Izzie up wide stairs to the top of the house.

"I would prefer to share with my sister," said Anne when Lady Stanley opened a door and showed her a bedchamber.

"That is not necessary. This house has many chambers," said Lady Stanley, sounding a little insulted. "There is space for you to have a bedchamber each even though my sons will soon join us as well. But if you insist," she conceded at last as Anne stood firmly outside the door, "though you will have to share the bed."

As Lady Stanley organised the servants to unpack their few belongings and bring washing water and more logs for the fire, Anne joined her sister by a window that Izzie had thrust open to look out.

"Noise," she breathed in excitement. "All I can hear is noise." Yet it wasn't a complaint. She looked round at Anne with brightened eyes. "The city is alive!"

All night long the noise kept Anne awake. Not just the chiming of the church bells and the singing and brawling of the drunkards in the streets, but other sounds that she couldn't identify: the barking of what sounded like a thousand dogs and, from a distance, a roaring and howling that she thought could only be the souls of the dead being tortured in purgatory.

"Those strange noises in the night," she whispered to Sir William as they sat down for breakfast next morning after hearing mass in the family chapel. "What were they?"

"Ah, those were the king's wild creatures," he replied. "But there is no need to be alarmed," he said, reaching for her hand. "Perhaps you and the lady Elizabeth would like to accompany me on a tour of the animal houses at the Tower?"

Anne stared back at his enquiring face. She'd had no idea that there were wild animals in London. She had heard that the Tower had a dungeon that was feared by many, but she did not know that the captives were guarded by ferocious animals.

"Is it safe?" she asked, imagining lions and wolves roaming at will.

"I will look after you," he said, moving a little closer and increasing the pressure on her hand. "The animals are all confined in cages so you can come to no harm. Except for the bear," he added. "His keeper takes him on a thick chain down to the river so that he might catch fish for his own dinner."

Anne stared at Sir William, unsure whether to believe him or whether he was teasing her and trying to make her afraid. Her instinct was to refuse, but the invitation to see these animals intrigued her. Perhaps, she thought, if she was to be his wife she should allow herself to get to know him better and a visit to see this menagerie appealed to her.

When the meal was finished, Sir William told Anne and Izzie to bring their cloaks.

"We will go by water," he said. "I have summoned the Stanley barge and sent word to the keepers to expect us."

When they stepped ashore near the west entrance to the Tower the smell assaulted Anne's nose. Everywhere there was a stench of rotting food and faeces. At the Lion Tower the keeper greeted Sir William and allowed them in through the gate and she held a corner of her cloak over her face and breathed through her mouth to prevent retching at the reek of the caged animals. But the stink didn't seem to bother either Sir William or Izzie, who rushed forward for a closer look.

"Nan!" she squealed in delight. "Come and see."

Behind wooden bars, that looked rather insubstantial to Anne, the amber eyes of a wolf gazed back at her. Rather than being the fierce snarling beast she had expected, it looked surprisingly subdued and even afraid. In the next cage was the bear that Sir William had spoken of. The thick metal chain that was fixed around the creature's neck clattered as it moved. Its paws were huge and ended in long, curved claws and she hoped that it wouldn't be let out whilst they were visiting. Suddenly a roar reminiscent of the ones she had heard in the night echoed across the courtyard and she found herself clinging to Sir William's arm in fright.

"Now that is the lion," he laughed, patting her hand and drawing her towards the wildcat's lair. Anne watched as the animal with a huge mane of reddish hair prowled backwards and forwards behind the bars, snarling and showing crisp white teeth that she had no doubt would tear her to pieces given the chance.

"It seems very angry," she said as she watched it turn and turn again in its small enclosure, praying that it wouldn't escape.

"It is quite content," said Sir William. "It has food and water and shelter. What more could it want?"

"Its freedom?" she asked, as she saw its mate at the back of the cage, gnawing on the bone of some other beast that had been fed to it.

"Come, Lady Anne." She felt his hand on her back and wasn't sure whether he meant to protect her or push her nearer to the cage. She didn't want to get closer but her resistance only increased the pressure of his hand. "You are quite safe," he told her. "They cannot hurt you." She glanced up and found him smiling down at her with a mixture of affection and impatience. She looked away and back at the pacing lion, suddenly feeling sorry for it in its captivity.

"Look!" exclaimed Izzie who was standing with her hand to her mouth outside another enclosure. Anne turned to see a spotted cat mount a female from behind, holding it tightly with its forepaws as it thrust into it. Izzie's eyes were sparkling at the unexpected entertainment and beside her Sir William laughed in an unsettling tone.

"It is disgusting," said Anne with distaste as she moved out of the reach of Sir William. And as she heard his laughter, now directed at her, she averted her eyes from the act on the other side of the bars, staring instead at the urine stained stream of water that flowed from the cage.

"The natural world can afford much pleasure if you allow it to," Sir William told her as she walked away from the animals and back towards the gate. Anne sensed him staring at her body again as he spoke. She would never experience any pleasure with him, she thought.

When they got back to the house, Lady Stanley called them to the solar where bolts of materials in an array of colours were spread across the coffers. There were wools and velvets, and silks brought from far Eastern countries, as well as martens' fur and dark brown sable.

Izzie rushed forward to finger them all, picking up some and holding them to her face. "They are all so beautiful!" she exclaimed. "Are we really to have gowns sewn from these?"

"My husband does not want you to appear in public wearing inferior gowns," said Lady Stanley. "He desires you to have clothing that reflects your status."

"Is it allowed?" asked Anne, her fingers tracing the softness of richly dyed indigo wool of the finest weave she had ever seen. It was a royal colour and she wondered from which merchant it had been bought.

"Of course it is allowed. The Stanleys may wear whatever they choose!" said Lady Stanley and Anne was reminded that she was sister to the traitor, Warwick. "See what a fine collar this would make," she went on, taking a pellet of marten fur and draping it around Anne's neck before gathering up a swathe of dark green velvet. "With this it would look very well."

Anne clasped the soft materials as Lady Stanley unrolled an azure blue silk and swathed it over Izzie's shoulder. These were the finest and most expensive cloths she had ever seen and, although they had always been well-dressed at Hornby, she had never had anything to compare with these.

"You must choose with haste," urged Lady Stanley. "The seamstresses must begin work at once if your gowns are to be ready."

On the morning of the coronation, the Stanley household was awake early with servants running up and down the stairs with hot water, basins and freshly laundered linen. The previous evening bathtubs had been filled for everyone to bathe in rose-scented water and, feeling fresh and fragrant, Anne pushed back the linen sheets of the bed and began to dress in her new chemise and the pale green silk kirtle. A girl helped her step into the darker green overgown and fastened the wide belt with gold thread that held up the voluminous folds of the skirts. She slipped her feet into fine stockings, with delicate garters, and then into soft leather shoes that the girl tied with laces around her ankles. Her hair was combed back from her face and fastened up underneath an embroidered hennin before a short veil of the palest cream linen was pinned into place.

"You look beautiful!" said Izzie, in her own blue gown with dark fur trim. Her fair hair was held back from her face but being younger was allowed to fall loosely down her back and she wore a blue cap that matched her gown.

Close by, the bells in the wooden tower of St Paul's church had begun to ring and, where there had been anticipation, a feeling of foreboding settled around Anne as she remembered that the purpose of the day was to place King Henry back on the throne as a puppet king – when the real king and his brother were exiled from their country. Thinking of Richard she glanced at herself in the burnished mirror and thought how joyful she would have been to see herself like this as a bride, about to be married to the man she loved. She watched her expression change to one of sadness and regret that the best time of her life could already be past.

"Let me see!" said Izzie, pushing her aside to take her place. Anne watched her sister smile at her reflection then meet her own eyes through the mirror. "The Stanley sons and cousins have come," she said with a touch of apprehension. "By the end of the day we will have met our future husbands."

They came down the stairs, clutching their billowing skirts.

"You look quite beautiful," whispered Sir William as she laid her hand on his brown velvet sleeve, fashionably slashed to reveal glimpses of a white silk shirt beneath. He escorted her to the Stanley carriage with its covered canopy in the crimson and blue Stanley colours. A moment later Lady Stanley joined them with her two elder sons.

"Where is Lord Stanley?" asked Anne as they moved off, out onto the street to the half-hearted cheering of the assembled crowd.

"He has gone with my brother to bring the king from the Tower," said Lady Stanley. "They will parade him through the streets of London for everyone to see – in defiance of those who rumoured that he no longer lived, or that he had become too mad to attend his own coronation."

Anne said nothing but couldn't help recall the things Uncle James had said about the king. The thought of her uncle made her worry anew about where he was. Had he and Uncle Robert fled as well? And if so what would happen to Hornby Castle?

They made slow progress through the crush and when they reached the church Anne realised she had to get down and walk through the crowd to the door. She hesitated, hanging back and wishing that she could stay in the carriage.

"Come!" said Sir William, handing the reins of his horse to a squire. "I will clear a path for you." And with his switch and his tongue he lashed people right and left so that they stepped back onto one another's toes to make way for them.

St Paul's was a magnificent building. When Anne went inside and saw the light shining down from the lantern tower above the nave she thought it was like divine radiance, and she crossed herself and made a silent prayer for the safety of those she loved.

She had expected some reverence once inside the church, but she was disappointed. It was barely more peaceful than it had been on the streets. People were talking and laughing and standing on tiptoes to look around to see who had come and who had chosen to stay away. How quickly people's allegiances altered, thought Anne. They considered only their own fortunes. Only a few months ago most of these people would have sworn their loyalty to King Edward, but now they supported Warwick and Margaret of Anjou without question; or at least without any public question.

A hush moved across the church, beginning at the door and making its way eastwards like a wave. Izzie gripped her hand and Anne peered towards the doorway to try to see what was happening.

"It's the king," whispered Izzie as the turning of heads gave way to bows and curtseys.

Anne watched as the procession came closer. A man, whom she thought must be the Earl of Warwick, led a shambling figure in a long, faded gown of blue velvet. The man stared about him in incomprehension; his eyes wild, confused and a little fearful as they darted from face to face. Lord Stanley followed him and when they reached the chancel steps he urged the man towards the throne that had been placed ready for him and nodded to the priest to bring forward the incense and the oil.

So this was the king, thought Anne. How right her uncle had been when he described him as mad and not fit to rule. The man seemed to have no understanding of what was going on and Anne felt sorry for him. The crowd, now silent, watched as the head, hands and breast of the king were bared and anointed. The crown of Edward the Confessor was replaced on his head and he was handed the sceptre and the orb. Then he repeated the vows, prompted by the priest, as a child might speak the words of a lesson not comprehended – and the atmosphere of jubilation and anticipation that had held London in its grasp seemed to fade as the congregation watched. Anne, it seemed, was not alone in her fear for the future.

With a fanfare of trumpets, the king was led away and Anne felt Sir William touch her arm. She glanced up and saw that he too looked troubled at the events he had just witnessed.

"It is time to go," he said. "There is a banquet to attend. Stay close to me and I will see you safely to the hall."

They walked in procession through the gathered throngs to the palace at Westminster, where, under the high hammerbeam roof, the bewildered king sat on another throne, his thin hands gripping the arms of the chair as he stared around, and it was the Earl of Warwick, with Lord Stanley close by his side, who was greeting the assembled guests.

"These are my wards, the lady Anne Harrington and her sister Elizabeth," said Lord Stanley. "From Hornby Castle," he added as Anne looked up at Warwick, the traitor she had heard so much about. He studied her for a moment.

"What of Hornby?" he asked, turning his attention back to Lord Stanley. "Is it in your possession yet?"

"James Harrington still holds it," said Lord Stanley with a shrug of irritation. "He fled back there and claims it is his. But," he added with a slight smile, "I will ensure he does not hold it much longer."

"Good man!" laughed Warwick, patting Lord Stanley's shoulder with resounding slaps. "Now all you need to do is marry your wards wisely and it will be Stanley property for ever."

"Indeed, that is my intention."

Anger rose in Anne as she listened to the men. Their casual talk of marriages made the blood fire her cheeks, but they turned away to greet some other nobles and she was left standing alone with Izzie, of no more consequence than a horse for sale at the market.

The celebration continued until it was very late. The king fell asleep on his throne, his head lolling to one side and a trail of saliva running from the corner of his mouth down his chin. Izzie joined in the dancing, quickly learning the steps from a succession of attentive admirers whilst Anne stood by and watched and politely refused all invitations to join in.

"Do you not like to dance?" asked Sir William, coming to stand beside her and bending to whisper in her ear. His beard touched her cheek and she resisted the urge to push him away.

"I am tired," she said, "and my legs ache."

"Then let me find you a seat," he said, leading her towards a bench at the edge of the room. Anne sat down, her toe tapping to the rhythm of the music despite herself and she wished that she could enjoy the day as much as Izzie, who seemed to be finding delight in each turn and clap of the carole.

Sir William sat down beside her, his legs spread wide and his knee touching hers, following it even when she moved her leg away.

"How delightful you look in your new gown. You will make a wife that a man will be pleased to have on his arm – and in his bed," he remarked as his hand closed over hers for a moment then brushed across her thigh. He had been drinking heavily and his breath smelled sour as he bent towards her and kissed her cheek. Anne tried to move from his grasp but she was trapped by the dancers who were skipping past in a never-ending chain. "I have asked my brother to consider me when choosing a husband for you, Anne," he told her, his hand now squeezing her leg just above the knee. "I think that you will enjoy having me as a husband as much as I will enjoy having you to wife."

Anne could think of nothing worse than having to endure his attentions in the bedchamber and knowing what would be expected of her made it even harder. She tried to move away but he edged ever nearer and it was with a feeling of relief that she looked up to see Lord Stanley standing before them, even if his stare of displeasure betrayed his belief that she was content to allow Sir William to touch her in such an inappropriate manner.

"It is time for my wards to leave," he said in a level voice that did not quite disguise his anger.

Outside the night was cold and Anne shivered as she looked up at the clear, star-filled sky. Lady Stanley looked tired and tense, but Izzie glowed with energy and seemed not to notice that Anne remained silent as they travelled back along the quiet streets. "I wish I could stay in London forever," she enthused and Anne formed the opinion that her sister had drunk far more wine than was seemly for a young lady.

The next morning as Anne watched Izzie groan and hold her head because of the pain and the sick feeling in her stomach, a servant came up with a message that Lord Stanley wanted them.

As Anne went down the stairs she guessed what the interview would be about. Lord Stanley was not a man to take chances and she knew that her marriage was the only way he could secure the ownership of Hornby Castle.

The family was gathered in the solar that overlooked the river. Lord Stanley was warming himself with his back to the fire and Lady Stanley sat near him on her high-backed wooden chair, her hands folded on her lap. Neither looked as if they had been up late the previous night and Anne was aware that by comparison she looked tired and drawn. She had lain awake until dawn, crying and praying that she might be delivered from this fate, and the mirror in the bedchamber had reflected a white-faced girl with down-turned lips and dark circles under her reddened eyes.

"I hope you slept well?" said Lord Stanley. "I have something important to say," he went on without waiting for any answer to his query. "As you know it is my honour to be your guardian. And although the appointment was made by the Yorkist, Edward, our present true king, Henry, God bless him," and he paused to make the sign of the cross before continuing, "King Henry has agreed that my guardianship should continue."

Anne thought that it was scarce possible for the king to understand or agree to anything and she surmised that it was the Earl of Warwick who spoke on his behalf, although the detail made no difference.

"As your guardian," continued Lord Stanley, "it is my duty to match you with suitable and loving husbands. And whilst we are gathered together, here, for these most joyous celebrations, my wife and I..." he paused to nod towards Lady Stanley who similarly inclined her head in agreement... "we have decided that it would be an additional pleasure to arrange your betrothals. Elizabeth," he continued, holding out a hand towards Izzie, "you will be wed to my nephew John."

Izzie smiled for the first time that morning and her aching head seemed quite forgotten as she placed her hand on that of the boy who had stepped forward and given her a formal bow. Anne recognised him as the same boy who had spent much of the previous evening with his hand on Izzie's waist teaching her dance steps.

"You will be betrothed now, but not formally married until John is fourteen," said Lord Stanley as he watched the couple with satisfaction. At least Izzie seemed happy with the arrangement, thought Anne. She supposed that she ought to be glad. It was better than having to deal with a sister who was weeping and fearful at the prospect of her marriage.

"And Anne..." began Lord Stanley and she glanced around the room to see if Sir William was nursing as bad a headache as he deserved, but was surprised to find him absent. How could her betrothal be announced without him, she wondered, as she allowed Lord Stanley to take her hand. "Anne, I will welcome you as a daughter of my own."

Confused at his words, Anne looked at the two boys standing beside their mother. George, the eldest son and Stanley heir, was only a few years younger than herself and Anne was surprised that Lord Stanley thought she was important enough to merit such a match. "Anne," he continued. "You will be betrothed to my son Edward."

Anne stared at the thin, pale boy. He could be no more than seven or eight years old. He was just a child. "But..." she began in dismay, wondering if this was a worse or better fate than becoming the wife of Sir William.

Chapter Five
November 1470 ~ October 1471

Anne bid a distraught farewell to her sister, and Izzie clung to her neck until Lord Stanley became impatient and told them both to stop being so foolish. Then she was ushered into the carriage for the long journey north. It was cold and lonely as the first of the autumnal frosts iced the lowland fields. But Lathom House looked inviting as they approached and Anne hoped that living there would not be as bad as she imagined.

When she was shown to a chamber with a soft bed and blue hangings she relaxed a little. The windows were wide and let in plenty of light; the view of the parkland, though not impressive, was pleasant enough and she decided that if this was to be her new home then perhaps it would be bearable, although being parted from her sister still made her ache with distress.

Although the vows of a pre-marriage contract had been exchanged before a priest in the small chapel at Stanley House before they left London, Anne's guardian was not content and she was soon married to Edward Stanley at Burscough Priory.

Wearing a new gown of blue, covered with a fur-lined cloak against the chill of the damp November day, she stood beside him at the door of the church as the prior gave them God's blessing. Edward's voice sounded childlike as he made his vows and as they knelt on the chancel steps to solemnise their union with the holy mass, Anne found that she could look down on the top of his blond head. But this was, at least for the time being, a marriage in name only to secure her inheritance for Lord Stanley. It would not be consummated until Edward was fourteen years of age. That was still six years away and Anne knew that as some of his brothers and sisters had died in childhood there was the possibility that he might not even live that long. In the meantime he was to train as a knight and she was to live at Lathom as a companion to Lady Stanley.

Her uncle still held Hornby and the irritation and anger on Lord Stanley's face when he returned from North Lancashire filled her with a mixture of trepidation and glee. He had supposed that once she and her sister were in his power that James Harrington would meekly hand over the keys, but he had not taken into account her uncle's tenacity or the fact that the Earl of Warwick had other matters more pressing to concern him and was not minded to give time to what he had dismissed as a petty dispute.

Sir William had been invited to her wedding but had ridden off from the house in London with a scowl on his face the day after the coronation.

"He has gone to France," Lady Stanley told her one afternoon as they sat together embroidering in the fading light of the chamber. "My niece is to be married to Edward of Lancaster, the Prince of Wales."

It was a moment before Anne, half-heartedly jabbing at her fabric with a blunt needle, realised the significance of this news.

"The Earl of Warwick's daughter, Anne Neville?" she asked, remembering that this was the girl whom Richard had expected to marry.

"Yes. They are to be married next month at Angers Cathedral. She will be the next queen of England."

"How old is the prince?" asked Anne, wondering if it was a marriage that would be consummate or just another thread in the net that Warwick was weaving around himself.

"He is seventeen," replied Lady Stanley, her eyes fixed on her work. "And my niece Anne is fifteen – much the same age as you. It is a good age for a marriage. Hopefully she will soon bear an heir for the prince – a boy first if she is blessed." Lady Stanley paused and, after fixing her needle to the shirt she was stitching, she laid a hand over Anne's in an awkward gesture of affection. "Your husband will grow up too," she said. "Be patient and give him time. He will become a good man. And you are still young. There is time for him to father your children."

Anne stared at the white, bejewelled hand and then moved hers away from beneath it. She would never permit Edward Stanley to touch her. She had already decided that.

They remained at Lathom for Christmas and her young husband came for the festivities. Anne watched as the small boy, accompanied by a squire, rode his overlarge bay horse up to the house. Having slid down the length of the horse's flank to the ground he ran towards his mother. Lady Stanley wrapped him in a warm embrace before kissing his travel-stained cheeks and smoothing down his fair hair. Then she held him before her at arm's length and declared that he had grown at least six inches since she had last seen him. He laughed at her exaggeration, clearly delighted, until his eyes strayed to Anne and a look of distaste suddenly replaced his joy at his homecoming.

"My lord," she said, stepping forward from the doorway where she had been watching. He bowed his head towards her.

"Kiss your wife!" encouraged his mother. "She has waited patiently for your return."

Anne bent awkwardly and proffered her cheek to the boy who put his lips to her skin; his face was as soft and smooth as her own. Then he turned away to talk to his mother who put her hand on his slender shoulder as they went inside. Anne followed, excluded from the family reunion. She had never felt so alone. She wondered where Richard was celebrating his Christmas and whether he ever thought about her – or if he had forgotten their time together as a transient memory of a summer day is lost in the darkness of winter's battle for survival.

Christmas at Lathom was a more lavish affair than anything Anne had seen before. But she did not find much joy in the celebrations, just a gnawing discomfort at the house being filled with cheerful strangers of whom she knew nothing. Her husband spoke to her only a handful of times. They were seated together at table and so he could not avoid her then, but other than clumsily serving her or giving her formal greetings he acted as if she didn't exist, except for his resentful glances. The only person he wanted to be with was his mother and, although Anne continued to sit with Lady Stanley in the afternoons, she began to feel she was as invisible as a servant to be ignored by both mother and son.

She took some small comfort from the feasting with its rich and spicy foods, the warm sweetness of the mulled wine, and the musicians and actors who came to entertain them, but the best day was when her sister Izzie came with her betrothed, John, from his parents' home in Cheshire to celebrate the Twelfth Night.

Anne had been waiting for the visitors all day, returning again and again to the thickly glazed window of her chamber to watch for them coming. She had not seen Izzie since they were parted in London and she missed her desperately.

At last they came. Izzie was riding on a dappled grey palfrey, wrapped against the cold in a dark blue cloak, her eyes sparkling and her face glowing pink. Anne paused a moment, jealously, before all thoughts of herself were forgotten and she ran to enclose her sister in her arms.

"Izzie, you look so well. You look so happy," she whispered, holding her close and enjoying the familiarity of the physical contact.

"Why wouldn't I be happy?" she asked as she wriggled from Anne's grasp and glanced towards John with a look of satisfaction.

"Then I am happy for you," said Anne as she led her sister inside and showed her to the bedchamber that they were to share for the duration of the visit.

"Are they kind to you?" she asked as Izzie threw her cloak across the bed and, without waiting for a servant to assist her, began to pull linen and stockings out of her travelling coffer and drape them around the room until it resembled the untidy chamber at Hornby where they used to sleep.

"Of course," she said as she stripped off her soiled clothes and washed, not even seeming to feel the cold. "And the house is comfortable, even in wintertime, and there is plenty to eat..."

"And your betrothed?"

Izzie paused with the wet cloth in her hand and smiled widely. "He is wonderful," she said and Anne saw that her sister was in love.

"You're fortunate," she said as she folded the soiled clothes that had been cast aside. At least one of them had found happiness, she thought, as she watched her sister draw on clean stockings over her smooth long legs.

Downstairs the Yule log was still burning in the hearth and the hall was decked with evergreen boughs. One of the kitchen boys whose usual job was to turn the roasting meat was crowned King of Misrule and allowed to choose the games – although Anne noticed that he did nothing without first looking to Lord Stanley for a nod of approval. She guessed that he had been given instruction on what he could and could not suggest and nothing too riotous took place.

The visitors stayed until after the feast of the Epiphany and although Anne was glad to be with her sister again she couldn't help but notice that Izzie showed little interest in her own situation. Apart from a brief acknowledgement that Anne had had a lucky escape from Sir William and that Edward was still too young to be a real husband to her, Izzie's talk was all of John and her new life. And although Anne was relieved that Izzie was content, it seemed that the Stanleys had stolen her sister away from her, and as she waved goodbye, one morning in January when the hoar frost still clung to the trees around Lathom House, she felt more isolated and alone than she could ever have imagined.

The motion of the boat on the shifting waves was making Robert Harrington feel queasy as a strong wind filled the sails and drove them toward the English coast. The Duke of Gloucester was standing in the prow with the cold wind tangling his dark hair across his face. His hat had blown off three times and he now held it in his hand as he watched bareheaded for sight of the small harbour where they would make landfall.

Robert's stomach heaved and he leant over the rail and watched the spellbinding movement of the grey water slapping against the wooden hull. He wondered how much longer his guts would withstand the constant motion, and it was with relief that he heard an excited voice shout that a fishing village had been sighted through the low coastal mist. Standing at the very end of a strip of narrow land that jutted out from the Yorkshire coast it looked unprepossessing. Yet they could hardly have sailed a fleet of ships straight into Hull and the king's orders were to come ashore discreetly. Their small force, although backed with men, money and goodwill from Burgundy, was not yet numerous enough to fight and their objective was to take a quiet toehold on England and trust to God and their Yorkist supporters that Edward could reclaim his throne from Warwick's puppet king.

Rumours had abounded at the Burgundian court, but credible sources spoke of the Duke of Clarence's discontent that the crown had not been placed on his own head. The king's sister had sent letters, conveyed by trusted messengers, urging Clarence to accept Edward's right to be king and to be reconciled with him. No promise had been forthcoming, but there was hope. Though it would need more than hope to keep them alive and see them prevail, thought Robert, watching the startled fishermen look up from mending their nets as the fleet of boats approached out of the fog.

The duke was first off the boat, scarcely before it was secured to the iron ring sunk into the wharf. He bent one knee to the wet ground and crossed himself in thanks to God and then ran his slender fingers through his salt-coated hair. "I will not run a third time," he vowed. "From this day on I will fight for what is rightfully mine, for my king and for my country."

"Yes, my lord," replied Robert, after giving similar thanks to have reached the shore without his stomach disgracing him. He turned to watch as planks were laid from ship to shore and the grooms began to coax the snorting, anxious horses onto dry land. The sickness was now replaced with the fluttering feeling that came before a battle. Not fear exactly but apprehension and Robert, watching the duke greet and hand largesse to the awestruck villagers, hoped and prayed that all of the north would be as pleased as these poor Yorkshiremen that Edward Plantagenet had returned.

Robert longed to see Isabella again. He hoped that she had not believed any rumours she might have heard about his death. Although it had been possible to correspond with some trusted lords in England, letters to a squire's betrothed were not a matter of importance and he had been unable to let her know that he was safe and would return to claim her as his bride.

Word had come that the queen had given birth to Edward's firstborn son at Westminster and had named him for his father. Well, first legitimately born, mused Robert, as he pondered on the king's roving eye for any pretty woman who would bestow a favour on him. Although it was said he was entranced by the queen and loved her passionately, marrying her in defiance of Warwick who had been negotiating for a match with a French princess, it had not prevented him from pursuing several dalliances amongst the court at Burgundy. His sister Margaret and his brother-in-law had seemed indulgent, regarding it as an endearing weakness in his character that had no matter, but young Diccon had, on occasion, frowned darkly at Edward's lack of self-control and on one evening in particular as he and Robert had sat in an alcove of the great hall, absenting themselves from the rest of the court, the duke had spoken about the lady Anne.

"I am aware that your brother sent her to my bedchamber as a bribe," he said. "It was not necessary. I had already taken you both into my service."

"But you did not send her away."

"I tried," explained Richard. "But she was anxious that your brother would be angry with her. I slept on a pallet that night and she alone in my bed."

"So she remains a virgin?"

Robert wondered if the duke was experienced himself. Diccon had always excluded himself from bawdy talk at Middleham, preferring the company of the women's chamber to men's ribaldry. Perhaps he was in need of a more knowing woman than a fifteen year old girl.

"No," admitted Richard. "She came to me willingly enough the next day. I would not have taken her against her will," he said, looking up at Robert with his clear blue eyes. "It is not my way to force a woman for my pleasure," he said, his glance straying across the hall to where Lord Hastings had a servant girl pinned against the wall and was smiling in apparent pleasure at her reluctance to allow him to plunge a hand inside her unlaced gown. "I think your brother had hopes of a marriage," he said after a moment.

"And what are your thoughts?" ventured Robert.

"To marry for wealth rather than love," he replied, and having set his cup down he said that he was tired and would go to his bedchamber. When Robert rose to accompany him the duke told him to remain, that he had no need of his services that night. And as Robert watched him walk away he thought that he had touched a raw wound and wondered just what feelings the Duke of Gloucester had for his niece.

For Anne, each day seemed interminable in its tedium and she could not recall the last time she had been free from the prying eyes of one servant or another.

Now that the worst of the winter was over she was at least allowed to take some exercise in the garden with some of the other women and although the spring weather remained cold, and often snowy, the lengthening of the days had provoked the birds into prospecting for nest sites. Watching them in the treetops and listening to the cawing of the rooks, Anne reflected that almost a full year had passed since she had spent those days with Richard at Hornby Castle. For both of them so much had changed.

Hearing the sound of hooves in the distance, she hurried up the slight incline towards the house to see if it was a messenger approaching. Was there news from Hornby, she wondered. Lord Stanley was there, still trying to wrest it from her uncle, though the last she had heard was that Uncle James was still resolutely clinging to the castle despite the Stanley assault.

The messenger must have ridden hard from the north, she thought, as she watched him leap from his lathered horse and, after flinging the reins at a boy, run to beg admission to the house. Anne hurried after him and found Lady Stanley peering at a letter.

"This is bad news," she said as Anne came in, breathless.

"Bad news?"

"My husband writes to me of trouble," said Lady Stanley, her mouth forming a thin line as she looked up and met Anne's eyes.

"Hornby?" asked Anne.

"No, not Hornby. The Yorkists have landed in Yorkshire. Edward Plantagenet has ridden into York and laid claim to his rights as the duke." She shook her head. "This could be dangerous," she said.

Was Richard with him, wondered Anne. Was he back in England? Could she sense his presence and feel him coming nearer to her with every passing moment? A shaft of sunlight broke through the heavy cloud and pierced the glass of the window.

The next evening Lord Stanley arrived with a small party of men. The gathering gloom was reflected in his dismal face as he stood to warm his hands before the fire, still dressed in his mud spattered boots and coat.

"This is not good," he muttered to his wife. "It is not good at all. They are raising support across the country and men are gathering again under Edward's banner."

"But people know that Henry is their rightful king," said Lady Stanley, handing wine and refreshments to her husband.

"The people have seen and heard nothing of Henry," said Lord Stanley. "Many have already realised that your brother is the real ruler. And I have heard rumours that there are plenty who would like to see Edward restored to the throne. Even my own brother has ridden to support him."

"Surely not?" exclaimed Lady Stanley and Anne glanced up from the bench beneath the window where she was sitting with her needlework. She wondered how much Sir William's betrayal of the Lancastrian cause was to do with his simmering anger at his brother over her marriage, and how much to do with his judgement of who would eventually prevail.

"I sent spies to York to discover what is happening. Edward is moving south. He has raised support at Wakefield and now marches towards Nottingham where Harrington has pledged to meet him with six hundred men. I need to gather an army."

"Then there will be more fighting?"

"Almost without a doubt, my lady, almost without a doubt." He turned from the fire, his cheeks pinkened from the blaze. "Be thankful your husband is too young to fight," he said to Anne. "I would not like to see you widowed before you have provided him with a son."

The next day he was gone again, leaving an air of disquiet lingering around the house. Even Lady Stanley could not sit still, but watched constantly for messengers. Anne waited too. The days grew longer and warmer as Lent passed with its frugal, meatless meals and incessant prayers in the priory church. Lady Stanley, she knew, prayed for victory for her brother, Warwick, and the Lancastrians. But Anne's prayers were for the Yorkist army.

"God keep him safe," said Lady Stanley as she made the sign of the cross.

"Amen," replied Anne, thinking of Richard.

James Harrington looked at the long line of men that stretched into the distance with warhorses, palfreys, baggage carts and pack animals. He had pledged six hundred men to the king and had not been disappointed by the response to his call. Every armed and able-bodied man from miles around had gathered under the Harrington knot. Stanley had withdrawn, taking his damnable cannon with him, and surely with the backing from Burgundy it would only be a matter of time before Edward was back in control of his country. And surely, this time, he would reward the Harrington's loyalty by giving him the legal possession of Hornby Castle. He gave a smile of reassurance to Joan who was seated in a litter with the children and their nurse. This latest siege had been hard on her and, as she was terrified of being left alone again, she was to travel with them as far as his lands at Brierley, in Yorkshire, where she would at least be safe from the Stanleys. He knew that she still held herself responsible for the loss of his nieces, but once his initial anger had faded he had admitted that neither she nor his steward had been to blame. The fault had been that of his younger niece and his only regret was that he had not beaten her soundly on the first occasion she had been discovered outside the castle walls. His reluctance to do so as she had cried and begged his forgiveness had been their undoing.

Coming out from the Duke of Gloucester's tent at their temporary camp near the town of Nottingham, Robert saw the black and white Harrington banner planted firmly in the ground in the midst of tents that had appeared like overnight mushrooms. He went across, slipping on the churned mud, to seek his brother. He was relieved that James and his men had arrived safely. During their own march down from York, Warwick's brother Montagu and his army had watched them from a distance, though he had not offered any challenge when he saw their numbers.

When he saw him approaching James hurried to meet him, clasped his arm, and then hugged him in a brief and uncharacteristic show of affection.

"Hornby?" asked Robert.

"Still in our possession and God willing it will remain so," James reassured him. "Although I cannot say the same for our nieces." He gestured Robert to a folding stool by his campfire and told him what had happened.

"Lord Stanley may have turned his coat but Sir William has declared for the king," Robert told his brother. "He was one of the first to join us with a force of men in Yorkshire."

"Then it would not surprise me to see Lord Stanley change his loyalty yet again. He runs with both the hares and the hounds," said James, contemptuously.

At Leicester Sir William Norris joined them with three thousand men raised from the estates of Lord Hastings. Then the king's forces marched on Coventry and the Earl of Warwick swiftly retreated inside the city walls. Despite a challenge he refused to come out and fight and Edward impatiently ordered them to by-pass the city and ride on to Warwick where he proclaimed himself king.

It was there that a herald came, wearing familiar murrey and blue livery, but with a bull badge sewn onto his tunic.

"From our brother George, the Duke of Clarence," said Richard as he watched the man being escorted towards him.

"My lord," said the messenger, going down on one knee. "I bring greetings from your brother. He craves to be reconciled."

Robert watched as Richard kept the man waiting for a reply, his face betraying no emotion. At last he gave a brief nod. "Take him to the king," he said to Robert.

After hearing what the messenger had to say both Edward and Richard gave orders for their men to ride out in battle array. "If this is some trick of Warwick's we will not be lured into his trap," remarked the duke. "And if my brother Clarence has truly seen his error then let our overwhelming force be a reminder to him that he has made a goodly choice."

They were about three miles beyond Warwick, heading towards Banbury, when an opposing army was sighted in the distance. Riding at the side of the Duke of Gloucester, Robert Harrington stood in his stirrups and watched. Clarence's forces had also come prepared for battle and there was an unease filling the air like the heaviness that precedes a thunderstorm.

As they watched, a figure on a bay destrier accompanied by three other men on horseback broke from the ranks on the far side of the field and came forward. They reined in midway between the two forces and the king signalled to Richard to accompany him.

"Wait here," said the duke to Robert as he gathered the reins and touched his spurs to his horse's flanks. "But at the first sign of trouble come quickly."

Robert nodded and watched as the two men rode forward to meet with their brother. The gathered army fell silent as if holding its collective breath. Robert could hear the voices carried on the breeze, but was unable to make out the words. His horse shifted beneath him, sensing his disquiet, and he reached forward to stroke its neck to calm both himself and the animal.

The Duke of Clarence dismounted and knelt before the king. The king also got down and raised up his brother and embraced him and kissed him. The Duke of Gloucester likewise greeted his brother, though Robert thought that his kiss was made with more reluctance.

Anne woke early on the morning of Easter Sunday and after dressing and making her own private prayers she walked with Lady Stanley to mass in the priory chapel. The mist played games through the trees, coming and going and making it difficult to see and Anne was surprised when the high stone walls of Burscough suddenly loomed in front of them.

As the priest recited the prayers Anne thought about Jesus being raised from the dead after his banishment into hell for three days. Was it a blasphemy, she wondered, to hope that Edward, the rightful king, would likewise be restored to his throne. She bowed her head and concentrated harder on her devotions, a little ashamed that her thoughts were not on the wonder of the everlasting God, but more fleshly concerns, as she came before the priest to receive the host.

As they walked back to Lathom House, hungry for a breakfast of fresh eggs and bread and butter, the sun began to burn off the mist from the lowland hollows. It warmed them as they made their way along the damp grassy path, holding up their skirts to prevent them becoming wet. And by nightfall Anne had discovered that the mist had favoured the Yorkists.

Standing in the hall, steaming and swathed in an aroma of sweating horse, the messenger from Lord Stanley described how Edward Plantagenet had met with the Earl of Warwick in battle at Barnet. The mist had been thick and some of Warwick's men had mistaken the stars and streamers of the Earl of Oxford's banners for the suns of the king's livery and had fought against their own side. When he saw that they would be defeated Warwick's brother Montagu had switched allegiance and, seeing that he could not prevail, the Earl of Warwick had fled into nearby woods. One of Edward's men had seen him and a force had been dispatched to pursue and kill him.

Lady Stanley wept for her dead brother and bade Anne accompany her to the priory to light candles for his soul. In the church Anne gave thanks to God that it was her own prayers that had been heard. Richard was safe. It had been a good Easter Day. The sun of York had risen again.

"Do not be too sure of this Yorkist victory!" spat Lady Stanley at Anne, through her tears. "I cannot believe that those who are my own cousins have murdered my brother! There will be retribution!"

Anne expected Lord Stanley to come home, to admit his defeat and to keep from the sight of the king. She thought that he would give up his futile attempts to take Hornby Castle and one night she dreamed that Richard rode to Lathom House on his grey stallion to rescue her. But the weeks passed and the spring blossom frothed onto the branches of the apple trees in the orchard and still no one came. There were just rumours and mutterings that Anne heard in snatches through open doors and windows as she wandered about the house, restless and lonely. Lady Stanley had withdrawn into herself since the death of her brother. She seemed unsure and afraid of what would happen to her now. Even the news, which had been sent secretly, that a force led by Margaret of Anjou had arrived in Weymouth and, joined by those Lancastrians who had escaped at Barnet, was marching towards Wales to gather the support of Jasper Tudor, was not enough to dry her constant tears.

From Lord Stanley there was no word until the first week in May when a messenger came with news of another battle at Tewkesbury, where King Edward had finally cornered and defeated the remaining Lancastrians.

"We are summoned to London," Lady Stanley told Anne, tearfully. "Though I dread what is to become of us. King Henry is dead and so is the Prince of Wales and I fear for my husband," she said.

Yet the news broke into Anne's world like sudden sunshine after a fierce storm. Not even the thought of the debilitating travel sickness or the strange beds and the greasy food at inns along the way could spoil her eagerness to arrive back in the crowded, noisy, smelly city.

At last they drew into the courtyard of the Stanley's town house and Anne got down with relief, taking deep breaths of air – although she barely noticed how foul it was as she caught sight of her sister waiting to greet her.

"Izzie! I did not know you would be here!" she cried as she hugged her and kissed both her cheeks.

"I have been here more than three days waiting for you. We thought you would surely catch us up along the road, but you have travelled so slowly."

Anne looked at her sister's face, flushed with excitement, and wondered what she knew. The only words Lady Stanley had spoken had been filled with doom and dire warnings about their fate. She seemed to have resigned herself to being locked in the Tower on her arrival and remaining there for the rest of her short life, but Izzie's face spoke of celebration and privilege rather than imprisonment.

Anne turned as she heard someone else arriving and saw Lord Stanley ride into the courtyard and dismount to greet his wife who was still sitting in the carriage.

"Come, my lady, allow me to assist you. What ails you?" he asked when he saw Lady Stanley's tear-streaked face blinking at the evening sunlight that fell across the shingled rooftops.

"I am pleased to see you in good health and with your freedom, my lord," she replied in a trembling voice when he had given her his arm and helped her out. "I had grave concerns as to whether I would find you alive, let alone at liberty."

"Oh hush," he told her. "Did you not know that I would fight for the winning side?"

"The winning side?" she asked as she gazed at him in bewilderment.

"Yes. With the assistance of the Stanley armies, King Edward, God bless him, has re-taken his rightful place on the English throne."

Anne watched as Lady Stanley continued to stare at her husband. "You fought for the Yorkists?" she asked. Her voice rose as she spoke and she raised her hand to her forehead as if she might fall into a fit. But then she regained her composure and turned away from him to enter the house. Lord Stanley followed with a slight smile playing around his lips.

"Have no fear, daughter," he said as he passed Anne. "You are safe and welcome in London. We are here to celebrate!"

"Come in," said Izzie as Lord Stanley followed his wife to their private chamber. "There is so much I have to tell you."

Anne followed Izzie up the stairs to the bedchamber and, after washing her hands and face and taking a drink of wine, she lay on the bed and listened as her sister prattled on about herself and John and all the things they had done since they had arrived in London.

"And then we saw Gloucester," she said.

"The Duke of Gloucester? Did he look well?" she asked, sitting up.

"Well enough for a man who's just killed a prince and a king," remarked Izzie with distaste. "I always told you that I disliked him and now I have good reason."

"What are you talking about?" asked Anne. She had been about to reply that Richard could never kill anyone, but she had swallowed back the words because she knew they were untrue. At Hornby she had seen the glint in his eye as he unsheathed his sword with a determination that left her in no doubt that he would delight in using his weapon should the opportunity arise.

"They say that after the battle at Tewkesbury the Prince of Wales fled on foot," said Izzie. "Gloucester went after him and cut him to death with no more hesitation than killing a deer at the end of a hunt. They say he did it because he was jealous that the prince had married Anne Neville. They say he wants her for his own wife and killing the prince made her a widow."

"What nonsense!" said Anne, but the stab of jealousy was sharp and she found herself rubbing at the imaginary wound to her heart.

"Don't tell me you still have feelings for him. After all this time?" said Izzie, watching her sister. "Oh you must forget him, Nan," she said with a serious expression. "He killed the king as well. King Henry, the Lancastrian king. When he came back to London from Tewkesbury he went to the Tower and plunged his dagger into old Henry too."

"Who has told you these things?" demanded Anne, picturing the feeble old king cowering in fear before a glinting blade held by a shadowy figure that she would not imagine as Richard.

"Everybody says so. Lord Stanley says..."

"And you give him credence?" interrupted Anne, angry that her sister accepted the lies of the Stanleys despite no evidence for what they told her. But what Izzie said created a sore that festered in the back of her mind. Richard was capable, she knew, even though she refused to believe he had done such things.

When Anne came downstairs to supper and saw the bulk of Sir William Stanley sprawled in front of the fire she was thankful, for the first time, that she was a married woman. Her young husband, Edward, may have ignored her when he arrived earlier but at least that was preferable to the leering gaze of his uncle as he stared at her breasts, which were just showing above the fashionable yellow gown that Lady Stanley had chosen for her.

"Marriage agrees with you," he commented, knowing full well that her marriage was nothing more than a legal contract. "Do you have a kiss for your husband's uncle?"

"I do not think that would be seemly," she replied with as much composure as she could manage.

"Oh come now, Anne. We were friends at Skipton. Besides, I have had a trying time these last few days," he remarked in a clumsy effort to win her sympathy.

"And why is that?" asked Anne, her curiosity aroused despite her resolve to distance herself from him.

"I escorted the former queen to a chamber in the Tower and had to tell her that her son was dead," said Sir William.

Anne felt an unexpected sympathy for the lady. She doubted that Margaret of Anjou would have received much compassion from Sir William. But it was Edward of Lancaster's widow, Anne Neville, who interested her more. She too had been brought to London, though she had not been taken to the Tower but was in the custody of the Duke of Clarence and his wife, who was her sister. She wondered if Anne Neville grieved for her dead husband, and if it was true that Richard planned to marry her.

"But now," continued Sir William, "my brother has invited me to feast with him, to celebrate our victory. I was made a knight banneret by King Edward on the field of battle at Tewkesbury! Your uncle was knighted too," he said. "He is Sir Robert Harrington now."

"Not that it will do him good. Or his brother," said Lord Stanley, coming into the hall. "The king has assured me, daughter, that Hornby is still yours. You have nothing to fear. I intend to keep your inheritance safe. In fact," he continued, "the king has requested that you and the lady Elizabeth attend court. He is keen to meet the two heiresses who have been the cause of so much strife."

The thought of going to court and meeting the king didn't excite Anne as much as the hope that Richard would also be there.

"Your uncles are summoned too," went on Lord Stanley. "The king has decided to tell them in person that Hornby Castle is not theirs."

Anne didn't reply. Lord Stanley, with his inscrutable eyes, made her even more afraid than Sir William. At least with Sir William she had some idea what he was thinking; Lord Stanley was a riddle.

They dined with all the family gathered at table. There was laughter and boasting from the men about their prowess on the field of battle, and for their part the ladies and younger children were required to listen and be astonished. Everyone seemed joyful at the eventual outcome, except for Lady Stanley, who sat beside her husband but did not look at him or speak to him – and on the one occasion that his arm brushed hers as he turned to gesture to a servant she cringed from his touch.

Anne spent a restless night, turning in her bed, with fleeting dreams of Hornby and Richard jumbled in incomprehensible visions. Soon after sunrise a servant woke her and brought clean linen and stockings. Anne told the girl to bring her the gown of a midnight blue, that covered her almost to the neck. It had a cap of matching material and Anne asked the girl to pin up her hair beneath it. The effect she saw reflected back at her in the mirror was what she had hoped for – demure, refined, but not unattractive.

The court was gathered at Baynard's Castle, just upriver from Stanley House, and those who had assisted Edward in the recent turmoil were invited to a great feast there to celebrate the king's reclamation of his throne. Anne followed Lord and Lady Stanley, in their jewelled and magnificent robes, down to the steps at the water's edge where the Stanley barge was waiting for them, its canopy flapping in the breeze. Her husband, Edward, walked beside her. He had almost reached her height, but still seemed small as he hunched his shoulders and kept his eyes downcast. Behind her came the Stanleys' eldest son George, and then Izzie and John giggling together as usual.

Lady Stanley's disapproval that she had chosen not to wear the yellow gown was still evident in her frown as she watched Anne take her seat.

"You look like a novice, not a Stanley," she had muttered when Anne had come down the stairs, and her eyes had fallen with more warmth on Izzie who wore a gown of pale green silk, cut fashionably low, with wide slashed sleeves that gave a glimpse of her lemon kirtle beneath.

It was only a short distance from Stanley House to the royal residence and Anne watched with excitement as the high walls drew nearer and the oarsmen manoeuvred the boat up to the landing stage. The barge rocked as they all stood up and Anne, looking up at the towering palace rather than where she was placing her feet, stumbled as she stepped ashore in her soft leather shoes.

She followed in the wake of the Stanleys, up the wide stone steps and through a series of chambers until they reached the huge hall where there seemed to be hundreds of people milling around in their best, brightly coloured clothing. The rising hum of conversation was almost as loud as the musicians and Anne found herself staring open-mouthed at the splendour of the high arched windows filled with stained glass and the lavish tapestries that adorned the walls.

The crowd parted like an ebbing tide as a pageboy showed them to their places at a long table covered with the whitest linen she had ever seen and set with silver cups and platters and flagons of wine. As soon as she was seated Anne's eyes searched the room for Richard, but the royal party had not yet arrived and the elaborately carved chairs behind the table on the dais were still empty. Then the royal trumpeters sounded a fanfare and the guests rose from their benches to bow and curtsey as the royal party entered. Anne saw a tall fair man wearing a jewelled crown who must be the king. With the tips of her fingers on his sleeve walked a woman wearing purple velvet set with jewels. Then came a man who must be the Duke of Clarence and a small dark woman, his wife Isabel. Anne's heart beat faster when she saw Richard, dressed in a blue doublet that she knew matched the colour of his eyes. He briefly acknowledged the assembly with a nod of his head and as soon as the king had taken his place he leaned forward to speak in an urgent manner to his brother.

Once the royal party was seated, the trumpets and drums announced the first course and the servants carried in the food, serving the royal table first before bringing overflowing platters to the other tables. The musicians continued to play as the guests ate their way through innumerable dishes, interspersed with huge intricate subtleties that made the diners gasp as they were carried in – a peacock with its huge tail displayed and a swan that concealed a pie filled with live songbirds, which flew in alarm to the rafters of the hall as soon as they were released. And even though there were tumblers and jugglers who strolled between the tables for their entertainment, Anne watched Richard. She willed him to look in her direction, but he remained deep in conversation.

The food could have been horse bread for all that Anne tasted it. Her nerves had dulled her appetite and she could only nibble on some of the tastier morsels as she waited for the feasting to end, hoping that when the time came for her to be presented to the king she would not stumble again, and Richard would at last notice her. But the banquet seemed endless and every time Anne thought it must be finished, more food was borne in.

At last the king gave a signal and the platters were cleared. The jugglers stopped, the minstrels were silenced and an expectant hush fell over the hall as the king turned to beckon Lord Stanley forward. In turn he crooked a forefinger at Anne and Izzie to follow him and Anne slid out from behind the table to approach the dais. She knew she should keep her eyes respectfully lowered but risked an upward glance and met the keen blue gaze of Richard who was looking directly at her. Her stomach fluttered and her heart began to race. She managed to give him the vestige of a smile before Lord Stanley took her elbow and pushed her forward.

"Your Majesty, may I present my daughter, the lady Anne Stanley." It was the first time she had heard her new name spoken and for a moment she hesitated, thinking that someone else was being presented first. "Make reverence!" whispered Lord Stanley angrily and Anne, gathering her senses along with her skirts, sank to the ground aware of a flush suffusing her cheeks as she stared at the king's pale leather boots and the fur lined hem of his gown.

"Lady Anne," she heard him say.

"Kneel before the king," muttered Lord Stanley in her ear and as Anne moved forward she saw Richard watching her with an amused half-smile.

"Your Majesty," she managed to say as a large, be-ringed hand was extended before her and she leant forward to give it a tentative kiss before becoming aware of Izzie beside her.

"Stand up. Stand up!" ordered the king after Izzie had paid obeisance. "Let me look at these two heiresses who have caused such argument."

Anne could see the king clearly now and she was amazed that these two men were brothers. The king was fair-haired and tall, but as he met her gaze she noticed that his eyes were the same shade of blue as Richard's.

"So you are Anne? The elder of John Harrington's two daughters?"

"Yes, Your Majesty," she replied lowering her eyes.

"Then you are the owner of Hornby Castle," he said.

"But..." began Richard.

"I have decided!" replied the king in a voice that made Anne quake as he held up a hand to silence his brother.

"Yes, my lord," replied Richard with an unfathomable expression and he began to fiddle with the small jewelled knife he used to cut his food.

"Anne. You are your father's eldest child and I will not deprive you of your inheritance. I have appointed Lord Thomas Stanley as your guardian and he is a goodly and pious man who will guard your interests well. He has already taken you as his own true daughter and your marriage with his son is beneficial to you and to your lands. It is an arrangement with which I am content. And your sister, the lady Elizabeth," he continued, "will have Melling. There is to be no more dispute in this matter. Call forward Sir James Harrington and Sir Robert Harrington!" said the king and Anne peered down the hall as her uncles came forward wearing the livery collars of the Duke of Gloucester with their white boar pendants.

She exchanged glances with them both and her Uncle Robert smiled, but Uncle James' face was set in an expression of simmering anger and she saw that he winced as he knelt before the king.

"Now it is time to give up your trouble making!" the king warned them. "You must surrender Hornby Castle to your niece, Anne Stanley. I shall send Sir Ralph Assheton to oversee the arrangements. It is my last word on this matter," he said, glaring at the men before him and then at the Duke of Gloucester.

Anne watched sadly. After everything that had happened the king would still not change his mind. He had handed Hornby to Thomas Stanley, a man who had fought against him less than a year ago. And the Harringtons, who had never swerved in their loyalty to the Yorkists, had lost the lands and the castle that had been theirs for generations.

"Now, let us have some dancing!" declared the king, gesturing to the musicians to take up their instruments. "Come Mistress Harrington," he said, winking at Izzie. "Give me your hand whilst you are still an unmarried woman and I cannot fear the wrath of your husband!"

Izzie giggled as the king came down the steps with his hand outstretched and servants rushed to stack the trestle tables away. Anne saw Uncle James look round for her and she went quickly to him, escaping the restraining hand of Lord Stanley.

"Uncle James," she said, finding that she had tears in her eyes at the sight of him. "Are you well?"

"A little bruised from battle and a wound that pains me when I kneel," he remarked, "but apart from that my body is well, though my heart aches at the loss of Hornby."

"I am sorry," she said, as he leaned to kiss her cheek. "How fares my aunt and my young cousins?"

"They are well. They have already gone to Brierley and I may soon join them there... Your Grace," he said suddenly, with a nod of his head, as his eyes fell on someone behind her and Anne felt her skin tingle at the awareness that Richard was close by.

"I am sorry, James," he said as he reached to rest his hand briefly on her uncle's shoulder, his sleeve brushing Anne's arm. "You fought bravely at both Barnet and Tewkesbury to return my brother to the throne and I feel that you deserve better. But my loyalty must be to the king in this, as in all matters."

"I am grateful to Your Grace for your interventions on my behalf."

"You are a good man, James Harrington; a true and honest friend, as is Robert. And Anne? Are you well?" he asked, looking at her.

"I... I am well," she stammered under his shrewd gaze.

Behind them the dancers swirled onto the floor as the musicians picked up the tempo of their tune.

"I do not care to dance," Richard said, watching Izzie with her hand in the king's. "I feel the need for some fresh air. Will you accompany me?" he asked her.

"I would be honoured," she replied and with a backward glance at Lord Stanley's stony face she placed her hand on his extended arm and allowed him to lead her out of the hall and through an ante-chamber to a door that opened into a courtyard.

"So, you are married to one of Stanley's sons," he said as the door thudded shut and the sound of the music and clapping faded.

"A marriage in name only. The boy is yet a child. Richard..." She pulled on his arm to make him stop and face her. "Richard..." She reached out her other hand and caressed the soft fabric of his doublet, remembering the hard muscles beneath. "I have missed you," she said at last, looking up to search his face for some reciprocal feeling.

"Not here," he said, glancing up at the surrounding windows. "Come with me!" He took her hand and led her to a secluded walled garden where fruit trees were growing along wattle supports. He turned her back to a space between two apple trees and pressed her hard against the rough stone with his body. Anne could barely breathe. He smelt the same, though it was not a scent she could ever have described. His breath was cool across her cheek in the moment before his lips rediscovered her mouth and as his hands began to caress her she slipped her arms around his slender waist and held him even closer.

"I want you," she whispered, as he paused for breath. "I have waited so long and yearned for you so much."

"We cannot," he replied as his lips moved from her mouth to her cheeks and eyes and his hand brushed against her breast. "You are a married woman."

"It is not a marriage. It is not consummated and was made without my true consent."

He took her wrists and kissed the palms of her hands in turn and then he paused and glanced around the garden. There was no one there; only the faint sounds of music and laughter from inside the castle. With a decisive movement he grasped her skirts and gathered the folds, crushing the cloth between their bodies. She felt his knee between her legs as he fumbled with his own clothes.

"These regal trappings do not lend themselves to this pleasure," he complained as he struggled to free himself.

"At least you do not wear your armour, sir," said Anne laughing at their boldness. Then she felt his warm hands on her bare thighs above her stockings and she was held hard against the stone wall.

"Forgive me, my lady, but we must make haste if we are not to risk interruption," he said as she felt him press against her. He was forceful and for a moment it pained her, yet it was what she had craved for over a year and she didn't want it to end, even though her heart pounded with the fear that they would be discovered with their nether parts bared for all to see. He drew a sharp breath and after a moment he kissed her cheek and withdrew from her to rearrange his clothing.

"We had best go in before we are missed," he said as she smoothed down her wrinkled gown.

"A moment," she said. "There is something that I have to ask you; it troubles me."

"Speak your mind," he said as she hesitated.

"Richard, I have heard stories." He said nothing but held her steadily in his gaze.

"They say you killed Edward of Lancaster," she said and almost regretted her words as she watched his eyes grow icy.

"In battle there are many deaths. It is not a fit subject for a lady to consider."

"He died in battle?"

"Yes."

"Did you kill him?" she asked, needing to hear the truth from him.

"I have killed many men in battle, Anne. If I do not kill them then they will kill me. Would that be preferable to you?"

"No, of course not."

"You have never witnessed a battle and be thankful for that. It is not a glorious thing. It is filled with the stench of blood and death and men's screams of agony as their entrails spill from their bodies and their brains from their heads. I am never proud to take a life. I pray that God will forgive me for breaking His commandment. But it is a necessary evil, and a man who fights against his king is beneath my contempt."

"I'm sorry," whispered Anne as she looked at the ground, filled with contrition by his reprimand.

"No," he said more gently, as his fingers raised her chin so that she was forced to look at him. "It is I who am sorry to be angry when we have so little time together."

"Richard...?" Her voice trembled, but she knew that she must dare to ask him one thing more if she was to have peace in her mind. "The king? King Henry? They say you murdered him in the Tower..." She froze as dark displeasure flashed across his face.

"You forget your place, I think, to ask me these things!"

"I'm sorry," she whispered again, brushing away an unwelcome tear with the back of her hand. She saw that she had made him very angry and she was afraid.

"My brother was merciful for many years," he told her, "but that mercy was used as a weapon against him by those whom he had trusted. What folly it would have been to let Henry live. Surely you can see that?" He took a step closer to her and she would have shrunk from him if she hadn't already been trapped against the wall with his arms imprisoning her on either side. "What would you had rather happened?" he demanded. "That he was cut by the blows of some inadequate executioner, dying in agony? Or that he had a quick and merciful death?"

Anne sobbed and covered her face with her hands, not able to look at this man who had just known the intimacies of her body.

"I wish I had not asked," she cried as she remembered the sad, bewildered man who had sat on the throne in St Paul's.

"Because it makes you dislike me?" She shook her head, unable to speak. "Anne," he said as his temper subsided and he took her wrists and pulled her hands away from her face. "Look at me. Look at me!" he repeated and waited until she obeyed, meeting his stern eyes.

"We must sometimes act at variance with our own wishes to show our loyalty," he explained. "I give my loyalty to my brother, the king. What he commands, I do – and though I may question him, as I have over the matter of Hornby, he is still the king. His word is law and I must obey."

He released her then and walked away without waiting to see if she had understood or forgiven him. Anne watched him go. She had known that he was capable, but to hear it from his own lips was still shocking. Yet she could not say that he was wrong. She could not say that it had stopped her loving him.

She picked up her cap from where it had fallen to the ground, shook the dirt from it, and pinned it in place. Then, smoothing down her gown once more and wiping her face with the palms of her hands, she attempted to recover her composure before going back into the hall.

Inside, she glanced around the hot and crowded room, at the dancers and the groups of people standing in conversation. He was close to the dais and engaged in talk with a group of men she did not recognise.

"Where have you been?" hissed Lord Stanley from behind her. "I have arranged for the barge to return both you and Lady Stanley to the house, for I am heartily displeased with both of you!"

"I... I was hot. I stepped outside for some air," she protested.

"Your cap is askew," he told her as he looked at her with disgust. "You will go back now and I will speak to you later!"

He did not allow her to protest and there was little she could say. He took her arm roughly and, as she glanced back towards Richard who was still deep in conversation, he escorted her out to the riverside where the Stanley barge was waiting with Lady Stanley already seated under the canopy. He handed her aboard and barely waited until she had sat down before signalling the oarsmen to proceed.

"My grief for my brother displeases my husband," said Lady Stanley as their eyes met. "I am sorry if your pleasure has been cut short to accompany me home."

Anne did not admit that she had displeased Lord Stanley as well. She was just thankful that her companion did not notice her crumpled gown, or the way her eyes remained fixed on the wall of Baynard's Castle as they were rowed away upriver.

Robert Harrington knew that it was the Duke of Gloucester who had recommended him for honours after the battle at Tewkesbury and it pleased him greatly, but he was disappointed that Diccon had still not been able to change the king's mind about Hornby. To have knelt before the king to be knighted was one thing, but to kneel before him to be told that his brother's claim to Hornby would never succeed had been humiliating and Robert had retreated to the far end of the hall to seek some solitude from the inquisitive eyes of the other guests.

He was relieved to see his nieces were safe, but as he watched Izzie dancing with her betrothed, John Stanley, Robert felt a twinge of conscience that he had not yet managed to visit Isabella at Balderstone. He had sent her a long and loving letter but he feared that even that might not be enough to reassure her. Now that this matter with Hornby was over he hoped that Diccon might at least recompense him with some leave to go north and arrange his wedding.

A door banging behind him made him look round and he saw the duke come in with a dark look on his face. Their eyes met for an instant but Diccon strode across the hall as if determined to avoid him. Robert felt sorry. The king's decision over Hornby had humiliated him too. He would speak with him later, thought Robert, who had learned long ago that Diccon in a bad mood was best left well alone.

James approached him with a face as gloomy as the duke's.

"I will not give it up," he said. "That castle belongs to the Harringtons and I will not stand by and see it handed to Stanley. At first light I will ride north and stock it with men and provisions and let the devil take anyone who tries to wrest it from me!"

"And what of your loyalty to the Duke of Gloucester?"

"I doubt he will gainsay me," replied James and Robert surmised that his brother was probably correct.

Anne lay in bed and gazed at the darkness beyond the small window. She could hear the lions roaring but now that she knew where the sound came from she found it strangely comforting. And she was in need of comfort.

She heard Izzie and a servant tiptoe in and close the door softly. In silence her sister was undressed and the servant dismissed.

"I'm still awake," she said as her sister came to the bed.

"Are you unwell?" asked Izzie. "Lord Stanley said you had returned early."

"I'm not unwell. I was sent back – in disgrace," she replied.

"Disgrace! Whatever did you do?" asked Izzie pulling back the hangings and then striking the flints to reignite the candle on the bedside coffer.

Anne hesitated but she wanted to talk to someone about what had happened and she hoped that since her own betrothal her sister would understand her feelings. "I went into the garden with the Duke of Gloucester," she told her.

"I hope that you didn't let him kiss you," she said, though Anne sensed that she craved the details despite her attempt at disapproval.

"Yes, he kissed me," she said. Izzie jumped onto the bed beside her sister.

"Just kissed?" she asked, with her head on the bolster beside Anne's.

"More than kissed," she admitted. "He... We..."

"Nan!" exclaimed Izzie, sitting up and staring at her with a shocked expression. "You don't mean...? What if someone had seen you? Have you no shame? You're a married woman. It's a sin!"

"Then I shall confess," shrugged Anne. "I shall confess that I love him. I love Richard, Duke of Gloucester!"

"Hush!" Izzie's hand smelt of fruit as it covered her mouth to silence her. "You must be more careful, Nan," she said. "This is a dangerous game that you play. And I told you about the things he has done. I wouldn't want him to touch me. And why make Lord Stanley angry? No good will come of it. You must forget him. Promise me that you will forget him, Nan."

"I can't," she said.

Next morning Lord Stanley called her down to the solar.

"You have displeased me immensely," he told her, his narrowed eyes displaying his contempt. "I will not have a daughter of my house talking in secret with Gloucester. You will go back to Lathom with Lady Stanley and you will remain there until your husband comes to claim you."

"Yes, my lord," she replied with resignation, wondering if her snatched moments with Richard had been worth such a severe penalty. She decided that they had. Her only regret was that they had not parted as friends. She bitterly regretted angering him and would have liked the chance to tell him that she understood and did not think badly of him, but another meeting was out of the question and even a letter was impossible as she was not allowed out of the sight of one of the Stanleys or their trusted servants as her belongings were packed ready to leave.

Before noon she and Lady Stanley were in the carriage heading north. Izzie had hugged her and told her that she hoped she would be allowed to come and visit her soon.

"Please," Anne had whispered as she clung to her sister. "If you see Richard, tell him that I understand." Her sister had nodded and kissed her cheek, but Anne suspected that she would not do as she was asked even if she got the chance.

The carriage ride made her nauseous as usual and with every mile that she was parted from him it grew worse. It was hot and the flies buzzed around their heads, attracted by the horses and the drying pools of water that formed in the sudden overnight thunderstorms. At least it will end when we reach Lathom, thought Anne. It was the only reason she was glad to arrive, but when she eventually crept to her bed to lie down the sickness continued.

She blamed it on her grief. Her body might be at Lathom but her heart and soul were in London with Richard. She longed to know what he was doing at every moment of the day. She thought about him every morning as soon as she awoke and his name was on her lips as she made her evening prayers.

It wearied her and as the weeks passed her stomach rejected everything she ate. At first Lady Stanley seemed too concerned with her own poor health to notice that there was something wrong, but Anne looked up to see her staring at her one afternoon as she sat with a piece of sewing on her lap that had not been touched for weeks.

"You are ill," she remarked. "Your humours are seriously disturbed. Your stomach rejects your food and yet it distends as if you are never from the table. You may need a bleeding to restore your balance – if the planets are favourable."

"I am well," insisted Anne.

"No. I have been too deep in my own grief to see. Something troubles you. I will ask the physician to come."

Despite Anne's protests, Lady Stanley was resolute that the physician should see her.

"You need have no fears," Lady Stanley reassured her. "The physician comes from Chester and he is well-qualified. He has attended me and other members of the family on many occasions with good success. I know you are hesitant. You have never had the privilege of consulting such a learned man before, but there is nothing to fear. The physician will make you well."

He came the next day; a small, squat man with dark hair and the face of a mole. Anne recoiled from him on sight. She had never had need of a physician before – she had always consulted Mistress Payne at Hornby.

Lady Stanley brought the man into her bedchamber and he began by taking her wrist to feel for her pulse.

"I am not unwell," she insisted. "It is the changes of air that affect me and the long journeys. I will feel better soon."

He didn't comment except to ask that she produce a sample of her waters in one of his glass flasks and he waited outside the bedcurtains with Lady Stanley whilst she blushingly complied.

"A little cloudy," he commented holding it up to the window. Then, having inspected her urine, he insisted on her lying on the bed and raising her gown to uncover her nakedness whilst he pressed his cold and clammy hands to her bare belly, leaving Anne feeling violated.

"Your husband will be pleased," said the physician at last, having asked her questions about her monthly phases. "Did you not realise that you are with child?" he asked as if she was witless.

Lady Stanley exclaimed in astonishment. The physician turned to her as if to say something but seemed to think better of it and, after accepting his fee in a small cloth purse, he wished them both a good day and went out to his waiting horse.

A letter was written immediately to Lord Stanley and sent by messenger the same morning. Lady Stanley did not speak of the subject to Anne but instructed that she was to keep to her bedchamber until Lord Stanley had given instruction on what was to be done.

Anne did not object. She needed time to think about what the physician had told her. Her mind had been so filled with worries about her sour parting from Richard that she had given no thought to the chance that a child might spring from their brief union. She wished now that she had asked Mistress Payne about the ways to prevent a man's seed taking hold. The village girls who worked in the kitchens at Hornby had often discussed such matters as they scrubbed the tables and swept the floors, but Anne had only listened idly, never thinking that the knowledge might be useful.

A few days later Anne was sleeping on her bed following the dinner that the servant had brought. She had eaten a little of the white bread and sipped at the pottage and for once it had stayed down and she felt a little better. At first she wasn't sure what had wakened her, but the voice she recognised from below filled her with dread. Lord Stanley himself had come.

The house was filled with the sound of his shouting and Anne waited, listening at her door, as Lord Stanley rebuked his wife.

"I left her in your care! You only had to watch her! How can this have come about? What villainous servant or village boy has availed himself of a daughter of my house? When I discover who is responsible I will personally thrash him until he begs for mercy!"

Anne quaked as she listened to his words and prayed that he did not intend to use her likewise. She doubted that being with child would elicit his compassion as the child was not of his blood and it would only please him if a beating tore it from her womb.

A moment later she heard a servant approaching and turned to the small mirror to put on a coif and pull her modest gown into order. She took a deep breath and, although she could feel the trembling of her chest as she slowly exhaled, she thought of Richard and took strength from him. She had not sinned, she told herself, the sin was with Lord Stanley who had forced her into a marriage to steal her inheritance. She would go and face him with dignity despite her fear.

When she walked into the hall and saw his grim face, her courage almost deserted her.

"So, you carry a child?" he demanded without preamble.

"Yes, Father," she replied meekly.

"I did not realise that I was taking a common strumpet into my family when the king gave me your guardianship," he said, his lips as narrow as his eyes, whilst his wispy beard trembled with rage. "I do not suppose he will be pleased to hear this. And neither can we pass it off as your husband's child since he is but nine years old." He paused again to glare at her. "So," he continued, "whose child is this that I am expected to take as a cuckoo into the house of Stanley? Who have you defiled yourself with whilst in my care and as a daughter of my house? Who is the father?"

"The Duke of Gloucester," she replied and watched as the calculations of his mind began to make sense of what he knew.

After a moment he stalked from the hall without another word and, going to the private solar, slammed the door shut behind him. Anne stumbled to a bench on shaking legs, one hand covering the child in her womb as if to shield it from harm.

"You are to return to your bedchamber," said Lady Stanley when she came in a moment later, "and you are to remain there until my husband decides what should be done with you. He is very angry," she added, unnecessarily.

Anne was thankful to retreat and close the door behind her. Later she heard Lord Stanley's messenger leave and he rode off himself early the following morning. She thought that once he had gone Lady Stanley might allow her downstairs, but no one came to her door except the servants with her food and to bring fresh water and take away her soils.

Balderstone in summer looked different. Robert was only able to catch glimpses of the manor house through the trees as he approached. But Isabella was watching for him and was waiting in the courtyard. It was so long since he had seen her that she seemed almost a stranger. But a beautiful stranger, Robert thought, wanting to pull the cap from her head and touch the fair curly hair that he glimpsed beneath it.

Her smile was warm and welcoming as were her lips when he pulled her against him.

"I'm right glad to see you," he told her, breathing in the scent of her body. "Pray God the king is secure and we can be wed at last."

"There were days this winter past when I doubted the day would ever come," she said.

"Surely you did not think me unconstant?"

"Never that. But there were dark days when I feared that you were lost to me," she admitted.

Although Robert would have liked to take her to the church and wed her that very afternoon he knew it was not possible. Harvest time was approaching and Isabella wanted to see everything gathered and stored before she left her mother to travel to his lands at Badsworth.

Robert felt irritated at her reluctance. Her mother would have to manage alone once Isabella was his wife. But she had waited for him and he owed it to her to wait a while longer, though he ached with the suppressed desire for her. They set a date for October and Robert returned in good humour to London.

Back at court, he was surprised to see the tall, broad-shouldered man in the ante-chamber of the Duke of Gloucester's apartments. His hand felt for the leather covered handle of his sword as he swallowed down his bile and civilly greeted William Stanley.

"You desire to speak with His Grace?" he asked as if such a thing were beyond belief.

"I do."

"Then I will convey your request," replied Robert, doubting that Diccon would agree.

"It is about Anne, your niece," said Sir William.

"What of her?" asked Robert, pausing. The man had an air of disquiet about him.

"There is something the duke should know... and maybe you as well," he said and the urgency in his tone made Robert think that something was amiss and he hurried to find Diccon to beg him to admit the man and hear what he had to say.

The Duke of Gloucester was sitting at a trestle table with letters and documents spread across it. A line was creasing the space between his eyes at the bridge of his nose and he was in low conversation with a trusted lawyer.

"My lord," said Robert, loath to interrupt.

"What is it?" asked the duke, although his tone was not one of rebuke.

"Sir William Stanley is here and craves to speak with you." The duke raised an eyebrow. "He says it concerns my niece, Anne."

"Fetch him in," said the duke after a moment. "Take these and try to make some sense of them," he said to the lawyer, and as the man left the chamber Sir William brushed past him.

"Stay," said Diccon to Robert as he made to leave. "This may concern you also."

"Indeed it does," replied Sir William and then he stood, turning his hat in his hands, before he began to speak. "You know that the lady Anne is at Lathom House in Lancashire under the care of my brother and his wife." He hesitated again and then looked at the duke with an expression filled with jealousy and contempt.

"She is with child," he said.

Robert did not believe it. The boy, Edward Stanley, was far too young to father a child and it was well over a year since Anne had been with Diccon at Hornby.

"Are you certain?" demanded the duke, his steely eyes fixed on William Stanley.

"Aye, Your Grace, and from what my brother tells me the lady has claimed that you are the father."

"And why do you come to me with this?" asked the duke, only betraying his emotions by walking to a chair and sitting down.

"Because my lord brother plans to have the child taken away when it is born and put in the care of the nuns at Chester. Anne is to be told that it is stillborn. I do not do this for you," he added, glaring at the duke. "I do it because I care for the lady Anne and would not like to think of her so ill-used."

Gloucester was on his feet with his fists clenched and for a moment Robert feared that he would strike Sir William. He stepped forward with a hand outstretched and when Diccon looked at him he saw that he was struggling to control his temper.

"Gather men, enough men!" the duke told him. "I intend to take the lady into my care!" Then with a tight-lipped face he strode from the hall to his private chamber and shut the door behind him. Sir William turned to Robert with a look of inquiry.

"It will be done, my lord," he reassured him. "And thank you for bringing us this news."

"As I said, I do it for the lady Anne," repeated Sir William with a brief nod before he left.

Anne's anxiety grew. She needed to know what was going to happen to her and although she imagined all manner of ways that she might send a message to Richard, not one of them was practical. And even if she did manage to get a letter to him how could she be certain that he would not be displeased? He had been angry with her when they parted and he might simply deny that the child was his.

Then, one morning, she heard hooves and the grinding wheels of a carriage outside. A banging came on the door that reverberated throughout the house and she heard raised voices downstairs – men's voices. As Anne listened, afraid that Lord Stanley had come to take her away somewhere, she thought that she recognised one of them. She pressed an ear to her closed door. She could not be sure what was being said, and though she longed to believe that it was Richard she could scarcely believe that he had come to Lathom.

Then she heard footsteps on the stairs and she shrank back, unsure what was about to happen.

"This chamber?" demanded the voice.

"Yes, Your Grace," she heard Lady Stanley reply as the door was opened. Anne recoiled as he came in, his face darker than the persistent clouds. She glanced at Lady Stanley, standing behind him, and then back at Richard.

"Get out!" he bellowed at Lady Stanley. "As soon as my men are fed we will leave, as you request. And my lady will go with us!"

Lady Stanley gave him a hesitant curtsey and hurried away. Richard closed the door.

"Anne," he said. "Forgive me for not coming sooner."

Her hands fastened into fists around the cloth of his tunic and all the tears she had been holding inside for weeks came tumbling and convulsing from her in relief. He said nothing but held her against him until she could cry no more.

"I've soaked your clothes, my lord," she choked at last as she raised her face to his. He kissed her swollen eyes then held her for a moment at arm's length, studying her shape.

"I have only just had the truth from William Stanley," he told her.

"Then you are not angry with me?" she asked him.

"Anne! No!" His face was anguished as he drew her to him again.

"But you were angry with me when we parted," she said.

"No. I thought that you despised me for what I had done. I wasn't sure I would find a welcome from you."

"Of course I welcome you. I have longed for you. I wanted to send word to you, but I didn't know how..."

"Hush, hush," he soothed as she began to cry again. "I am here now."

"But what about Lord Stanley?"

"I will deal with him," he replied. "What matters now is your welfare and the welfare of our child." He glanced down and then cupped his hand around her burgeoning stomach. "He grows strongly."

"How do you know it is a boy?"

"You were made to bear my sons," he replied, kissing her wet cheeks again.

"Where will you take me?" she asked.

"To Pontefract Castle. You will be safe there. And you will be cared for. I once promised you that I would do my utmost to keep you from Stanley's control. It has been far more difficult than I ever imagined, but I will keep that pledge, as far as I am able, until the day I die," he told her.

When she came downstairs Anne was glad to see that her Uncle Robert was one of the men who had accompanied Richard. He also embraced her and reassured her that she would be safely conducted to Yorkshire. The horse litter that Richard had brought was large and filled with furs and well-stuffed pillows to cushion her from any jolting, but they had not travelled far before the sickness beset her again.

"Stop. Stop!" she called as the juices flooded her mouth and the bitter fluid rose in her throat. As soon as the horses had been halted she scrambled to the ground, heaving. Gentle hands held her head and it was a moment before Anne realised that it was Richard who had got down from his horse and knelt beside her.

"This is not a fitting thing for you to see," she told him, wiping her mouth and feeling ashamed.

"I have seen much worse in battle," he replied as he helped her to her feet. "Besides, I have been remiss in not finding a woman companion for you. So until that can be rectified I must assist you myself," he said as he handed her his own fine linen handkerchief to wipe her face.

Chapter Six
October 1471 ~ February 1472

At last they approached Pontefract and Anne pushed back the curtain of the litter to watch as the castle, standing on a hill a short distance from the town, grew closer. The encircling sandstone walls and towers looked formidable as they drew up the slope to the west gatehouse.

"You will be safe from Lord Stanley here," said Richard, leaning down from his horse. She smiled up at him. Although the journey had been trying and tiring at times, his unwavering kindness had allowed her to take some enjoyment from it and they had grown to know one another better in the privacy that it had afforded.

Richard urged his horse on ahead of the litter as they clattered under the arch of the gatehouse, through the bustling outer bailey where people paused in their tasks to watch them pass, and beneath the Constable Tower into the huge inner bailey where as soon as they halted Richard was at her side.

"Let me help you," he said, reaching out as she stepped unsteadily towards him.

"A moment," she said as weakness overcame her.

"I will assist the lady," he said, waving away both her uncle and an approaching servant. "Can you walk?" he asked, "or shall I carry you?"

"I do not think that would be seemly!" she said, shocked at his suggestion. "I'm sure I will manage. I do not think..." she began, as the bailey began to darken around her and she felt him lift her from her feet and carry her up some steps.

Inside, he put her down on a chair near the fire and knelt before her to unfasten her cloak and rub her hands between his.

"Bring a little wine," he told someone and she felt his hand cradle the back of her head as he lifted the cup to her lips. She sipped and felt the warmth revive her a little. Her vision steadied and she saw him watching her with concern.

"What will people think to see the brother of the king kneeling before me?" she asked, half-serious in her concern that the retainers of Pontefract should not judge her harshly.

"They can think what they please," he replied. "Anne, you made me afraid. Do you feel a little recovered now?"

"I... I am better."

"Shall I send for a physician?"

"No!" she protested fearfully.

"Well, colour is returning to your cheeks," he said, smoothing her face gently with his thumb. "Rest here a while and I will make sure your chambers are ready."

"Everything is as you ordered, Your Grace," said the constable, who was watching anxiously from the other side of the hearth.

"Do you feel able to walk now?" Richard asked her.

"Yes. I do not need you to carry me again," she replied, still embarrassed at his open show of affection for her in front of these strangers. "But I would be grateful for your arm," she said as she stood up. He smiled and rather than simply offering her an arm to lean on he grasped her firmly, pulling her close to the warmth of his body.

"Come," he said. "I will take you upstairs."

They ascended the stone steps one by one and walked along a short passageway to a door. Inside was a pleasant room with a large oriel window that overlooked the inner bailey. A fire blazed in the hearth and there were comfortable chairs and tapestries, and even a rug laid on the boarded floor that Anne thought too expensive to put her feet upon. There was a large bed, with dark green hangings fastened back, and, beyond, a second bedchamber and a small garderobe set into the outer wall.

"Is this all for me?" she asked, staring around the luxurious apartment.

"I thought the smaller chamber could be used for the nurse and the baby when he is born," said Richard. "But in the meantime I will arrange a companion for you. I thought of your mother but I am told she is heavy with child herself at Dudley Castle and cannot come. So I have asked your uncle if his betrothed, Isabella Balderstone, can come and attend you. He speaks of her often and I believe she is a kindly woman and only a few years older than yourself."

"Thank you," said Anne. "I am grateful."

She watched him as he stood with his back to her, staring down into the bailey. After a moment he turned to look at her. "I cannot stay with you long," he said. "There is a matter in London which I must attend to."

"When must you go?"

"Tomorrow."

"Richard." She reached for his hand, but he didn't come to her. "Can you not stay with me for a few days at least?" she asked, not wanting to be parted from him. He studied her for a moment and she thought he was going to relent, but then his eyes seemed to grow distant.

"There is something I have to do," he said. "It cannot wait. Now that I have you safe, I must return."

She wanted to ask him what it was that was so important, but she was learning that there were things that it was better not to question him about, like the time when she had asked him about the old king, Henry. And she wondered how many other things there were that it was better not to know.

"Stay with me tonight?" she asked.

"You are unwell. You need to rest."

"I need you," she told him and watched his serious face turn to a smile.

"I will come to you later," he promised.

Anne rested and ate a little of the supper that was brought. Then a girl came to turn down her bed and asked her if she needed any help to undress. Anne sent her away, then sat on the small stool by the fire and waited for Richard.

At last there was a brief knock and he came in.

"I have spoken with your uncle," he told her. "He will send a messenger to bid Isabella to come. He sends his greetings. I told him you were too tired to be disturbed tonight but that you will speak to him tomorrow before we leave."

"Thank you."

"Would you rather I left you to sleep... I can see that you are weary. Shall I send for someone to assist you with your gown?"

"No," she said. "I only need you." She watched as he prowled the room, reminding her of the caged lions at the menagerie. "What is wrong?" she asked, feeling her lip tremble as she spoke. "Are you displeased with me?"

"Anne," he said, coming to her and kneeling at her feet again and resting his head on her lap.

"What is wrong?" she asked as her fingers touched his dark hair.

He sighed and then looked up at her.

"You do know that I love you?" he asked after a moment.

"I did not know for certain. I hoped you did. I love you," she told him, feeling a rush of desire for him that overcame all her weariness and fatigue. "Lie with me," she pleaded and he lifted her onto the bed and helped her to take off her clothes before pulling her close and gently loving her.

As promised Isabella Balderstone arrived a week later. She was a quiet woman, with dark grey eyes and blonde curly hair that crept out from around the edges of her coif. She was shy at first and a much meeker companion to Anne than Izzie had ever been – and although it was pleasant to have someone who agreed with all she said and consented to her suggestions, Anne missed the fierce debates she enjoyed with her sister.

They stitched clothes for the baby, walked in the gardens, played music and sang a little and the days passed, though throughout each one, as her body grew more rounded with their child, Anne wondered what Richard was doing and when he would return.

She devoured each snippet of gossip she heard from servants and messengers about what was happening at court until she overheard some talk that disturbed her. It preyed on her mind until one afternoon, as it grew too dark to sew, she put her stitching aside with a sigh and decided to confide in her friend.

"I've heard some talk... about the Duke of Gloucester," she began. Isabella did not look up but continued to embroider a delicate flower on a gown for the baby.

"What have you heard?" she asked after a moment, continuing with her work.

"That there is trouble between him and his brother, the Duke of Clarence."

"Ah that."

"You know of it?"

"I've heard some whispers."

"And you get letters from my Uncle Robert," said Anne. She had seen Isabella reading them and with every one that came she felt a jolt of disappointment that Richard did not write to her.

"He writes to me, yes," said Isabella, her eyes still downcast.

"Does he ever mention the duke?"

"He is in his household, so much of his news reflects the duke's affairs. But there is nothing that need concern you."

"You know something," said Anne, looking closely at her. "There is something you are keeping from me – something that concerns Richard."

"The duke is a busy man. He has affairs that he must attend to. If there is anything he thinks you should know then I am sure he will tell you himself."

Anne stood up. Her back was aching with the weight of the child and she found it difficult to sit in any position for long. She walked up and down the chamber to ease the pain, pausing to look out at the darkening afternoon and the threat of snow to come. The penitential season of Advent was wearying to her with its short daylight hours and pervading cold and she would be glad when Christmas came.

She sighed and eased herself back down onto the chair by the fire. "I am fearful that the duke will fall out with his brother again," she said. "Do you know what it is they quarrel about?"

"Land," replied Isabella. "You know how much the Duke of Gloucester needs land and how he loves the north."

"Yes," said Anne, remembering how he had once spoken of his plans for the future as they lay together. "I know he loves those wild places. He told me that Middleham Castle is even more remote than Hornby."

Isabella cried out after stabbing her finger with her needle and quickly set the tiny gown aside to prevent it being stained with her blood.

"Does he argue with Clarence about Middleham?" asked Anne.

"I cannot say," said Isabella. "Excuse me." Anne stared after her as she hurried out. It was so unlike her companion to be flustered. She frowned. It was the mention of Middleham that had brought it about, she was sure. What was it that she was keeping from her? Anne went back to the window and stood looking out. Whatever it was that Isabella knew she was determined to discover it. She turned and looked at the closed door. Isabella slept in a chamber just opposite hers. Then Anne dismissed the thought. She would not demean herself by reading Isabella's private letters. She would write to Izzie and ask her what she knew. She and John were spending much of their time at the Stanleys' London house and if there was anything to know she could rely on her sister to find it out.

Robert grimaced as the raised voices carried out through the closed door. God knew, the wood was thick enough to have muted the argument but every word was clear.

"You will tell me where she is!" demanded the Duke of Gloucester.

"She is in my wardship and her whereabouts are no concern of yours!" shouted back the petulant voice of George, Duke of Clarence.

The brief display of brotherly affection after the reunion at Banbury had not lasted long, thought Robert. And neither had the hopes that the duke might take his niece to wife. It was another Anne he was seeking now: Anne Neville, the widow of Edward, Prince of Wales and heiress to half of Warwick's vast estates. Diccon wanted to marry her. But his brother, reluctant to share the Warwick wealth with anyone, would not reveal where he was keeping her hidden.

"I will find her!" raged Gloucester. "I will find her if I have to search every house in London!"

Robert knew that Diccon's threat to search every house was no idle one. They had already looked in all the places the duke thought his brother might have hidden the heiress. Clarence was keen that Anne Neville should take vows at a convent and allow her portion of the Warwick lands to be administered by him. But Diccon was not willing to give up his chance of taking the share that had long been promised him. The death of Edward of Lancaster at Tewkesbury had provided him with the opportunity he had thought lost, and he was not prepared to lose it a second time.

Before Anne had chance to send the letter she had written to her sister there was a sudden buzz of activity.

"The duke is on his way!" Isabella told her, hurrying in. Anne knew that the excitement in her voice was because she would soon see Robert. Their planned marriage had been postponed again as Richard had needed her uncle in London, and although Isabella never complained Anne knew that she craved the day when she would be his wife. "A messenger has arrived to bid the servants make preparations," she said. "They will be here before nightfall and plan to stay for Christmas."

Anne felt all her anxieties fade. She had convinced herself that Richard intended to stay in London but the news that he would be with her before the end of the day filled her with joy. The baby within her kicked. "Your father comes," she told the child as she cupped her hands protectively around it. "He comes because he loves us."

They waited, their sewing neglected, watching impatiently from the tower. It darkened and began to snow in the late afternoon and Anne grew anxious again. Then, at last, she heard the sound of a horn in the distance. Isabella said that she could see them coming, and they both hurried down to the hall.

The retinue came into the outer bailey, the horses slipping on the wet cobbles, and Anne watched from the top of the steps as Richard rode in under the carved gateway on his grey stallion, accompanied by Uncle Robert. She was half-way down, oblivious to the weather, by the time he had dismounted and handed the reins to a stable boy with a word of thanks. Her heartbeat and the fluttering of her stomach and the leaping of the baby merged as one as he looked up at her.

"My lady!" he said.

"Your Grace," she stammered, trying to curtsey on the narrow steps as he bounded up them two at a time to take her arm and steady her.

"Come inside," he told her sternly. "I would not like you to tumble in your rush to greet me. See how the lady Isabella waits inside," he scolded as they reached the doorway where her companion was standing. Isabella smiled and curtseyed to the duke but her eyes quickly returned to Robert Harrington who followed them up the steps.

Richard pulled off his gloves and cupped Anne's face in the palms of his cold hands as he leant to kiss her gently on the mouth. Then his gaze fell as he caressed a hand over her belly. She smiled as she felt the baby kick at his touch.

"He grows strong and well. And you?" he asked as he looked up again at her face. "Are you well?"

"Yes, I am well," she assured him, her fingers brushing the light dusting of snow from his shoulders. "Come to the fire and warm yourself. Shall I call the servants to bring mulled wine?"

"Indeed," he replied as he unfastened his cloak. "The journey was long and cold, but I am pleased to be here with you." He tossed the cloak aside and, pulling her close to him, he kissed her again – a longer, more leisurely kiss whilst their child was held tight between their bodies. "I have missed you," he said, then turned with a smile to her uncle who was standing with Isabella clinging to his arm.

"Uncle Robert," said Anne with a slight curtsey, remembering her manners. He bowed his head towards her.

"Bring the packages, Robert!" called Richard. "I have brought you gifts, my lady, and I see no reason you shouldn't have at least one now – though I shall make you wait until the Twelfth Night to open the others," he teased. He took the saddle bag that her uncle had carried in and unbuckled it. "This, you may have now!" he said, handing her a small package. "And also I carry a letter from your sister Elizabeth."

"Thank you." She looked down at the small parcel, wrapped in a cream coloured silk cloth. It felt hard and weighed heavy in her hand. She glanced up at his smiling face as she unfastened the knot that held it and spread the cloth aside to reveal a lozenge shaped brooch of gold, set with a large, oblong emerald and hanging from it three small pearls.

"It's beautiful," she said, wondering at the costliness of such a gift. She had never owned anything so lovely.

"It is to thank you for the gift you have given me – the gift of a child, and to keep you safe in childbirth. I did intend to keep it until later. But you looked so exquisite as you came down the steps to greet me that I had to give it to you now." Anne looked up from the jewel in her hand and smiled at him again. He seemed as delighted to present the gift as she was to receive it. "Let me pin it to your gown," he said. He took the brooch from her hand and she felt a spasm of desire for him as his hands brushed her breast as he fastened the ornament to her collar. "Now thank me again," he commanded as his arm stretched around her thickened waist and he pressed his lips more urgently to hers. She raised her hands to the hard muscles of his upper arms, her fingers stretching out and exploring his neck and the feel of his hair as he continued to kiss her hungrily, despite the lack of privacy. After a moment Anne pulled away from him.

"Later, my lord," she promised him and he laughed.

"Later indeed," he replied and took some wine from a waiting servant.

In her bedchamber, after she had told Isabella she had no need of her and her friend had gone eagerly to find Robert, Anne picked up the letter that Richard had brought from her sister. She had not seen Izzie since the spring in London and as it was not yet time for supper she broke the seal and sat down at her small desk to read what news her sister sent:

To Anne Stanley, at Pontefract:

Well-beloved sister, I greet you well and recommend myself to you. I pray this finds you well.

I am in good health and the preparations for my wedding to John Stanley on St Stephen's Day progress well. I'm sure you will be glad to know that we love one another and that I am looking forward with much delight to our union. I hope you will be also pleased to know, if you have not already heard, that our mother was safely delivered of a baby girl to be named Dorothy.

Sadder news is that Lady Stanley died at Stanley House not two weeks past and was buried in the chancel at the church of St James and St John at Garlickhythe. Lord Stanley grieves for her and everyone in the house here is much saddened at her loss. Her health had failed and I think she also still grieved for the loss of her brother.

I'm sure that you have been craving news from me for some time and I pray that you do not think I am remiss or neglectful in not writing to you oftener. The truth is that you have much displeased Lord Stanley and he has forbidden that I correspond with you, so this letter has been sent discreetly through the kindness of Sir William whom you must acknowledge still cares for you, although he has been wed to Elizabeth Hopton in Shropshire.

Sister, I must be the bearer of grave news. I know of your delicate condition and would not have you disturbed except that there is something you must know which concerns the father of your child, the Duke of Gloucester.

You already know my thoughts on him, but do not judge me harshly for what I must say. The duke is to be betrothed to Anne Neville, despite the opposition of both the king and his brother George, Duke of Clarence. Clarence contrived to hide the girl from the duke, but so determined was he that he scoured the city without rest and discovered her disguised as a kitchen maid in the household of one of Clarence's friends. He has taken her to the sanctuary of St Martin's le Grand in London and has compelled her to promise to marry him so that he can protect his claim on the Warwick lands...

The letter blurred and Anne could read no more of it. She pushed it aside and with her face in her hands she sobbed huge shuddering tears that shook her body as she tried to convince herself that such a thing could not be true. Yet she recalled Isabella's reluctance to speak about Middleham and other idle words of gossip she had overheard and she had to acknowledge that her sister probably wrote the truth.

She did not know how long she had been sitting there when Isabella came to seek her.

"Everyone is waiting for you. Are you unwell?" she asked coming across to Anne and touching her shoulder gently.

"Yes, I am unwell," she replied, without looking up as she pushed the letter under her Book of Hours that lay open on the desk. "Please beg forgiveness from the duke. I cannot come down to supper."

"Do you need a physician? Shall I help you to bed?"

"Just go! Leave me alone!" shouted Anne, and after a moment she heard Isabella leave the room, shutting the door gently behind her.

Anne shook with the effort of containing her sobbing and her anger. Her tears had long since ceased and yet she was still wracked with shuddering convulsions that she could not control. How dared he come and take her in his arms and kiss her as if he loved her and keep from her this news that he had chosen to marry Anne Neville.

She heard her door open again and looked up to tell the servant to go away, but it was Richard himself who came in without knocking and closed the door behind him. She turned her head away as she heard him cross the chamber and stand beside her.

"Anne?" he said, and she felt his hand rest lightly on her arm as he crouched beside her. She shrugged off his touch. "Are you ill?" he asked. His voice was filled with concern, but when she tried to stand up to move away from him she felt his grip tighten and he pulled her around so that she was facing him. "Tell me what is wrong," he said. She shook her head, unable to speak or meet his eyes. He pressed his palm to her forehead and even though she tried to hate him she found comfort in his touch. "You seem feverish," he said. "I will send for the physician."

"No!"

"But you are unwell."

"I am not ill," she replied, hearing her voice tremble.

"Anne, you need not be afraid of the physician..."

"I am not afraid! Let me go! Don't touch me!"

He stood. Glancing up, she saw his puzzled expression. Then she turned and groped for the letter and threw it down on the floor at his feet.

"Did you think I would not know? Or did you think I would not care?" she shouted as he bent to retrieve the parchment. "And you can take this back!" She unpinned the brooch with trembling fingers and as he scanned Izzie's words she flung the gift at him, catching him across the forehead with a sharp corner so that when he raised his fingers to the wound he stared in surprise at the blood on them. His face darkened with anger and for a moment she thought that he might strike her.

"I will send for the physician," he said shortly as he placed the letter back on her desk. "We will speak about this later, when you are calm."

When he had gone Anne went to the bed; the bed where she had expected to have him hold her and love her. She was too tired to cry any more and her grief was making the child leap in distress. She lay down in the darkness without lighting a candle and waited until Isabella and the women came and undressed her and put her between the linen sheets. Then someone came with a foul, sour brew and held her head until she drank. She wished it was Richard, but he did not come back to her that night.

It was already light when she awoke and even the faint winter sunshine which crept through a gap in the bedcurtains made her head hurt.

"Do you feel any better this morning?" asked Isabella, looking down at her with a worried face. "The physician was concerned about you last night. He will come back later to see if you are recovered, but in the meantime said you must eat a little oatmeal."

Anne rubbed her sore eyes and saw the servant hovering with a tray of food behind her friend. "I don't want anything," she said.

Isabella waved at the girl to put the breakfast down on the coffer. "Bring some warm water. I will help the lady wash," she said.

"I will wash myself," murmured Anne. "I want to be left alone." But Isabella helped her bathe her face and braid her hair and even though Anne insisted she wanted to get up, her legs felt so weak when she walked to the latrine that she was thankful to get back into her bed.

Isabella was still fussing around her when there was a short knock on the door.

"Tell the physician I need no more of his stinking medicines," complained Anne as she still tasted the sleeping draft on her tongue. "I will soon be well if you will all leave me alone."

Isabella went to the door, but Anne saw that she quickly opened it wide and gave a curtsey that could not be for a mere physician.

"Leave us," said the Duke of Gloucester and, despite Anne's attempt at protest, her companion and the other women went obediently from the room closing the door behind them.

Richard came over to the bed. Anne stared at the tapestry of a hunting scene that hung on the far wall. She felt the bed move as he sat down and took one of her hands in both of his. His thumb gently caressed her palm as he waited for her to look at him and eventually she turned and found him watching her solemnly. There was a small scab on his forehead where the brooch had struck him and Anne looked away again. She tried to pull her hand from his but the grip tightened.

"I hope I find you calmer this morning," he said. "If I had known what news your sister's letter contained I would have kept it until I had spoken to you myself." Anne remained silent. She wanted to ask him if he really had intended to tell her about his marriage plans, but all she could do was sob at the thought of it. "Hush!" he said as he released her hand to wipe the tears from her cheeks. "Do not distress yourself in this way, Anne. It does not mean I love you less."

"What does it mean then?" she managed to ask, leaning her face to his palm despite herself.

"It is a marriage that will ensure my share of the Warwick lands. That is all."

"But I thought that the king had granted you a share of the Warwick lands?"

"Grants can be revoked. Clitheroe and Halton were taken back from me because of Stanley. But if I receive dispensation to marry Anne Neville I can create a contract that will mean I do not run the risk of losing Middleham."

"Middleham," repeated Anne, with a sudden burst of anger. "Is it all about Middleham? I was going to ask you if you loved her more than me. But the real question is do you love Middleham more than me. And the answer is yes," she told him without waiting for his reply. "You men are all the same with your greed for land and for castles." She pushed his hand from her face. "You are as predatory as the Stanleys," she accused him.

"Anne," he reasoned, "I am a youngest son. I have no lands that are mine by inheritance. Everything I own has been granted to me by favour – and can be taken away again on a whim. Would you have me penniless?"

"I would love you if you were a peasant!"

"No you wouldn't," he said. "If I were a peasant with filthy clothes and greasy hair you would turn away from me in disgust." She glanced at him and saw that he was gently teasing her. Then she averted her eyes again, unwilling to forgive him so easily. "But you turn from me in disgust even so," he said, standing up, "and I don't know what to say to make you dislike me less."

He bent to retrieve the brooch from where it had landed the previous night and, crossing to her desk, he straightened the letter lying there and placed the gift on top of it. "I came with the intention of telling you about my intended marriage," he said. "I hoped you would understand that it is something I must do." Anne watched him as he stood with his back to her. "If I were a peasant I might marry for love," he continued, "but younger sons like me must gain their own fortune and must make marriages that are advantageous." He turned and met her eyes. "I must marry someone. I must have land. I must have a legitimate heir. As the widow of a defeated prince, Anne Neville could spend the rest of her life in a nunnery – but then all the Warwick land would be claimed by my brother, who has shown no true loyalty to the king. I will not allow him to take Middleham from me."

Anne pulled up her knees and rested her forehead on them, holding the baby tightly. "What will become of me?" she whispered.

He came back to the bed and sat down again beside her and cradled her in his arms, pulling her close. She buried her face against him, breathing in his warmth and scent. He kissed the nape of her neck and rocked her gently as if she were a small child.

"Anne, I promised that I would take care of you and I will. But you are not free to be my wife – and my marriage means no more to me than yours does to you. It suits me to marry Anne Neville and it suits her to become my wife. At least I hope she finds me preferable to the cloistered life of a convent. She will have her ladies and her own household, and she will be Duchess of Gloucester. But that is all. I love you."

"But you will bed her," said Anne, not wanting to think of him with someone else.

"I hope she will provide me with a legitimate heir. But you must not be jealous, for I will have to close my mind to thoughts of you and your husband too."

"I will never let Edward Stanley lay a finger on my body," vowed Anne. He didn't reply and she knew that although he held her close and spoke of love, and although she carried his child, he would not refrain from Anne Neville's bed once she was his wife.

After a while he laid her gently back on the pillow, kissed her cheek and left her to sleep away her grief. When she woke again she lay and thought about what he had said. She had always known that he would not marry her and would seek a rich heiress. So why should she be so surprised that he was to marry Anne Neville now that she was free? Perhaps she had been unfair to him, she thought. After all, he had brought her to Pontefract. If he had not cared for her he would have left her at Lathom.

She insisted that the servant who was set to watch over her help her to dress. Then she went down the steps to the hall on unsteady legs. Richard was sitting near the hearth, talking with Uncle Robert and Isabella. They didn't notice her at first, but when Richard saw her he came quickly to put his arm around her and guide her to a chair near the warmth.

"You are still pale," he said, caressing her cheek with his hand. Anne held it against her face for a moment then turned her lips to his palm and kissed it. She knew that she must be content to have him as her lover; she only prayed that he would not forget her after his marriage, and that Anne Neville would not steal his heart from her.

Snow fell heavily during January, but Richard seemed content to remain with Anne at Pontefract and displayed no desire to go back to London to his intended wife. He spent his days with his secretary, writing letters and dealing with the administration of his northern lands. At night, he began to come to her bed again, despite the raised eyebrows of the women who thought it wrong when she was with child. And although the coming baby numbed her physical passion for him, she was glad to have him close.

Anne Neville was not mentioned again and she put away Izzie's letter. Yet when she woke sometimes in the early hours of the morning, her back aching from the heaviness of the baby, Anne's thoughts were all of her namesake and she felt the pain of envy keenly enough to bring tears that she cried silently so as not to disturb Richard.

She knew that when the weather improved he would leave, but she hoped that before that happened their baby would be born – and she prayed that it would be the son he always spoke of. Even if she lost his love, the child would bind him to her.

As the days lengthened and the northern cold intensified, the leap year of 1472 promised an extra day of winter and Anne woke in the early hours of that Thursday morning with a tightening pain around the baby and an intense aching in her back.

"What's wrong?" asked Richard, waking at her sudden gasp as pain struck her again. He sat up in the bed and pushed back the hangings to light a candle. "Is it time for the baby?"

"I think so," she said, looking up at his rumpled hair and the smile of anticipation that played over his face.

"You are afraid," he said, stroking her hair back from her face. "Don't be." He bent to kiss her forehead. "I have engaged the most reputable midwife, and I have a physician should there be the need. They will see the child safely born."

"Oh!" called Anne as another contraction grasped her body. "Richard!" She grasped for his hand as he turned to pull on his clothes. "Don't go. Don't leave me!"

"I need to send for the midwife. Isabella will come to you."

"But she knows nothing of childbirth. I wish my mother was here."

"The midwife will come. She will not be long. Be brave." He took her hand as he stood by the bed and looked down at her. Then he raised her fingers to his lips and kissed them. "Sweet Anne. I shall pray for you in your travail," he said.

"The brooch," she cried. "Bring the brooch." He turned to find it in the small wooden casket he had given her to keep her jewels safe and brought it to the bed where he sat down and pinned it to her nightgown. Then his hand strayed to her stomach as he caressed her and the child and he kissed them both.

As another wave of pain surged through her body, Anne closed her eyes and didn't see him leave as she prayed earnestly to Saint Margaret of Antioch that she would be safely delivered of the child, as the saint had been delivered from the dragon.

Isabella came to sit beside her and wiped her face with cool cloths. Servants were sent to fetch water, which was heated on the fire and, as the midwife prodded at her stomach and murmured in the corner of the room with her two assistants, Anne gave over the responsibility of her body to them and their superior knowledge. As her pain intensified the midwife pushed pillows behind her and helped her to sit up to ease the birth.

Anne had never known pain like it. Although the women who attended her rubbed her belly and back with fragrant ointments to ease the agony, she thought it was impossible to feel such pain and still live. She tried to make her peace with God, praying, amongst other things, for forgiveness for her unfaithfulness to her child husband, and she prepared to meet her death as yet another spasm of agony ripped through her.

Then she felt an uncontrollable urge to push the child from her body and as the midwife held her arm and encouraged her to bear down she panted and sweated in the overheated chamber and gradually the child was expelled from her – first the head, and then the body parted from her in a slippery rush and Anne gave thanks that she and the child were now separate beings.

"A boy!" the midwife told her as she scooped the baby in a cloth and wiped the blood and mucus from his face and nose.

"Let me see," said Anne, trying to ease her aching, bleeding body up from the bed.

"A moment," said the midwife and then Anne heard him cry as he took his first breath and one of the assistants tied and cut the pulsating cord that still attached him to her. The midwife bathed his tiny body in warmed milk and gave him a taste of honey on his tongue to soothe him before swaddling him in linen cloths. Then she placed him in Anne's arms. He had a head of thick dark hair. His face was red and puffy, and his little mouth, showing pink gums, let out cries that belied his tiny size.

"Is he complete?" asked Anne, looking in wonder at the small person who had, until minutes ago, been within her own body. "Has he fingers and toes?" she asked.

"He is perfect. A healthy boy," smiled the midwife as she ran a hand over Anne's hair. "You were a brave girl. You've done well and you have a son to be proud of."

The women delivered Anne of the afterbirth then washed her and put clean sheets on the bed. Isabella took the baby to show him to his father whilst they worked. Then he was put into the cradle, away from the light, and he was rocked until he slept and Anne, exhausted, leaned back and closed her own eyes.

She woke suddenly, unsure if it had been a vivid dream, but the pain and soreness as she moved confirmed that she had indeed given birth. She tried to sit up, anxious to see the baby, to hold him and know that he was safe. The curtains had been drawn around her bed and she pulled them back to look into the cradle. She felt a moment of panic as she saw it was empty. Then the figure standing at the window moved and she saw Richard, holding his son.

"Did I wake you?" he asked. "The midwife said you were exhausted and he was beginning to cry so I picked him up." He looked suddenly anxious. "Did I do wrong?" he asked.

"No." Anne smiled at the sight of them; the tiny baby nestling in his father's arms and sucking at his little finger.

"He's strong," said Richard. "And hungry I think. Shall I send for the nurse?"

"No," she replied as she eased herself up on the pillows and held out her arms for her son. "I will feed him." Richard gave him to her tenderly and watched as she uncovered her breast.

"Have you considered a name?" he asked.

Anne looked down at the dark head and soft cheek as the baby gazed up at her with bluish eyes. Her finger traced his tiny, perfect ear and then smoothed down a tuft of his hair. She had thought about his name.

"I would like to call him John, to remember my father," she said. Richard nodded and Anne knew that, for a moment, he too thought of Wakefield and the abhorrent events that had followed the battle there.

"John of Gloucester," he said, and Anne felt relieved that he acknowledged this child as his own. Whatever happened, whomever he wed, no other woman would have the privilege of being the mother of his first born son.

PART TWO
1472 ~ 1478

Chapter Seven
April 1472 ~ July 1473

Anne watched as Richard swung his leg over the back of the grey stallion and gathered the reins. The worst of the weather had passed. There were signs of springtime and he could not put off his return to London any longer.

He turned the horse in a circle, waiting for Uncle Robert and the rest of his household to be ready.

Anne shifted baby John into a more upright position on her shoulder as Richard drew rein beside her and he bent to kiss his son's head in a last farewell.

"Take care of him, Anne – and take care of yourself. You will both be in my thoughts and prayers."

Anne nodded, not able to speak. Every time he left it was hard, but this time was the worst. This time he was going away to finalise the arrangements for his wedding to Anne Neville and she had no idea when, or even if, he would return. His reassurances that he loved her and the baby, that he would take care of them and not forget them were all very well, but once he was in London would he really spare the time to think of her?

"Don't cry," he said as he circled the horse again. Anne looked up at him. The sun reflected off his polished armour and dazzled her so that she couldn't see his face. She shook her head, not knowing what to say. She had told him, more than once over the last week, that she did not want him to go; a bittersweet week when he had made time to be with her and the baby; a week in which she couldn't have asked more from him, but a week that she knew would end like this.

The horse shifted restlessly, pawing the ground with its hoof, wanting to be off, and Anne sensed that Richard felt a little of the same anticipation. She moved back from the horse as it trod near her, her hand shielding John's head from both the sunlight and the animal. She watched as Richard glanced at the gathered horsemen and judged that they were at last ready to leave. He leant from the saddle again to kiss her mouth in full view of everyone as she raised her face to him in once last attempt to implore him to stay.

"I love you," he said, then touched the horse's flanks with his heels and as it sprang forward he rode out of the castle courtyard, his arm raised in a last farewell. Anne saw Uncle Robert kiss Isabella before urging his own horse after the duke. Isabella waved and blew him another kiss as he rode underneath the gatehouse. They were to be married as soon as Richard could spare him and Anne was afraid that she might lose her friend, even though Isabella had promised that she would remain at Pontefract for as long as Anne needed her.

Robert twisted in his saddle for one last look at Isabella. The last few weeks had been both sweet and hard. To have been free to spend so much time with his betrothed yet to have abstained from full knowledge of her body had been difficult. There had been times when his self-control had almost deserted him. And Isabella too, with her soft and eager kisses, had often parted from him so reluctantly he knew that it would not have taken much persuasion for him to be allowed into her bed. But the date of their marriage was still not set, the autumn wedding having been put off so that he could attend on Diccon in London.

As the overexcited horses settled to a steady pace, Robert eased the tension on the reins and relaxed into the saddle. It was a fine morning with a hint of good weather on the horizon where patches of blue sky were showing between the pale clouds. Beside him, Diccon rode with his face set into a stern expression and his eyes on the road ahead of them. He seemed disinclined to talk and Robert knew that he had found it hard to leave Anne and his baby son behind. Robert remembered how Isabella had come to the chamber where he had been keeping company with the duke during the birth. Diccon had jumped from his seat as if stung when she had come in with the baby in her arms. And the expression of bewilderment and pride as he had peered at the tiny, wrinkled face of his son was one Robert would never forget.

As soon as he had been able, Robert had bade the scribe write a letter to his brother James at Hornby to tell him the news – and he had pressed an extra coin into the hand of the messenger who would ride with it.

"Tell him that his niece and the child are both well and that he is baptised John of Gloucester," he had instructed him, knowing that James would be well pleased that the duke's son was named for their dead brother.

Anne went back into the castle. John was asleep in her arms, unaware that his father had gone away, and he didn't wake as she took him up to the nursery and laid him down in his crib. He was a strong child who was growing quickly and Richard had never missed an opportunity to pick him up and toss him in the air to make him gurgle and laugh.

"Be careful with him!" Anne always told him, worried that he would let the baby fall.

"He'll come to no harm. He's a Plantagenet. He'll grow to be an excellent horseman and a fearless knight. A blessed son of York," Richard had said as he'd held the writhing baby high above his head. "I have great plans for his future."

"Not battles," she'd said as she'd taken her son from him and encircled the child in her arms, nuzzling her face against his soft dark hair. "I couldn't bear it if he had to fight in battles." She'd kissed John's cheek and allowed his perfect little hand to grasp her finger. The intensity of her love for him frightened her.

"He will love to fight," said Richard, watching them.

"Why must men fight?" Anne demanded with sudden anger as she realised that she would not be able to protect her son from harm forever.

Richard had taken her face between his palms and kissed her gently on the mouth.

"I fight to keep you safe," he had said. "I've fought for the king, and for England and for St George. And now I will fight for my son and for you, Anne Harrington."

A door slamming somewhere nearby disturbed her recollection and the raw emotion of loss rose from a place just below her ribs to her throat. She twisted the ring on her finger, as she had seen Richard twist the same ring on his own hand. It was fashioned from silver with a blue enamelled centre behind which was hidden a fragment of the true cross. He had pushed it onto her finger the day John was born and now Anne prayed that it would bring her hope and consolation in the difficult times ahead.

The next week her mood lifted when her mother came with her own baby girl, Dorothy, to visit her. She sighed and cooed over her first grandchild in adoration.

"Do you think it is wicked of me to have a child by the Duke of Gloucester when I am a married woman?" Anne asked her as they sat in the nursery and watched their children sleeping. She was still concerned that her mother disapproved of what had been done.

"If your marriage to Edward Stanley is not yet consummated it could be annulled. It is what your Uncle James desires, although Lord Stanley will not agree."

"Lord Stanley would never agree," sighed Anne, "even though he is very angry with me. He will not allow Izzie to speak of me or write to me – although she does write. Sir William sends her letters to me with his messenger," she said, stroking John's cheek as he whimpered and murmured restlessly.

"Izzie wants to leave Stanley House and go to the house at Melling," her mother told her. "It would afford her and her husband more freedom. But your Uncle James is still holding that property as well as Hornby Castle, despite the king's instructions to give it up. And he still has the support of the Duke of Gloucester." She paused and gazed at the children for a moment. "The duke is not a man to be thwarted when he makes up his mind about something," she went on. "And he is ambitious, Nan. That is why he means to marry Anne Neville. He will never be satisfied until he has wealth and power."

"Is that a bad thing?"

"Perhaps not. He seems to care for you, and he has acknowledged the child as his. You could do well from it."

"I'm not interested in profiting from it," said Anne. "Why must women always think of how they can profit from their marriages, or their lovers?"

"You love him," remarked her mother. "That's a dangerous thing to do. Love brings heartbreak often enough."

"You loved my father," she replied.

"Too much," said her mother. "Despite my present husband I still yearn for him every day. I see him in you, Nan, and sometimes I cannot bear to look at you because you remind me of him. I can see him in this baby too." She glanced down at her grandson. "Your father would have been so proud – so proud that you are the mother of a Plantagenet and that you named the baby for him."

"Richard thought it was a good name. He wanted to honour my father for giving his life for the Yorkists." She paused. "Mother, what will I do?" she asked. "What will I do if I am forced to return to my husband? You know that the

Stanleys will not allow me to stay here for ever. They want Hornby too much."

"Yes, they mean to have Hornby. It has become a matter of pride that they defeat the duke and your uncles. And Lord Stanley is a dangerous man to cross. I fear for you, Nan. You will need to be careful."

Richard returned in the summer as he had business on his northern estates. His household rode with him and suddenly the empty echoing chambers and corridors of Pontefract Castle were filled with strangers and noise.

"I am pleased to see you, my lord," she said as his shrewd eyes looked her over with a smile of approval.

"You look well, and have regained your figure," he replied, as he raised her hand to his lips. "How is my son?" he asked.

"He sits unaided for a time and takes some solid food."

"Then soon he will sit on a horse and I will take him hawking with me."

They went up to the nursery and Richard was pleased that John seemed to remember him. Anne watched as he lifted his son into the air and John kicked his legs and laughed as he grasped for the shiny boar badge that was pinned to Richard's doublet.

That night he called an end to supper after the second course had been served and grasping her hand had taken her up the steps to his bedchamber. But as he led her from the table Anne noticed the smirking and winking from some of his retainers. She pulled her hand from his as she realised what they thought of her.

"Your knights and retainers look at me as if I am a common harlot. They speak of me as Gloucester's mistress," she complained to him, remembering some uncouth conversation she had overheard earlier that day.

He frowned as he dismissed all his attendants and closed the door behind them. Then he came to her and took her in his arms and began to kiss her. She resisted. She wanted to speak with him candidly about her position at Pontefract and what her future held.

She was beginning to feel a prisoner there as she had once been a prisoner at Hornby and she was worried about what would happen to her after his marriage.

"What troubles you, Anne?" he asked, as she pulled away from him.

"Do you need to ask? My sister writes of your marriage plans, yet you tell me nothing."

"Don't spoil these times we have together," he said, his fingers tracing the contours of her face. "It is not a subject I wish to discuss with you. I have told you that I love you. Be content with that."

Anne didn't answer him. She doubted that she could ever be content unless she had the whole of him.

"Come to bed," he said, taking her hand and kissing first her palm before moving closer again and kissing her neck. Silently she damned the Stanleys. If matters had been different he might have chosen her freely to be his duchess, though in reality she knew that he would never have exchanged Middleham for Hornby. "Come to bed," he whispered again into her ear, and despite her misgivings she went with him willingly.

Next morning he woke early and got out of bed whilst she still slumbered in the warmth of their bodies. As he stood naked, she noticed that his spine curved slightly, making one shoulder seem more prominent than the other and giving him a slightly lop-sided appearance. There was not a portion of fat on him anywhere, just hard muscle and a scar on his right arm from a sword wound.

He pulled a shirt over his head and ran his slender fingers through his hair.

"When I have attended to my correspondence I think I will take a hawk from the mews and go hunting. Will you come? Or are you still afraid of riding?"

"I will come," she said. She had been practising her riding skills under the tutelage of a stableman and become fond of the little dun mare that he had chosen for her. And although riding and hunting did not hold the same appeal for her as they did for Richard she would have agreed to almost any outing to keep herself in his company.

"And I will speak to my men – on the subject of showing you respect," he promised. "I will not allow you to be insulted."

The fine days of riding out to hunt songbirds and hares with the falcons jingling on their wrists, and the happy nights that followed, soon passed. When letters came from London that made him sigh in annoyance she knew that it would not be long before he left.

"Just for a while," he said, but made no promise about when he would return.

The cause of his annoyance was revealed when Isabella received a letter from Robert Harrington some weeks later.

"Gloucester is disputing with his brother Clarence about the Warwick lands," her friend told her as they walked in the garden. "Robert says that the rows are becoming so intense that men are considering wearing their armour to attend court. Apparently, Clarence became so infuriated with his brother's demands for half the Warwick estates that he challenged him to a fight for them. But someone informed the king who intervened and made them relent, for the time being at least." Anne frowned. She could imagine, all too well, Richard threatening his brother with a dagger and a sword.

"The king has promised to hear their cases in a court of law and says that they must abide by his decision," said Isabella.

Anne wondered if Richard would still marry Anne Neville if the king ruled in favour of Clarence and told him that he could not have Middleham Castle after all. She felt a flicker of hope, but knew, deep down, that after Clarence's rebellion, Edward would favour Richard in this matter.

"Does Anne Neville remain in the nunnery?" she asked, tempted to pray that the woman might find a vocation and stay there.

"No. She is in the safekeeping of her uncle, the Archbishop of York."

Anne was pleased when the bickering went on. Richard would not risk marrying Anne Neville until the matter was settled and he could be sure that Middleham would remain his.

He came to her again as he travelled north to York and stayed for a few nights. He was loving to her and John, as always, and if she had not known about his marriage plans Anne would never have doubted that she was the only woman he desired.

He never spoke to her about what had happened in London. It was as if he separated the two worlds in which he lived with no coincidence between them.

But it filled Anne with anxiety. She needed to know what would happen to her when he married and whether she would be able to remain at Pontefract, and on the last night of his visit she could keep silent no longer.

"I have heard of your disagreements with your brother," she said as she sat combing out her hair in his bedchamber. She watched as he paused. He had sent everyone else away and was sitting on the edge of the bed, taking off his hose.

She waited, holding the comb in one hand and a strand of hair in the other, and watched him. Her heart beat a little faster as his brows drew together and she wondered if it would have been better if she had kept her silence.

"I think the dispute between my brother and myself has become the chosen subject of London gossip," he said as he came across to her. "George remains totally unreasonable. He will not see that he must allow Anne Neville her share of the Warwick estates." He took the comb from her hand and began to draw it through her hair.

"Are you displeased with me?" she asked.

"What makes you ask that?"

"I always seem to ask questions that you will not answer."

"Which questions?"

"About our future. About what will happen to me when you marry..."

He put down the comb then gathered her hair in his hands and bent to kiss her. The kiss was insistent and his hands held her head firmly until she finally responded and kissed him in return. Then he lifted her and carried her to his bed where he covered her mouth with his mouth and her body with his body and eventually she lost herself in the moment and he had still not answered her concerns.

The leaves on the trees that grew around Balderstone Hall were fading to orange and yellow as Robert waited for Isabella outside the porch of St Mary the Virgin. It was here that they were to be married in the presence of both their families – although Anne remained at Pontefract. The Duke of Gloucester would not allow her to travel into Lancashire lest she fall back into the hands of the Stanleys.

James stood beside him. Confident that Hornby would not be attacked by Lord Stanley in his absence, he had left the castle. He had accepted the offer of the king to allow the matter to be considered by an independent council of arbiters and had agreed to a huge fine of three thousand marks to accept their decision. It was a sum that Robert doubted his brother could pay if the court did not find in his favour and he did not share his brother's optimism that he would be successful. If only points of law were to be discussed and matters of loyalty put aside, then the castle did belong to Anne and he feared that James would never be content with such a ruling.

The piping and bells of the minstrels who accompanied his bride made him look round. Isabella was beautiful. Her hair was loose and uncovered for the marriage and sprang brightly around her face from beneath a chaplet of late roses. He greeted and kissed her. She was scented with the herbs in which she had bathed and her breath was warm on his freshly shaven cheek as she eagerly greeted him in return.

"At last," he whispered as the music ceased and they turned to the priest.

As the autumn of 1472 turned to winter at Pontefract, Anne felt the subtle, fluttering movements of a new life in her womb. She had been waiting for Richard to visit her so that she could give him the news of another child, but when the Christmas season came and went and he did not come, she was forced to acknowledge that she was far from his immediate concerns and she decided that she must send him a letter.

She sat down to write such personal tidings in her own hand, but as she composed her letter she heard a great commotion outside in the courtyard and, dropping the quill with a splash of ink, she hurried to the great hall just as he came in, well wrapped against the cold.

"Your Grace!" She curtseyed clumsily before him as he pulled off his outer coat and tossed it to a pageboy she didn't recognise. "I did not expect you."

"It appears we have arrived before the messenger," he glowered. "Send the lazy wretch to me when he does arrive," he ordered. "I would like to learn what has kept him along the way!" Anne twisted the ring on her finger as she watched him go to the fire to warm himself.

"My lady, I apologise," he said after a moment. "The journey has been arduous and my patience sorely tested. I miss the good sense of your uncle as he and his new wife amuse themselves. Bring wine, and something to eat!" he bawled at the young page who fled, looking terrified, to do his bidding. "I should not have shouted at the lad," he said as he watched him go. "He is a good boy and I have no wish to appear a tyrant, but the cold has numbed my very soul, I think." He held out his slender hands to the blaze of logs and then rubbed them together. "Feel how cold I am!" He touched her cheek with the back of his hand and laughed as she recoiled from the iciness. "And how are you, my love? I am truly sorry you had to spend Christmas alone. If it could have been otherwise I would have made it so, but..." He studied her hard for a moment then reached to turn her to face him, holding her arms with his cold hands and looking at her figure. "This is not from feasting," he commented as one hand swept across her stomach. "Anne?"

"I am with child, my lord," she said and watched as his face softened into a wide smile of pride and satisfaction.

"I said that you were made to bear my sons."

"Or daughters. You are not displeased?" she asked warily.

"Anne, why must you always think that you court my displeasure? Just because I cannot be always with you does not mean I love you any less. Come!" He held his arms wide and she accepted his embrace with relief. "When do you expect the child?" he asked, kissing her face.

"Around Maytime. Will you...?"

"I will make sure that I come to you," he reassured her. "And now, let me see my son. Does he walk yet? What words can he say?" He took her hand and they went to the nursery where John was playing with little farmyard figures on a rug before the fire. When he saw Richard a smile lit his face and he lifted his arms to his father who picked him up and tossed him in the air as he screamed in delight. "He knows me."

"Of course he knows you," said Anne, with relief, as she watched her son close his chubby hands around the fur of his father's collar and say something that Richard always swore was 'Papa'.

His cold and hunger were forgotten as he played with his son and Anne delighted in watching them together. Later, when they had said prayers and both kissed the boy goodnight they went to a late supper, and afterwards he asked her permission to come to her chamber.

"My bed has been too cold these winter nights," she replied.

"Then you would have me warm the sheets for you? I thought I employed servants to do that."

"Not in the way that you warm them, my lord!" she laughed.

He took her to bed and gently eased himself into her burgeoning body as she clung to him, loving him more at each ripple of joy. Eventually they slept, warm in each other's arms and for a time at least Anne felt safe.

The weather worsened and the snowdrifts piled themselves against the castle walls. Richard was anxious to get back to his affairs in London, but Anne was glad that the weather kept him at Pontefract. And, as he realised that there was no chance of heading south again until a thaw set in, he relaxed in her company.

"Does my uncle still hold Hornby?" she asked him one morning as they were playing with the baby.

"For the present, although I fear he may be forced to give it up. Why? Are you in need of the place?"

"It would be nice to go home," she said, wistfully.

"But this is your home now. It's far grander than Hornby."

"I have pleasant memories of Hornby," she said, thinking of the day she had first gone to his bedchamber, and wondering how long she would be allowed to remain at Pontefract after his wedding and where she would go if Hornby was claimed by the Stanleys.

"Anne," he said after a moment's silence. "I will have to return to London soon."

"I know," she said, sadly.

James had been called to London for the arbitration and now he watched as the Duke of Gloucester came towards him with sorrow and disappointment clouding his eyes. "I'm sorry," he said. "You will be informed officially, but the tribunal has found against us. Hornby will go to Stanley after all."

It was many years since James had cried but he found it difficult not to do so now and it was a moment before he could compose himself enough to speak.

"Your Grace, I am indebted to you for all your support."

"I only wish the outcome could have been what you desired... what we both desired," said the duke gloomily. "But we will soon go to war with France," he continued and James noted the gleam in his eye. "It is better for the country if all Englishmen pull in the same direction rather than squabble amongst themselves. And Anne will have the castle. With God's blessing she may bear another son who will inherit it in time."

"A son with her husband?" asked James.

"I will not compel her to remain my mistress when I am married to Anne Neville," said Richard.

Late in the spring of 1473 Anne felt a dull ache in her lower back. It intensified as the evening wore on and as she laboriously climbed the stone steps to her chamber that night she felt wetness and realised that the time had come.

This time Richard was not there to take her hand and reassure her. Isabella was attending to some affairs on Robert's estates at Badsworth and the only companion that she had was John's nurse. She came running at Anne's sharp cry and quickly sent one of the kitchen maids to fetch the midwife.

Anne wept with pain and fear – and because Richard had not come as he had promised.

"You must send a message to the Duke of Gloucester," she gasped between the pains of her contractions.

"You can send word to him when the child is born," said the nurse.

"No. Tell him now. Tell him to come," she sobbed, wanting no one else's arm around her but his, though she knew that many days would pass before he could reach her even if he rode north as soon as he received the letter.

At last the midwife came, with her assistants; the same ones who had attended John's birth.

"What's this mistress?" she asked gently. "Do not be distressed. It'll do the babe no good. Dry your tears," she said, handing Anne a cloth, "and we'll soon have this baby in its cradle."

Once more Anne gave herself up to the women and in the early hours of the morning of the sixteenth day of May she bore a little girl, smaller than John had been but with a similar head of thick dark hair.

"She has her father's hands," said Anne, caressing the long, slim fingers when the midwife laid the baby in her arms.

"What will her name be?"

"I don't know. I hoped for another boy. The duke wants sons."

"He will be smitten when he sees this little one," smiled the midwife. "For all they say they crave sons they always make a special place in their hearts for daughters."

Anne smiled up at her. "Thank you," she said. "You have been so kind to me, again. I will make sure the duke rewards you well."

Richard came within the week. Anne was still confined to her chamber. This time she was unable to feed the baby herself and a wet nurse was brought; a young wife from the town whose own baby had not survived. It pained Anne to watch this stranger suckle her newborn to her breast, but as soon as the baby was fed she took her from the girl and held her close to her own body as she slowly walked the chamber until she was lulled to sleep. It was a practice frowned upon by the nurse who thought the baby should be tightly swaddled and put in the crib, but Anne defied her and was pleased when the woman demurred.

Richard came straight up when he arrived. His footsteps echoed outside her door. She smiled at his infectious laugh as she heard him teasing Isabella that it would be her turn next, and she wondered at the strength of the love she felt for him. She had tried so hard to quell her feelings, to put her passion for him aside, but it seemed that it was stronger than ever and when he came in and his eyes met hers she could not prevent herself running to him.

"What's this, my love? I thought I should receive a frosty welcome for my tardiness," he said as his arms surrounded her and she felt herself crying on his shoulder as she had when he'd come to take her away from Lathom House. "Oh Anne! Don't cry. You make me feel ashamed."

"I cry with joy to see you, my lord. You have a daughter," she said, wiping her cheeks with her hands and watching his face as he turned to the cradle, his arm still around her waist, to look at his sleeping child.

"Did you choose a name for her baptism?"

"She is called Katherine."

He bent to pick the baby up and the nurse looked disapproving as he cradled her wearing his travel-stained clothes. Anne saw his face soften with the affection that the midwife had predicted and she knew that this little scrap of humanity would always be special to him.

On a sunny morning later that summer Anne rose early and went across the bailey to the chapel of St Clement to pray. It was the day that Richard would marry Anne Neville at Westminster Abbey and she felt bereaved. She knelt at the altar before the steady flame of a beeswax candle and knew that by the time it burnt down he would be the husband of another woman. She knelt, relishing the pain in her knees and her back as she watched and prayed all through the day. No one disturbed her – not even the nurse who had come to say that little Katherine cried for her mother. The whole of Pontefract Castle knew what was taking place and they left Anne alone to grieve.

When the candle was finished and the evening shadows began to creep from the high windows across the chapel walls, Anne rose and walked stiffly back to her apartments. She climbed to the nursery where she lifted her sleepy daughter from the crib and, resting the baby's tiny head in the crook of her neck, she paced up and down the chamber still weeping silent tears. There was no one there to comfort her; her uncles and Isabella had gone to London to attend the wedding – and although Isabella had apologised again and again for this betrayal Anne had hugged her and told her to go and enjoy the day. She was to return north with the Gloucesters as they travelled to Middleham Castle. But Richard and Anne Neville would stay at Nottingham. She would not see him.

Chapter Eight
November 1474 ~ May 1477

The letter that her Uncle Robert brought to her from Richard was formal, written by a secretary, and only signed in his own hand. It told her that he intended to come to visit his children.

"I cannot face him," she said to her uncle when she had read the brief message. "It is too hard. Please may I stay with Isabella at Badsworth until he has been and gone?"

"The duke will be sorry not to see you," said her uncle. "He asked me to send him an account of your well-being with my reply. He still loves you, Anne."

"And I love him," she replied, turning away to hide her hurt. "That is why I cannot see him," she said as she turned the letter in her hands so that her eyes would not rest on his signature.

"He does not need your permission to come," her uncle reminded her. "His diplomacy in asking your agreement to his seeing the children is laudable and I think you do him a disservice to run and hide."

"But it is too hard," she said again as tears flowed at her uncle's harsh words. "How can I bear to see him now?"

"I think that my brother James should never have given you to the duke," said her uncle with a touch of bitterness. "We knew that he would never marry you and it was done for our benefit rather than yours. I'm sorry for it," he said. "I will write to say that you are at Badsworth."

When she returned from her visit Anne found that the children had new clothes and toys and that John kept telling her, "Papa came!"

"His Grace was saddened not to see you," remarked the nurse, and Anne left the nursery without a word and walked the castle grounds with her hood pulled over her face to hide her tears.

He sent gifts at Epiphany for the children and a beautifully illustrated book for Anne. He sent his regrets that he would not see her, but she knew that he meant he regretted that she would not see him. Whenever he sent word that he was coming to Pontefract, Anne made arrangements to visit Isabella and left John and Katherine with their nurse. It hurt her to know that he was only within a few miles of her, but she knew that it was nothing to the hurt she would feel if she saw him and had to be parted from him again.

Isabella seemed to understand and allowed her to talk and weep all through the days of her visits. She had her own baby now, a son named James. Anne was his godmother and she consoled herself by nursing him on her lap until it was time to return to her own children.

Early in the New Year she heard from her sister again. Izzie was with child for a second time and wrote that she would name the new baby Anne if it was a girl.

She wrote of how London was in a flurry of preparation for the war with France and repeated the news that she had already heard from Isabella that her Uncle James had at last agreed to relinquish Hornby and was to ride to France as a knight of the body to the king.

A week later when John was sitting at a desk in the nursery and Anne was teaching him to form his name and Katherine was playing with a doll at their feet they all looked up at the sound of horses' hooves. The nurse put down her sewing and went to enquire who had come. Expecting it to be a messenger from one of her uncles, Anne picked up Katherine and took John by the hand to follow the nurse down the steps to the great hall. But as she went down she could hear that the numbers of horses and men that were arriving were in far excess of mere messengers. From a narrow window she peered through the thick glass and could just make out a long train of loaded baggage carts and ranks of archers with their bows on their backs as they marched into the bailey.

She hesitated, wondering if it was safe for the children to remain with her. Then she froze as she heard Richard's voice in the hall. Her heart beat so fast she thought it would run out of control like some skittish horse and she let go of her son's hand to steady herself against the cold stone of the wall. Released from her grip, John ran on ahead of her and she had no choice but to follow him.

"Papa!" called John as he ran across to Richard who bent to embrace him. "What have you brought for me?"

"Wretched boy! Do you love me only for my gifts?" demanded Richard, ruffling his son's dark hair with an affectionate smile. He looked across at Anne and scrutinised her with his stern blue eyes before coming to gently pinch his daughter's cheek. "Are you well, little maid?" he asked her. Then he turned to the nurse. "Take the children to the nursery," he said. "I will come to see you in a little while," he promised them. "But first I must speak with your mother."

Silently the nurse took Katherine from Anne and led a reluctant John away. Richard put down his gloves on the table and drank from the cup of wine that a servant had brought.

"Leave us!" he said to the men who had followed him in. "Go and find yourselves some food from the kitchens and make sure the horses are stabled and that the men find suitable ground to pitch their tents. Sit down," he said to Anne as they left, "you look pale."

"I did not expect you," she said.

"No," he told her with a glint of disapproval in his eyes. "If you had expected me you would have fled to Badsworth."

She stared up at him, unable to wrench her gaze from his face. He looked the same, though why she thought his marriage should have changed him she couldn't explain. As he watched her his severe expression softened.

"Are you well? You look–"

"I am surprised, that is all."

"Am I so daunting as to make you tremble so?" he asked. She looked down and clenched her hands tightly on her lap to try to steady herself but she could not. "I have enquired about you often," he said.

"So my uncles tell me."

"Anne, why do you avoid me?" he demanded.

"I... I..." She looked up at him again, at his blue eyes under the dark expressive eyebrows, the prominent nose, the strong chin. "I love you." She had said it before she realised her thoughts were on her lips. "I'm sorry," she said and moved to stand up, thinking that she must go away from him.

"Did I give you permission to leave?" he asked. "Sit down!" And she sank back onto the stool, not daring to look at him now.

"My lord, I apologise," she whispered. He was silent for a moment then she heard him sigh.

"I am on my way to London to join the forces for the invasion of France," he said, "but I wanted to speak to you about Hornby Castle. The king has been unmoveable on the matter and was much angered by your uncle's occupation there. You know my views, Anne, but the matter is settled now." She glanced up at him but he wasn't looking at her. "This is no time for squabbles. Your Uncle James has accepted a position with the king to compensate him for his loss and your Uncle Robert will remain in my service. As to Hornby it will pass to the heirs you give your husband."

"I will bear no Stanley heirs," she told him. "The only children I want are the ones that you have given me."

"Anne, do not be so hard on yourself. You are young. You –"

"Would you like to think of me in another man's bed? As I have to think of you with another woman," she burst out.

"That is enough!" he reprimanded her. "You do not speak to me of my wife in that manner!" A fresh shiver ran through her at the coldness of his rebuke. There was a long silence between them until he came across and laid a hand on her shoulder. "Do not be unhappy because of me, Anne," he said more gently. "When I leave here I will continue to London and the army will set sail for Calais. If I do not return..."

"Richard!" She reached to clasp his hand, but he withdrew it. "Do not speak of such things."

"If I do not return," he continued, "the children will be provided for from my household and I have arranged a small annuity for you as well. I wanted to reassure you on this matter before I leave. I... I needed to see you," he confessed with a tightness in his voice.

She looked up and his eyes revealed his feelings.

"When do you leave?" she asked.

"At first light tomorrow. Whilst you and the children are still abed," he said, meaning that he did not want her to watch him go. She nodded.

"My prayers will be with you. I will pray each night for your safety," she told him.

"I will see the children now," he said. "I have indeed brought gifts, though I hope I have no need to buy their affection. Will you take supper with me tonight?" he asked. "Please, Anne. Let us be friends," he said when he saw her hesitation.

"I will," she agreed after a moment, finding that she was already looking forward to having his company.

"And you will not hide from me in the future? You will be here when I come to visit the children?" She nodded her assent and he left her to go up to the nursery.

At supper he spoke of the coming war.

"Many feuds apart from the one between Stanley and your uncles have been settled," he told her. "The king believes that we all need to pull together against a common enemy rather than fight amongst ourselves and that now is a good time to try to recoup some of our land lost in France. It will mean wealth and prosperity and peaceful living in England if we succeed."

Watching him tearing at his bread as he spoke Anne could see the excitement in his eyes at the prospect of war and she feared for him, as she had so many times before when she knew that he was fighting. But she refrained from saying anything to him. It was not her place now and he didn't seem to notice her meek demeanour, or at least he didn't comment on it or tease her as he once would have.

It was still early when he said that he would go to his bed. "May I wish you goodnight?" he asked her. Anne stood up, hoping for at least a kiss on the cheek, but he took her hand and raised it to his lips and then he was gone. She knew that he would look in at the children before he retired but she did not follow him.

At first light she heard his army gathering at the castle gate and she went to the window, but it only overlooked the inner courtyard, which was empty. She waited until the sounds faded into the distance then returned to her bed and buried her face in the pillow, wondering if it was possible to feel more sorrow than she did at that moment.

All through the long hot days of that summer of 1475 Anne thought of Richard. Both she and Isabella watched and waited for news and when, at last, letters came they were almost too afraid to open them for fear of what they might contain. But as it turned out they had no need to fear. The war with France was over. In fact it had never begun. Not a shot had been fired, or sword unsheathed. Duke Charles of Burgundy had been reluctant to assist the English, owing to pressing concerns elsewhere, and Edward had made a treaty with the French. He had met with King Louis at Picquigny near Amiens and the French king had offered him seventy-five thousand crowns and another twenty-five thousand each year for as long as they both lived. He had also offered the marriage of his eldest son to one of the king's daughters.

Safely home, Richard came to see her on his way to Middleham.

"I am to be a father again," he told her. "My wife writes that she is with child and I pray that it will be a son."

Anne stared at him as he sat on a small nursery stool with his daughter on his knee.

"I am pleased for you," she said at last as she watched him kiss his daughter as tenderly as he used to kiss her.

The following spring, 1476, word came that a boy had been born to the Duke and Duchess of Gloucester at Middleham.

"There is much rejoicing," Uncle Robert told her when he came to visit, "though it is a fragile babe, much like its mother."

"What does the duchess look like?" asked Anne with sudden curiosity.

"She's pretty enough and nice natured," he said. Anne nodded, wondering if she would have been more content to hear that Anne Neville was ugly and bad tempered. "The baby is like her, small and fair. They have baptised him Edward," said her uncle.

"The duke is pleased?" she asked.

"Of course. He dotes on the baby."

Anne nodded, jealous of this new child that had been born legitimately. Yet it was his child too, she reminded herself, and because it was a part of him she could wish it no harm and she added little Edward to her daily prayers.

"The duchess's sister Isabel also expects another child," her uncle told her. "This will be her fourth. They hope for another boy this time."

But the son born to Isabel in October was sickly and late in December a series of events began that shocked and bewildered Anne.

Uncle James had been given leave by the king to attend his own estates and she and the children had been invited to Brierley for the festive season. Anne was looking forward to being with her family again to celebrate the Nativity and set off in a happy mood on Christmas Eve, after saying mass in the chapel at Pontefract.

The journey was brief but cold and she was pleased to arrive at the manor house and be offered spiced wine and a chair by the fire to warm herself. Uncle Robert and Isabella with their baby, James, had come as well. All it needed, reflected Anne, was her sister to make the reunion complete, but Izzie and her husband were still in London and were hoping to be summoned to court.

Uncle James had just come to greet her when a messenger arrived. The man looked frozen and her uncle bid him warm himself in the kitchen and take some food before he returned. Then he sat down beside her to read and she watched his expectant face grow serious as he scanned the words.

"What is it?" she asked, forever fearing that she might receive bad news about Richard.

"Isabel Warwick is dead," he told her. "She died two days ago. Her little son still lives, but is sickly. This is sorry news indeed, so close to Christmas."

Anne thought about her own experiences of childbirth – the pain, the fear, the danger of bleeding and of childbed fever and she was thankful that she had survived twice. She hadn't known Isabel Warwick but she was saddened by the news of her death and felt sorry for her other children, Margaret and Edward, who had lost their mother.

But it wasn't until Isabella received a letter from Robert in the early spring that Anne realised how momentous that piece of news had been.

"There is talk of war again," sighed Isabella as she read extracts of her letter to Anne. "The Duke of Burgundy has been killed and the French king is threatening to seize his domains. Duchess Margaret has written to Edward and asked him to send an army, but he refuses, seemingly reluctant to forfeit his French pension." She paused and turned the letter over. "There's also more trouble between the king and George of Clarence. He has a fancy to marry Margaret's step-daughter, Mary, but the king will not hear of it. Robert thinks it would give him too much power. Edward still does not entirely trust him. There is to be a great council meeting in Westminster to discuss the crisis."

A few weeks later, Uncle Robert came to Pontefract and told them more.

"The king is furious," he said. "There is a rumour that Clarence had two astrologers cast the king's horoscope to try to ascertain when he will die; they say that they discovered the next monarch's name will begin with a 'G'."

"For George, Duke of Clarence?" said Anne in shocked surprise. "But casting the king's horoscope is treason in itself. Why would he do such a thing?"

Uncle Robert shook his head. "The dispute over the Warwick lands has strained the relations between the king and his brother. They no longer speak directly, just send one another ill-tempered messages. And I also hear that Clarence and his followers are spreading leaflets around London encouraging people to rise against the king."

"So, he still wants the crown for himself," said Anne. "I know that Richard found it hard to accept his disloyalty when Warwick rebelled. I don't suppose he's pleased by this turn of events."

"No, the duke is sorely displeased with his brother and I can see trouble ahead," said her uncle gloomily. "Especially when Clarence asserts that the king is not his father's son, but the son of a French archer and that he, Clarence, is the rightful monarch."

Easter fell on the sixth day of April in 1477 and the Great Council broke up. On his way north, Richard stopped to see his children, and Anne.

"My brother Clarence has gone to Warwick Castle," he told her as they strolled along the wallwalk in the warm spring sunshine. "And my sister Margaret still appeals for help in Burgundy, but the king is mindful of his treaty with the French. It's all a mess," he commented, with a faraway look in his eyes as he gazed down over the town of Pontefract. "I don't know how this affair with George will end. He tries the king's patience so severely with his claims that the crown is rightfully his that I can see no solution."

Anne put out a hand to touch his arm in reassurance but she merely skimmed the fabric of his sleeve and then drew back. She longed to hold him and have him hold her and she suspected that he felt the same.

She knew that even the slightest touch between them might break their self-control. But she also knew how much it would hurt him to break the vows he had made to his wife and she did not want the guilt – or his accusations that she had tempted him.

Some weeks later Uncle Robert broke his journey north to Middleham from London with a serious and worried face.

"What is wrong?" asked Anne as he came into her solar where she was embroidering a little gown for Katherine to wear at midsummer.

"The king has had Clarence arrested and sent to the Tower, accused of treason," he told her. Anne stared at him in disbelief as he began to explain. "Clarence accused his late wife's attendant, Ankarette Twynho, of poisoning her. He said that she gave Isabel a drink of ale mixed with poison four days after the birth of the baby. When he returned to Warwick at Eastertide he sent armed men to bring the woman from her home in Frome to Warwick Castle. She was put on trial and although she pleaded not guilty she was taken to the gallows and hanged the same day. And that is not all. On his return to London, Clarence had his men spread leaflets about the city making all manner of wild accusations against the king. Edward fears that Clarence has become too powerful and too unpredictable."

"But surely the king won't execute his own brother?" asked Anne, stunned by the events that had taken place whilst she played with her children in the Yorkshire sunshine. "What does Richard say?"

"He is very angry with Clarence. You know that he cannot abide any disloyalty to the king. But what will become of Clarence now I cannot say."

Chapter Nine
June 1477 ~ September 1477

June 1477 brought more immediate trouble for Anne. As soon as the letter with the seal of the eagle's claw was placed in her hand she knew what it would contain. It was the letter she had been both expecting and dreading and she didn't need to read it to know that her husband, Edward Stanley, had reached his fourteenth birthday and she was summoned to Lancashire for her marriage to be consummated.

Her first thought was for her children. It did not surprise her that no mention was made of provision for them and she understood by this omission that they would not be welcome. She sat down on the stool at her writing desk and stared at the letter for a long time wondering what she should do. Then, after opening up the little wooden writing box and taking out a quill, she sharpened it, dipped it into the ink-horn, and wrote to Richard at Middleham.

A few days later a messenger dressed in his familiar blue and murrey colours brought his reply. He told her that he would take the children into his own household and that, if she desired it, he would arrange for her to enter the sanctuary of a convent rather than the obligations of her marriage.

She sat and held the letter. It was not written by a secretary but was in his own hand and she wept, not just because she would be parted from her children, but because whichever option she chose it meant that she would no longer have the meagre comfort she received from his visits to see John and Katherine whenever he had business at Pontefract.

She knew that his preferred choice was that she should go to the convent, but she was not ready just yet to cut herself off entirely from the secular world. Besides, in her letters, Izzie still implored her to return to the Stanleys so that they could be re-united. If she returned she might eventually be allowed to go back to Hornby with Edward Stanley. She would be able to visit her sister at Melling and Anne hoped that she would find consolation with Izzie that would be impossible within the walls of a nunnery.

After long consideration she wrote to Richard to thank him for his offer of protection but to say that she had chosen to acknowledge her marriage. He replied briefly that he would respect her decision and gave a date on which he would come for the children.

Anne sat in the nursery with John and Katherine, trying not to cry. She was bereft at the thought that she might never see them again and had been unable to explain to them what was to happen, other than to say that they were to visit their father in one of his other castles.

Her stomach lurched as she heard the horses coming but rather than going down to the hall to greet him she waited, not knowing how she could face what was to come.

Before long she heard his voice as he came up the stairs and John looked up from his game with the little carved horses and knights that Richard had given him.

"Papa?" he asked her. Anne nodded, her lips pressed together against her tears.

The door opened and he came in. He was dressed in dark blue and his hair was longer than it had been the last time she'd seen him. There was a shadow of stubble around his cheeks and chin as if he had not shaved that day and before he had chance to say anything his son had flung himself at him. "Papa!" he exclaimed and Anne was torn between the torment of losing him and thankfulness that he loved Richard so much; a love that was visibly returned as his father bent to hug and kiss him.

"How you have grown into a comely young man!" he told him and, keeping one hand on the boy's head said, "And where is my pretty daughter?"

Katherine had been clinging to Anne's skirts but when her father bent and held out his arms she ran to him with a smile and he picked her up and swung her around in a wide arc making her squeal and clutch at him. Then holding her in one arm and with his other hand on John's shoulder his eyes at last met hers.

"Anne. Are you well?"

"I am well, Your Grace," she choked as she made her curtsey to him, desiring with all her being to run to him as the children had, to be hugged and kissed and held as he held them. "And you?" she managed to ask, although it was an unnecessary question. He had the look of a man who was content with his place in the world.

"I am well," he replied. "Now," he said to the children, "do you want to come to the stables and see what I have brought for you?"

"A horse?" asked John, looking up at his father with an eager face.

"You'll see in a moment," replied Richard. He grasped them both by the hand and was about to take them out when he turned back to her. "Will you come as well?" he asked.

She nodded and followed them down the stairs. Both John and Katherine were quizzing their father about the animals he had brought. What size? What colour? What were their names? When could they ride them?

"Soon!" he laughed. "But first they need to rest and eat their dinner. They have walked all the way from Jervaulx Abbey and their legs are very tired. How would you like to come to Middleham Castle and live with me for a while?" he asked as the children danced on the ends of his hands.

"Yes! Yes, please!" they cried and Anne wept as she followed behind and listened to them.

He had brought a sturdy bay pony for John and a little dapple grey with pretty dark eyes for Katherine.

"Kate is too little to ride all the way to Middleham," said Anne as Richard lifted his daughter to sit on the pony's back and she leaned forward to hug her arms around its neck.

"I had no thought of her riding all the way," he replied. "I have brought a small litter for her to travel in if she becomes tired." Anne nodded, duly reprimanded. She knew that he thought she fussed over the children more than was good for them.

"When do you plan to leave?"

"I thought to stay a day or two. There are some matters I can attend to whilst I'm here. Unless that makes it too hard for you?" He turned to her in the gloom of the stable and Anne saw that he understood how difficult this would be for her.

"Please stay," she said. She knew that putting off the parting with the children would not make it easier when they did go and that parting from him again would be almost unbearable, but she gave in to the temptation of two more days; two more days with John and Katherine; two more days with him. And although she knew that he would not come to her as a lover, she hoped that he would spare some time to come to her as a friend before she finally gave herself up to Edward Stanley.

He nodded and rested his hand on her arm, sending a whirling surge of desire for him coursing through her body. "They will be well cared for. I promise you that."

"And your other son?" she asked after a moment, when she had regained control of herself. "How is he?"

"Edward is beginning to thrive, thank God," he told her. "We were fearful for him, but his health improves." He glanced back at their son and daughter. "I pray he grows as strong and bold as these."

"I pray so too," she said, and although she wanted to ask about his wife, in the way that she sometimes wanted to press the hurt of a bruise, she didn't and Richard said nothing about her although she knew that Anne Neville was never far from his thoughts.

The morning came when they were to leave and although Anne had expected the rain to pour down from a dark sky she saw that it was bright and sunny, and she was thankful for her children's sake that they would have a pleasant day to begin their journey. She dressed quickly and hurried to the nursery, determined to join John and Katherine at their prayers and see them dressed and fed one last time.

She kissed them both as soon as she saw them. They were excited about their journey to Middleham with their father and Anne tried to match their eager talk as they asked her questions she could not answer about the castle.

Richard did not come to them, although he had visited the nursery on the other mornings of his brief stay. Anne was thankful that he had realised her unspoken need to say goodbye to her children alone.

Too soon a servant came to say the coffers were loaded and the horses ready. She fussed over the children's clothing, making sure their hats were secure and their coats were fastened. But they were eager to set off and as soon as she released them from her arms they ran down to the courtyard and the ponies that they had been promised they could ride at least part of the way.

Richard was waiting. The morning sun illuminated him and Anne's heart skipped a beat at the sight. She watched as the children ran to him without hesitation and he lifted them to their saddles, making sure their feet were in the stirrups and the reins in their hands. John he trusted to ride alone; a squire was to lead Katherine's pony.

Taking a breath to compose herself Anne went to say her farewells, determined that the children's memory of her should be a smiling mother rather than one convulsed in tears. She tried to tell them that she loved them and would miss them, but their thoughts were already of their adventure and their new home and they seemed to have dismissed her from their lives already. Anne tried not to be hurt. They did not realise the enormity of the parting and she hoped that, when they did, they would not miss her too much.

Finally she turned to Richard who had watched as she had kissed and blessed both John and Katherine. He stepped forward and put his arms around her. His hands sought out the contours of her back as he pressed her close to him and his lips caressed her cheek. She clung to his familiar body, savouring the moment, until he put her from him and turned, without a word, to his horse. Through her tears she saw him wipe his own face before he mounted the stallion. He didn't say goodbye as they rode from the courtyard but Anne saw him glance back as they turned out of the gateway. She raised a hand in farewell, her silver ring catching the light. She didn't know if she would ever see him or her children again and she prayed that Anne Neville would be kind to them.

A few days later armed men from Lord Stanley came to escort her to Lathom. They transferred all the belongings she had accumulated during her years at Pontefract onto baggage carts and, after she had thanked the servants with handfuls of coins, Anne stepped into the waiting carriage. Accompanied only by an unknown woman from the Stanley household, she closed her eyes in private prayer as they rolled out from the safety of Pontefract's high walls and took the road westwards.

Lathom House looked unchanged as they approached and, although Anne's whole being drooped at the sight of it, she was glad that her prolonged and trying journey was over. No one came out to meet her. A groom helped her down and, as she stood shivering, a servant opened the outer door ajar. An ominous silence fell as she walked in. Lord Stanley stood waiting. He looked older and even more severe as his critical eyes surveyed her. Trembling, Anne curtseyed, her eyes straying as she did so to the woman dressed in black who sat in Lady Stanley's chair. So this was Lady Margaret Beaufort, she thought, widow of Sir Henry Stafford and Thomas Stanley's new wife. She was reputed to be a pious woman, but Anne thought that she looked merely sour.

Then she saw her husband, Edward Stanley. He had grown taller and his shoulders were broadening under a dark green velvet doublet. His pale eyes, under a fringe of thick fair hair, regarded her with as much distaste as ever.

The hostile silence seemed to last forever until it was broken by Lord Stanley. "Greet your wife," he told his son and Edward came towards her and took the hand she proffered. He touched it with his lips as though tasting some dish that had taken on a putrid air and after he had released it Anne wiped it surreptitiously on a fold of her skirt.

"The girl will show you the bedchamber," said Lord Stanley. "Bathe yourself well for you looked grimed with travel. Then you may come down for supper before your husband takes you to his bed."

Anne guessed that her own look of dismay must have matched Edward's expression at the prospect. She still felt sickly and was tired, and she had hoped to be spared the indignity of having to share a bed with the boy for one night at least. But it was not to be so. She inclined her head and followed the silent servant up the stairs to the chamber where she had been imprisoned until Richard had come for her. It looked menacingly familiar. Her coffers had been brought in but not unpacked. A bath had been prepared and after being helped from her dirty clothes she sank her weary, aching body into the warm scented water. The girl brought a soft cloth and began to help her to wash but Anne dismissed her, wanting to be alone and thinking to slip beneath the water and remain there. But moments later, choking and coughing, thoughts of her children and of Richard crowding her mind, she acknowledged that she could not commit that sin. She grasped at the wooden sides of the tub and as she pulled herself up her ring caught the candlelight. She twisted it around her finger and prayed fervently for strength. After all had she not chosen this outcome? Had she not thought that she could be stronger than this; that she could deceive and outwit these people and find some dignity? Women find other ways of wielding power. That was what Richard had said to her once when she had asked him why he thought she should not inherit Hornby. She hoped that he was right and that she could find some way to remain in control of her life, and that she would not regret deciding against his well-meant advice to commit herself to the convent.

She pushed herself up and stepped, dripping, from the tub onto a cloth that had been spread on the floor. Shivering, she wrapped a towel around her and went to stand in front of the fire to rub herself dry. As she did so she saw the blood and realised that her prayers had been answered. Marital relations were not permitted at such a time.

She lifted the lid of a coffer with a feeling of relief and found the stash of woollen cloths she kept. She bound one to her then slipped a clean chemise over her washed body. She called the servant and bade her bring the dark gown that she had sewn herself at Pontefract. If the new Lady Stanley, the Countess of Richmond, could dress like a widow then so could she. Anne added a plain white coif that completely covered her damp hair, allowed the girl to fasten her stockings and dark shoes and then went down the stairs to face the Stanleys.

Lord Stanley pointed wordlessly to the place where she should sit. The family priest led the prayers and then the servants brought the food; there was roast chicken and vegetables that Anne could not stomach. The pain of her bleeding intensified and she wanted to weep under the hostile glances of her companions.

Edward seemed equally unhappy. He ate little and made no attempt to join the talk as Lord Stanley and his wife discussed the Duchess of Gloucester and the delicate health of her son – a theme Anne thought they had deliberately chosen to add to her distress. They talked of the dangerous air that surrounded the isolated castle at Middleham and how unsuitable it was for young children. Anne said nothing, though she silently prayed that no affliction would visit John and Katherine there.

When the meal was over Lord Stanley looked to his son. "I think the time has come for you to take your wife to the marriage bed and do your duty," he said. The boy looked up sulkily and his glance met Anne's as he stood. He took the very tips of her fingers between his as the priest blessed their union. Then the priest and Lord and Lady Stanley accompanied them upstairs to a specially prepared bedchamber where they were helped to undress to their under linen and put into the bed under the watchful eyes of all present. Then more prayers were said for healthy heirs to the house of Stanley, rose petals were strewn and the bed was blessed with holy water.

Eventually they left, closing the door firmly behind them and no doubt posting a guard to ensure that there was no escape. Anne looked around the oppressive candlelit room with the shutters closed across the windows and fragrant apple logs burning in the hearth despite the stifling heat of the day. Her husband, looking very young and awkward, had leapt from the bed and begun to sweep the petals from the cover into his hands. He placed them in a neat pile on the coffer. He was visibly trembling and Anne saw that it was not with passion. Although he had grown taller than her, taller than Richard, he was still only a boy and she could see that he hadn't practised his skills on any wenches. He swallowed as he watched her from beneath his fringe and Anne realised that he was terrified of what she, a grown woman eight years older and knowing about these matters, might do. Suddenly she felt sorry for him.

"We cannot consummate this marriage tonight," she told him. "It is a time for me when it would be in contravention of the holy laws of the church."

He nodded, though she could see that he had no notion of what she meant. But his look of relief was quickly replaced by one of fear.

"My father will..." he began.

"Your father will believe whatever we choose to tell him," she said. "Why don't you sleep in the ante-chamber?" She pointed to the small adjoining room where there was a narrow pallet for the use of a servant and, barely staying to wish her goodnight, her young husband fled and closed the door behind him. Anne lay down, exhausted, reminded of the night when Richard had offered her a similar escape – and she wept for his arms around her now.

She slept fitfully despite her tiredness and was vaguely aware of Edward tossing on his bed too. He rose early and apologised to her as he rushed through the chamber although she had drawn the embroidered curtains around the bed.

When he had gone the servant girl came in with water for her to wash and to help her dress, and Anne said prayers of thanks before going downstairs.

In the hall she was astounded to be confronted by Sir William Stanley warming himself at the hearth. He was dressed in a rich ruby red and his beard and hair looked recently washed and trimmed.

"My lady!" he exclaimed. "How delighted I am to see you! I feared that being locked up in that dungeon at Pontefract would spoil your beauty, but I see that my worries were unfounded and that you have escaped the clutches of Gloucester looking as lovely as ever!"

"I did not expect to find you here at Lathom, sir. I hear you have a wife now," she replied pointedly, as her heart pounded in alarm at the sight of him.

"I hear your lover has a wife too," he replied with a slight smile.

"I no longer have a lover," Anne told him.

"If the position is vacant I would gladly suggest myself," he told her. "That boy must have been a disappointment to you. And I have my doubts about the Duke of Gloucester. I don't suppose his attributes are much to excite a woman. No, what you need, Anne, is an experienced man to teach you how pleasurable the bedchamber can be."

"I'm sure I have no idea what you mean," she replied, sitting down on the Countess of Richmond's chair where she picked up some needlework in a frame, thinking that she might have defended herself with the needle if it had been larger.

"Oh do not play the maid with me, sweet Anne," he said coming to squat beside her and resting his large paw-like hand on her knee. "I can guarantee you pleasure you've never known the like of," he whispered in her ear. "All memory of Richard, Duke of Gloucester, will soon be vanquished."

"I am a married woman, Sir William! The wife of your nephew. I beg you not to speak to me in such a manner!"

"The pleasures of the body are nothing to be ashamed of, Anne," he persisted, trying to take her hand in his. "It is a pity I could not teach you from your maiden state, but now that you have known the fumblings of mere untutored boys you will appreciate me even more. I beg you Anne! Say that you will come to me and you will not regret it."

Anne had never thought that she would be so pleased to see the pinched and disapproving face of her step-mother-in-law, but Margaret Beaufort's appearance was a blessed reprieve from the unwelcome words of Sir William. The countess frowned as she saw her work in Anne's hands and Anne put the tapestry down and got up from the chair.

As she did, Sir William caught her wrist in his hand. "Do not forget who smuggled out all those letters from your sister," he whispered, his breath hot against her ear. "You are in my debt, and I mean to collect what I am owed."

Anne pulled her arm from his grasp. Edward Stanley she could deal with for the time being, but she had not expected such a vigorous renewal of Sir William's attentions.

She followed the family to the chapel for mass and afterwards, when they were seated at the table, she saw Lord Stanley look from his son to her and back again.

"I trust you both did your duty?" he asked, cutting a slice of cheese to add to the bread on his platter.

"We did, father," she lied with a warning glance at her husband's shame-filled face.

"Then we shall have a Stanley heir before long. I hope you ensure it is a son," he told her.

"Oh I'm sure a Stanley heir can be assured," remarked Sir William, "one way or another."

Anne found herself choking on the breadcrumbs and quickly drank some ale to relieve her coughing. The Countess of Richmond frowned and when he saw no one else was looking Sir William winked at her, then slapped his nephew on the back with his open palm.

"Perhaps a little tuition is in order!" he laughed, whilst Anne wondered if Edward could become any redder.

"When do we leave for Hornby Castle, my lord?" Anne asked him when she could speak again.

"I think we should leave soon," replied Edward and Anne was grateful for the unexpected authority in his voice. "I am eager to inspect my new home."

"I thought you might stay here awhile," remarked Lord Stanley. "Hornby is a remote place, you know."

"I think we should go soon," repeated Edward. "It would not be wise to leave the castle unguarded."

"As you wish," said his father. "It will do no harm for you and your wife to be alone and get to know one another better. I trust you have no objections?" he asked Anne sourly.

"None at all, Father. I am eager to see my lands at Hornby again," she told him.

"But I will be sorry to be parted from you so soon," said Sir William. "Perhaps you will allow me to come and visit you?" He stared at Anne and she understood him very well.

"I think I must defer to my husband on that matter," she replied.

Sir William laughed out loud. "We will see," he said as Anne saw Edward look from her to his uncle in bewilderment. "You will not, of course, remain at Hornby all the time," he went on. "I'm sure you will be invited to London, to court." He smiled slyly, and Anne realised that he was determined to have her and that she was going to find it impossible to avoid him completely.

Within the week they were heading north. Lord Stanley had made it quite clear that he could spare no carriage for the journey, but Anne was happy to ride the dun mare that she had brought from Pontefract. The animal had been Richard's last gift to her and was docile and biddable and Anne found that journeying on horseback was easier than in a litter. It did not make her feel so sick and although her muscles ached with the unaccustomed exercise she enjoyed being in the fresh air.

She felt a flutter of excitement when she saw the top of the octagonal tower again and, as the road climbed, the whole of the grey stone castle came into view. They turned from the main road and she saw the river sparkling under the bridge as they rode across it and up through the market place where the stalls were busy with people buying and selling the produce from the surrounding farms. She felt a smile flit across her face as they turned in past the church. The heavy wooden gates stood wide open and the portcullis was raised. Only a few guards watched as they passed under the archway and up the steep slope to the inner bailey. Anne had never seen Hornby so undefended.

She dismounted stiffly in the courtyard and looked around for familiar faces, but all she saw were sullen-looking strangers. There was no sign of Cedric or Martha or any of the other people she had known since childhood.

"Where are my servants?" she asked, turning to Edward as he handed the reins of his horse to a groom and came to stand beside her. He shrugged.

"My father sent people from the estate at Lathom to get the castle ready."

Anne stared at the strangers who at least had the manners to avert their eyes when she looked at them and to give her some half-hearted curtseys.

"I hope that everything is clean and well prepared," she said, quietly determined that these people would obey her, even if they did wear the badge of the eagle's claw on their tunics.

She climbed the familiar steps, unwelcome memories of Izzie and Richard haunting her mind. Everywhere she turned she saw the ghosts of them lurking, teasing her with their absence.

The hall looked clean. The rushes were freshly strewn, the tapestries hung straight and a fire burned in the hearth. Anne continued down the steps to the kitchen where the cooks and kitchen maids looked up from their work at the sight of her. An unknown boy was turning a boar on a spit for their supper and from the adjacent buildings came the aromas of baking bread and brewing ale. She nodded at the strangers as they acknowledged her politely then returned up the steps, pausing to glance into the solar and seeing that it was as Uncle James had left it, as if he had only just stepped out and might return at any moment.

She went upstairs. In the main chamber the bed was made up and rugs had been laid on the floor. This was where her uncle and aunt had slept and she had never been there before. The bed was hung with dark blue curtains and the tapestries and rugs looked expensive. She wasn't sure if it had been like this before or if these things had come from Lathom. She crossed to the window, which was glazed with thick glass, and peered through into the inner courtyard.

"This is a pleasant chamber," said Edward who had followed her in. He walked across to an inner door and opened it to reveal an adjoining chamber, smaller, but with a bed and a narrow shuttered window that was set into the outer wall of the keep. "I can sleep in here," he suggested, "if you will bid the servants bring some fresh bedding. What's up there?" he asked as he peered up the narrow winding stairs.

"It leads up to the top of the tower. There are two small chambers where my uncle used to keep valuables and a larger one that was used as a lookout post."

She followed him up and found him examining the upper chamber in delight.

"This is perfect!" he exclaimed.

"For what?" she asked.

"For my work! I will have the servants bring my coffers up here and then I can unpack them." He paused and smiled at her. It was the first time she had seen him smile and his full mouth revealed his prominent white and even teeth. She was surprised to see that he seemed a pleasant and even attractive boy once the sulkiness was gone from his face.

"What is your work, my lord?" she asked, intrigued by the unexpected passion he showed and a curiosity that had been gnawing at her ever since they had left Lathom to know what was in the numerous coffers he guarded so carefully. At first she had thought them to be filled with coins or other valuables, but it was the fragility of their contents that had seemed to be her husband's concern as they were lifted on and off the wain.

"My experiments, and enquiries, into the nature of the universe..." He stopped as if he was embarrassed to speak of it. "My father did not approve of some of my ideas," he told her.

"Which is why you were keen to come here," she said, now understanding that it was his work not her or the castle which had driven him to be so bold in insisting that they did not stay any longer at Lathom.

"You will not object, or write of it to my father?" he asked, worry replacing his smile.

"No, of course not," she said as she reached out and touched his arm, "Edward, let us try to be friends. It will make our lives more tolerable." He didn't move away from her but met her eyes and looked thankful. "Neither of us asked for this marriage," she said, "but let us try to make the best of it, shall we?"

He nodded. "Thank you," he said and with a rush of the maternal affection that she had thought was reserved only for her children, Anne ran a hand over his hair and kissed his cheek.

"Don't worry," she said as he looked perturbed, "I will keep to the blue chamber and I will not interfere with you or your work."

The servants brought her belongings in and as she unpacked, helped by a young girl from the village, she heard men cursing as they manoeuvred Edward's coffers around the tight turns of the tower staircase.

"I feel as if I know you, but can't quite remember you," said Anne to the girl who had introduced herself as Lucy. She paused with some linen in her hand and watched the girl as she emptied one of the travelling coffers, spreading gowns across the bed and smoothing the fabrics with her hands as if she had never felt or seen anything so splendid before.

"I remember you, my lady. I used to come up to the castle with my mother sometimes, but I was always told to stay below in the kitchen. Though Martha would slip me something good to eat whilst I waited."

Anne studied the girl. She must be about fifteen years old, she thought, which meant she would have been a child of about eight when she last saw her. She had dark eyes and an elfin face and a graceful figure that was just blossoming into womanhood. "You are the wise-woman's daughter!" said Anne, suddenly seeing the resemblance.

"Yes, my mother is Mistress Payne," she said.

"I remember your mother very well," Anne told her. "She brought herbs and potions whenever I was unwell and was very kind to me. Does she still live in Hornby village?"

"Yes, my lady. And she still brews potions for people's ailments and helps with their childbirth."

"I wished for her when my children were born, though the midwife who attended me was very kind."

"You have children, my lady?"

"Yes," said Anne wistfully, thinking about John and Katherine and longing to know how they were and what they were doing.

"Did they die?" asked the girl, watching her curiously.

"No. They live in their father's household. I could not bring them here." She saw the puzzled look on the girl's face. "It is no matter. Let us get on with putting these gowns away," she said briskly, picking up the green one that Richard liked so much and wondering if she could ever bear to wear it again.

"You spoke of Martha," said Anne after a while. "Do you know what has become of her and Cedric?"

"Yes, my lady. They live in the village now."

"Do you know whereabouts?"

"Yes, my lady. I can show you if you like."

"Yes," said Anne, "please do. I would like to see them again."

It seemed strange to Anne, to be able to put on her cloak and outdoor shoes and simply walk out of Hornby Castle. Her young husband showed little interest in what she did and apart from mealtimes she rarely saw him. He spent all his time in the tower chamber, often working until late into the night, doing what she had no idea but, as she had promised, she did not interfere or question him about his work. She was simply thankful that he had something with which to occupy himself.

She walked with Lucy, through the market place and along a small lane to a stone built hut with a thatched roof. Even if she hadn't had a guide she thought that the familiar smell of Martha's baking would have led her there anyway.

"Lady Anne!" Martha came rushing out to greet her. She made a curtsey, then her delight overcame her and she kissed Anne on both cheeks. "I'm sorry!" she apologised for her forwardness. "I'm just so pleased to see you safe and well. That day when you rode off with that terrible man I didn't know what would become of you! I've prayed for you every night, my lady."

"Then I am grateful for your prayers. And here I am, safe and well," said Anne, as the elderly woman held onto her hand.

"Will you come into the house, my lady? I've baked some of my honey cakes for you."

"I can smell them, and nothing will make me go away without tasting them," said Anne, feeling, for the first time since her return, that she had really come home.

"But what of you, and Cedric?" she asked as Martha fussed around her. "Why did you leave the castle?"

Martha paused, with a cloth in her hand, as she piled the cakes onto a platter. "It was not from choice, my lady," she told her. "Lord Stanley's men came and told us we must go. They said the castle would be run by Stanley servants now and that we were no longer wanted."

131

"And how do you manage?" asked Anne, knowing that Cedric was far from able to work the land.

"We raise a few crops and vegetables and I keep some geese. I sell my baking on market day and we do well enough," she said, placing the warm cakes and a jug of ale on the small scrubbed table. Anne bit into a cake and a rush of childhood memories flooded her mind – sunny days and winter days in the kitchens, tasting cakes straight from the oven and watching the women work and listening to their gossip when she should have been upstairs in her own chamber with her needlework or her reading.

"If you are in any difficulty you must come to me," said Anne when she had finished her mouthful. "I will ensure that you do not go cold or hungry when the winter comes. Promise me you will not be proud and that you will ask for what you need."

"I'm grateful, my lady," said Martha. "Truly grateful," she added, as she urged another cake towards Anne.

After the visit, Anne walked back to the castle with Lucy, pausing to watch the river and the rooks in the trees, and breathing deeply of the familiar air. She could have been happy, she thought, if the children had been with her, and Richard; though she could have been happy anywhere with them.

As she approached the hall she heard music coming from the solar. Still wearing her cloak she walked towards the open door, enjoying the melody that floated from the room, and as she listened a voice began to sing. Pausing in the doorway she saw Edward, with the afternoon sun on his hair. He was sitting with his back to her playing on a clavichord. Suddenly, aware of being watched, he stopped and turned to her.

"Please, go on," she told him. "It was quite beautiful." And without saying a word his fingers returned to the keys and the music filled the room once more as Anne sat down to listen.

"There is a letter come for you," he said when the piece was finished. He handed it to her and recognising her sister's hand Anne excused herself and took it up to her chamber to read. Izzie wrote that she and John were at Melling and asked if it was possible for Anne to come and visit her. Anne wrote back immediately, telling her sister that she would come the next day.

The fortified manor house at Melling lay near the church and not far from the high walls that enclosed the priory. It was surrounded by a dry moat and grasses grew thickly beneath the lowered drawbridge as Anne, accompanied by Lucy, rode across. As a groom held the mare for her to dismount Anne saw Izzie come running out to greet her and she slid down from the saddle and caught her sister in her arms, both of them crying tears of joy.

"I thought this day might never come," wept Izzie. "I have missed you so much."

"And I you. Let me look at you!" Anne held her sister at arm's length. Izzie had grown from a girl into a woman since she had last seen her. Her figure had thickened a little, but her dark brown eyes and her face were just the same. "Where are your children?" she asked.

"Inside. Come and meet them."

Izzie grasped her hand and led her into the house where Anne saw a nurse holding a baby in one arm and a little girl by the hand. The child looked achingly familiar. She was only a little older than Katherine and Anne longed to pick her up and embrace her. But when she held out her arms the little girl stepped back and hid her face in the fold of her nurse's skirt.

"Jane, this is your aunt," said Izzie. "And here is little Anne."

Anne took the baby, enjoying the feel of a warm, heavy body in her arms as she kissed the small, fair head.

"You must miss your own children so much," said Izzie, watching her. "I could not bear to be parted from mine."

"It pains me every hour of the day and of the night," said Anne as she rocked the whimpering baby in her arms. "I feel that part of me has been torn away and the wound will never heal."

"Oh, Nan, what a mess you've made of everything," said her sister putting an arm around her. "You could have been happy, like me, if only you'd been patient and waited for Edward."

Anne pulled away from her sister and gave the baby back to the nurse. "I was happy," she said, "until the Stanleys came. Do not expect me to think well of them. I never shall!"

"Don't be cross with me," pleaded Izzie. "It is not my fault." She waved the nurse away. "Come to my solar and let us talk and not be angry with one another."

She led Anne upstairs, to a small room at the back of the house that overlooked a walled garden where lavender and thyme were growing; the scents wafted in through an open window on the summer breeze. Anne was quiet. She felt angry both with herself and her sister. She didn't want to argue with Izzie, but her continual spoken and unspoken disapproval of Richard hurt her more than she could explain.

"Come and sit down and tell me how things are at Hornby," said Izzie, patting the cushion on the window seat.

"All the old servants are sent away and replaced with Stanley retainers," Anne told her. "Cedric and Martha are living in a tiny hut in the village and many of the others have gone to look for work elsewhere."

"Surely not all the servants are from Lathom?"

"No. I have a maid from the village. Lucy Payne, the wise-woman's daughter. She has ridden with me today. But the cooks and kitchen maids are all strangers. It seems so odd. I keep expecting to turn a corner or look from a window and see you or Uncle James."

"And is your husband kind to you?"

"Edward spends his time in the top chamber of the tower conducting experiments. He is a philosopher. He sometimes plays and sings. He is a talented musician too," she said. "I think in time we may grow to be friends."

"You will become closer when you give him children," said Izzie. Anne stared at her sister.

"That will never be. Our marriage is not..." Anne paused, suddenly wondering if she could trust her own sister. Izzie had become so much a part of the Stanley family that she wasn't sure if she could speak openly to her any more.

"Not consummated?" asked Izzie, her finely shaped eyebrows raised in wonder.

"No. My husband does not seem inclined..." Misunderstanding, Izzie reached out to touch her hand.

"Be patient, Nan. He is still very young. With a little encouragement I'm sure he will come to you." Anne shook her head and got up to walk across the room and stare at one of the tapestries hanging on the walls. "Don't waste the rest of your life wishing for things you cannot have," said her sister. Then she came across to Anne and pushed something into her hand. "Uncle James left this for you. He wasn't sure if he would be admitted to Hornby."

Anne recognised Richard's handwriting at once, but before she read his letter she opened the two small parchments upon which John and Katherine had each written their name. John's was bold and well-formed and he had added a small drawing of himself on his pony with a hawk on his wrist. Below her faltering letters Kate had drawn some people. Anne recognised her attempts at Richard and John, but there were two other figures there; one must be the duchess and the other the Countess of Warwick, who also lived at Middleham. This was her daughter's family now. Tearfully, Anne thanked her sister and put the letters away until later when she could look at them privately.

Chapter Ten
December 1477 ~ March 1478

Anne and Edward were summoned to court at Christmas. Anne did not want to go, but the message that came from Lord Stanley made it clear that he would hear no excuses and young Edward bowed to his father's wishes. The coffers were packed and the horses brought and she reluctantly prepared herself for the long and arduous journey through the coldest of the weather. And when they arrived she knew that she would be expected to share a bedchamber with her husband and that when they went to court Richard would be there, with Anne Neville.

It took almost two weeks of freezing days and even colder nights to reach Stanley House in London. Once there, despite its large and plenteous chambers she and Edward were given only a small one, with no adjoining ante-room.

"I will sleep on the floor," offered Edward the first night, when the servants had gone. Anne looked at him, pale and shivering in the winter chill.

"We can share the bed. It is roomy enough," she said, knowing that there would be no temptation to either of them except to seek some mutual warmth. He smiled gratefully.

"Thank you," he said. "And you won't mention my work, my investigations, to my father – or my step-mother?"

"We are husband and wife," she replied. "They have no reason to be privy to our secrets."

She smiled as a look of relief spread over his young face. "Have you been worrying that I might have forgotten my promise to you?" she asked. He nodded and she was compelled to reach out and caress him briefly on the cheek. "I will not speak of your work," she reassured him.

"They would not understand," he said.

"Perhaps not. But I know nothing of what you do anyway, so there's little I can give away," she replied, although secretly she yearned to know what it was that kept him confined day after day with the bunches of herbs and roots that Lucy carried from her mother up the stairs to him.

"I am practising alchemy," he confided. "But I am afraid my step-mother will not approve of such work as she thinks it to be witchcraft, and she has a growing influence over my father."

"You are seeking to make gold?" asked Anne, wondering if the Stanley family did not have more than enough already.

"No, I am searching for the secret of eternal life," he confessed. Anne studied his face and saw that he was in earnest. She had heard that such a thing might be possible, but preferred to rely on the power of her prayers for the saving of her own eternal soul.

"Why would anyone want to live this earthly life forever, when there are such blessings awaiting us in heaven?" she asked him, genuinely puzzled.

"Man's life is only like the winding of a clock," he told her as he saw her interest and began to speak more freely. "It begins full wound and gradually ticks away until it is gone. Afterwards there is nothing."

Anne stared at him, not knowing how to respond to such a blasphemy. "But what of God, of heaven, of eternal life?" she whispered at last, scarce believing what she had heard him say.

"I do not believe that any of those things exist," he said.

She continued to stare at him in silence, unable to comprehend what she had just heard. Then a fear swept over her. "Edward," she said, reaching for his cold hand, "you must not say such things." Then she withdrew her hand and twisted the ring that Richard had given her; the ring that contained the fragment of the true cross where Jesus had died for their sins. "You must pray for forgiveness," she urged him. But as she spoke she saw his face, which had become for a moment open and trusting, close in on itself again as he withdrew from her. She was sorry that her response had been so hasty but she was shocked and feared for his soul. "I will pray for you," she offered.

"I knew you would not understand," he muttered as he walked across to the bed and lay down on the very edge with his back to her. Sadly, she blew out the candles and lay down beside him. They both lay still and silent all night, not speaking again and striving not to touch one another.

Lord Stanley had little interest in his son's affairs. The only topic discussed at the table that Advent was the Duke of Clarence. He was still imprisoned in the Tower and when parliament reconvened in January it was to hear the charges of treason against him and decide on his guilt or innocence.

"The facts speak for themselves," said Lord Stanley. "He is guilty and I am sure parliament will decide in the king's favour."

"What will happen then?" asked George Stanley, his eldest son. "Surely the king will not have his own brother executed?"

"He seems resolved to do so. Though people say that Gloucester sees the king every day to beg for his brother's life."

"That surprises me, given the history of their disputes."

"The Duke of Gloucester is a tolerant man," remarked the Countess of Richmond. "It will be his undoing."

Anne stared at the woman as she cut her bread into tiny pieces and placed them one by one into her mouth.

"How can tolerance be a bad thing?" she asked. The countess frowned at her.

"Treason is punishable by death. There can be no exemptions. Not even for a king's brother. Once you allow the law to be different for one man then law and order will break down entirely. Besides, it is parliament that will decide, not the king, so Gloucester's pleading is pointless anyway."

"Well said, my lady," agreed Lord Stanley. "It is for parliament to decide and they will find him guilty."

"And what of his punishment?" asked George Stanley. "The death for high treason is by hanging, drawing and quartering." Anne felt sickened at the thought of such a thing happening to anyone let alone a royal duke.

"Then he had better pray hard for his immortal soul," commented the countess and Anne's eyes briefly met those of her husband as she recalled his words of disbelief.

"Ah!" cried Lord Stanley as they heard the sound of horses outside. "Here is my brother at last, come from Chirk!"

The huge bulk of Sir William filled the doorway as he stood in his travelling clothes and looked around at the guests. When he saw her, he smiled in a self-satisfied way then reached up to unfasten his coat as if he had decided that he would stay.

"Wash your hands and then eat before the meal grows cold," said Lord Stanley, sending servants for fresh basins of hot water. "You can go to your chambers afterwards. Bring your lady forward. See how she shivers from the cold."

Anne watched as Sir William looked behind him at the small cowering figure who must be his wife, Elizabeth Hopton. "Don't waver like the wind, woman!" he told her. "Come forward!" Lady Elizabeth came towards the table. Her wide eyes looked huge in a pale face and she constantly glanced at her husband for his approval before she did anything. Anne felt sorry for her.

Sir William settled himself onto the bench next to her and rubbed his hands together as if to warm them. "I'm pleased to see you made the long journey from the wilds of north Lancashire," he said. "I was afraid you might not come."

"I came as commanded by my lord and husband," she replied. Sir William glanced at his nephew.

"If it pleases you to say so," he said before attacking his food with the knife that he had drawn from his belt.

She did her best to avoid being alone with Sir William. The house was busy and she usually managed to be in the company of her husband or her sister.

"For goodness sake do not leave me alone with Sir William," whispered Anne to Izzie as she got up to leave the window seat in the solar that overlooked the river.

"Do not be so foolish. What harm can he do you?" she whispered back. "The nurse wants me to attend to baby Anne. You will be quite safe."

Sir William looked up from his book as Izzie left and then put it carefully down on the coffer beside him.

"Where is your wife?" she asked him.

"In our bedchamber. She ails in the cold weather. In fact she ails in any weather and coldness is her constant state. Unlike you, dear Anne. You blossom even in the wintertime."

"What nonsense you speak, sir!" she remarked as she saw, in horror, that he was coming to sit beside her.

"Sir William, you must excuse me," she said. But his heavy arm dropped around her shoulders and his fingers tightened on her upper arm.

"Don't go," he said. "There are things we need to speak of."

"I have nothing to say to you, Sir William."

"Oh come, Anne, don't play games. I know what you desire. A woman like you, deprived of your lover and wasted on a boy for a husband..."

"No!" she told him, trying to slip from his grasp and finding that her voice squeaked in panic as his other hand enclosed her breast.

"How I long to feel you in your nakedness," he whispered in her ear, his breath warm and moist. "Do not tease me, Anne."

She felt tears stinging her eyes and she swallowed them back to try to keep some dignity.

"You must let me go!" she said with all the authority she could muster.

"No," he said, squeezing her until it hurt. "I am determined to have you. You owe me favours!"

She grasped at his hand, digging her nails into his skin to try to make him release her, but the more she struggled the more he tightened his grip and Anne began to think that he would force himself on her there and then.

"Uncle William!" Suddenly she was released and she sprang up from the seat to stand, trembling, by the window. Edward looked from his uncle to her and back again but she couldn't speak to make any sort of explanation.

"You should take control of your wife. She has been begging me to bed her, like the whore she is," remarked Sir William before stalking from the room. Anne sat down again, her teeth chattering.

"Anne?" said her husband.

"Please do not believe him," she managed to say at last. "It is he who attacked me." She felt a warm hand on her back and glanced up at Edward's sympathetic face.

"I am sorry," he said. "I will make sure you are not left alone with him again."

"Thank you," she replied, through tears of gratitude, realising that the boy was more astute than she had realised.

Edward was as good as his word and stayed near her as Christmas progressed. He had never been close to his father or brother, he told her, and he missed his mother. Anne recalled how he had always run to Lady Stanley when he came home and how she had felt excluded. But now that she was a mother herself she understood something of that close bond. She missed John and Katherine; Edward missed his mother; and they began to find some comfort in one another.

Anne discovered that the Countess of Richmond had a son as well. She had thought the woman, who lived like a nun, to be childless until she spoke of her dearest, most beloved Henry who was living in exile. Eager to know more Anne learned from Izzie that the countess had been married at the age of twelve to Edmund Tudor, Earl of Richmond, the half-brother of the old king, Henry, and that she believed her son was the true heir to the throne.

"Edmund Tudor wasn't legitimate, so there is no valid claim," said Edward as they talked later in their chamber. Anne listened with interest, always surprised at how much her quiet husband had learned by simply listening to those around him. "His mother was Katherine of Valois but his father was Owen Tudor, one of her household – and as you know such children are bastards."

"Yes," said Anne, thinking of John and Katherine. "Edward, does it concern you that I can give you no heir?" she asked him.

He shrugged his shoulders. "I am happy with my work," he said, but as she watched him getting ready to go to his side of the bed, Anne wondered for how long that would content him. He had shown much more maturity during this Christmas visit than she had previously thought him capable of and she saw that he was leaving his boyhood behind and becoming a man.

On Twelfth Night Anne bathed in a tub of scented water and dressed in the green gown that Richard liked her to wear. She pinned on the brooch he had given her the Christmas before John was born and she wore the silver ring on her right hand. Then, with her hair brushed and fastened up into golden nets, dainty slippers on her feet despite the frosty air and her fur-lined cloak pulled tightly around her shoulders, she joined her husband and the rest of the family to ride in their newly acquired coach to Windsor Castle for the banquet and dancing.

Her stomach fluttered as the houses rushed past under a bright, starlit sky and when they arrived she could hear the music of the minstrels and people talking and laughing as they gathered in the great hall. With her hand on Edward's arm she joined the throng and gazed around at the fine tapestries and the high walls that were garlanded with greenery of every kind. The tables were covered in pure white linen and elaborate salt cellars marked the rankings of where the guests would sit. Edward was listening to the minstrels with interest.

"They are not as talented as you," she whispered, standing on tiptoe to bring her mouth close to his ear. He smiled down at her.

"My hands itch to snatch their pipes from them and demonstrate how they should be played," he admitted. "Let us find our places," he said as a servant in the king's livery beckoned them forwards. "And let us hope it won't be long before the food is served. My stomach growls with hunger."

"Blame your father for cancelling our dinner time," said Anne.

"He and the countess might think it worth saving their appetites but Christmas is meant to be a season of feasting not penitence," Edward grumbled.

They were seated further down the hall than Anne would have liked. The top table was too far away for her to see clearly as the king and his family came in and throughout the courses her eyes strained towards the dais.

"He is there," said Edward at last, with a mixture of amusement and exasperation. "Now will you attend to your food?"

At last the platters of small delicacies, marzipan fruits and tiny spiced tarts were carried in and passed around as the servants hurried to clear and stack away the tables. People drifted towards the benches around the edge of the hall or stood talking in small groups with their friends.

"I will sit down," said Anne to her husband, pointing to a bench in a quiet alcove. "You join in the dancing," she urged him, as the musicians changed their tune to a rhythmic carole.

"Are you unwell?" he asked as he offered his arm to walk her to the seat.

139

"No," she reassured him. "I am well. Just not in the mood to dance," she said. "But do not let me spoil your evening. There are many pretty young girls who would enjoy partnering you," she urged, giving him a gentle push before settling herself to sit and watch.

The dancers lined up and began to step and stamp across the hall. Anne's foot moved to the beat of the music as she watched them pass before her; her eyes examining each one as they went by, looking for only one person.

"So this is where you hide yourself." Anne jumped as William Stanley sat down. "Were you waiting for me, my love?" he asked. "Or were you hoping for a tryst with another?"

She moved up the bench away from him as he leaned towards her, his hot breath smelling of wine and spices. He laughed and edged up beside her. "This is novel sport!"

"Leave me be!" she told him, knowing that he would not obey, but would make use of the opportunity to pester her. "Where is your wife?"

"Gone back to Stanley House with a headache. So I am all yours, now that your husband has deserted you for the comely ladies on the dance floor."

Anne got up to escape from Sir William. As she turned in confusion she stepped into someone coming towards her.

"I apologise..." she began with downcast eyes and had stepped aside before realising that it was Richard. His eyes were grim and the two men glared at one another for a moment before Sir William stalked off.

"I was not speaking with him by choice," she burst out, desperate that Richard might think she had been encouraging the odious man. "I did not want to be with him. He keeps trying to force his attentions on me."

"Where is your husband?" enquired Richard coldly.

"He is dancing."

"And you do not join him?"

"I... I preferred to sit and watch. I did not want to..." She hesitated.

"Did not want to what?" he asked.

"I did not want to come face to face with you in the dance," she admitted, going back to the bench. He followed her and sat down, but unlike Sir William he did not try to touch her though she did not move from his reach.

"Are John and Katherine well?" she asked after a moment.

"They are very well. Did you receive the letters?"

"Yes. Thank you." She paused. "Are they with you?" she asked, hoping that they had come to London and that she might have the opportunity to see them.

"No. They have remained at Middleham; Edward too. The journey was too long for him," he explained.

Anne nodded. "I yearn to see them," she told him.

"Perhaps in the summer, when you are back at Hornby, something can be arranged."

"Could it?" She looked directly at him then, but her eagerness waned when she saw the expression in his eyes.

"What is it? Something troubles you," she said, seeing his unhappy look. "Is it your brother?" she asked, remembering Lord Stanley's words about the Duke of Clarence.

"I cannot speak of it. I have pleaded with the king, but he will not listen. His mind is made up – or rather I might say he has had his mind made up for him." He glared at the passing dancers and Anne thought that he looked as if he hated every one of the household that surrounded the king. She put her hand on his to comfort him.

"Is there nothing more you can do?" she asked. But before he could answer they were approached by a slender woman in a blue gown.

"Richard?" she said as he pulled his hand from Anne's and got to his feet.

"My lady, this is Anne Harrington... Anne Stanley," he corrected himself as Anne got up and curtseyed, not able to take her eyes from the pretty girl with the oval face and clear blue eyes under arched brows. "This is my wife," said Richard, "the Duchess of Gloucester."

They stared at one another and the music and the dancers seemed to fade away. "My husband has spoken of you warmly," said Anne Neville after a moment. "I am pleased to meet you at last."

"And I you, Your Grace," said Anne, surprised at the friendliness of this woman whom she'd thought must hate her.

"I am sorry that your son and daughter are not with us. You must long to see them," she said. "But they are well cared for and I have become fond of them. They are good children."

"I am pleased that they are well-behaved. And your son?" she asked. "The duke tells me he has been unwell?"

"He has lately suffered from a falling fit and we thought the journey too arduous for him, so we decided it was better that all the children should stay at home together." Anne nodded. "Richard," said the duchess placing her hand on his arm, "the king is asking for you."

"I must go," he said to Anne. She nodded and curtseyed to him and the duchess, then watched as they walked away together. She wandered disconsolately towards the wall and began to pluck leaves from a garland that was hanging there, wondering how she would ever learn to cope with the life she had chosen for herself. Eventually her husband came to find her. He was flushed and glowing from the dancing and she forced a smile, telling him nothing of her encounters with his uncle or the Gloucesters.

Robert Harrington flexed his right arm in the new armour that had been fashioned for him. It seemed flimsy, but the smith had assured him that its curved surface would reflect a blow from a lance. He hoped the man was right. The armour had not been cheap and although his wages from the Duke of Gloucester were generous the payment was not entirely selfless. Although Diccon had never been fond of jousting himself, he still expected the knights of his household to do well, and Robert knew that the duke was expecting a good account from him at this tournament that had been arranged to celebrate the marriage of the king's second son.

"Who better to fight under the badge of the white boar than you?" he had

141

asked with a smile. "Now is your chance to prove yourself and show me that you really have those skills you tried to beat into me at Middleham."

Robert had been on the point of reminding him that he had never received a beating from anyone and that both his brother, the king, and the Earl of Warwick would have dealt severely with anyone who had dared to do so, but he held his tongue and merely agreed. With Diccon you could never be sure when he was jesting. He had the ability to keep a serious face and even those who knew him well could never be certain. The problem came when he was in earnest and a bold reply unleashed his temper.

Robert mounted the horse that wore a caparison of murrey and blue and settled into the saddle. He adjusted the weight of his shield on his arm and after shutting the visor on his helm he bent to take the lance from the squire. It was unfortunate, he thought, that his first opponent was Anthony, Earl Rivers. Not only was he the queen's brother and tutor to the Prince of Wales at Ludlow Castle, he was renowned for his skills at the tourney and, as far as Robert could remember, he had never been bested.

January was cold for such sport, he thought, as he circled the horse and, through the restricted vision of his visor, saw the newlywed children, well wrapped in furs, fidgeting as they waited for the joust to begin. Diccon was sitting with them and Robert made a private prayer that he would not let the duke down too badly.

He watched his opponent take his place at the far end of the field. Why couldn't the man stick to his books, thought Robert. It scarce seemed fair that such a learned man should excel in sport as well.

At the trumpet signal he touched his spurs to the horse and it leapt forward, unsettling his balance. He quickly regained his seat but it was enough for him to miss his target and feel instead the jarring thrust of the lance even if it did not knock him from the horse. He fought to bring the beast back under his control and turned it ready for the second run. He was vaguely aware of the cheering and shouting of the crowd, though the blood coursing through his veins was making such a singing in his ears as to almost deafen him to anything else.

He was a moment too hesitant to start and even as he lined up his lance he knew that he had misjudged. He was only vaguely aware of the hit and found himself on the ground struggling for breath and with the taste of blood in his mouth. Someone hauled him to his feet and pulled off his helm. Robert spat onto the grass and was thankful that the blood only seemed to be coming from a bitten tongue. Earl Rivers was holding his lance aloft as he galloped a victory run down the tiltyard and the crowd was cheering. The king had risen to his feet to applaud him and without making eye contact with Diccon, Robert limped from the field. No one bested Rivers, but even so he felt angry and humiliated. He knew that the duke detested the queen's brother and blamed him for the accusations of treason against the Duke of Clarence. He often remarked that the man grew too powerful for one who was not royally born. Robert knew that Diccon had been hoping to prove that a knight of his own household was better, and now he had let him down.

The squire unbuckled his gauntlets and handed him a cloth, to wipe his face, and a cup of ale. Robert drank, tasting blood more than anything and spat again. This matter with the Duke of Clarence had cast a pall over both the Christmas celebrations and this wedding tournament. Not that the king seemed troubled by it, he thought, as he watched Earl Rivers salute his sister and brother-in-law. It was as if Clarence, locked up in the Tower, was already dead to him.

James Harrington wondered whether it wouldn't have been better to keep hold of Hornby than to be reduced to this. The war in France had come to nothing and now here he was, guarding the king's door whilst he cavorted with one of his mistresses. He tried to shut his ears to the cries of pleasure from within the chamber. Not only did they make him ache uncomfortably for the chance of some release of his own, but he hated having to deceive the queen about what occurred in the king's bedchamber. Though she must be aware of what went on, thought James, as another shriek rattled the bedposts within.

James had spent the evening with the king, Lord Hastings and the Marquis of Dorset as they had become drunk enough to want a woman, but not too drunk to lose the wherewithal to satisfy one. Lord Hastings and the queen's eldest son delighted in encouraging the king and Edward seemed to lose all self-control when in their company. The result was that they had each chosen themselves a bedmate and it had fallen to James to stand outside the king's door and admit no one, especially not the queen.

At length the door was pulled open and Mistress Shore came out with a gleam in her eye and a handful of gold. She smiled broadly at James and he knew that it was his duty to escort her back to her husband's house in the city. As they walked in silence, their way lit only by the circle of light from the lamp that he carried, James glanced up at the keep of the Tower. In some chamber there, the Duke of Clarence awaited the decision of parliament on the charge that he had committed treason against the king. The evidence against him was conclusive and the duke himself had shown no remorse. It seemed that he truly believed he was the rightful king, and nothing would stop his claim other than his execution. James shuddered and averted his eyes as he heard one of the menagerie lions give out a predatory roar. Mistress Shore moved closer to him. She was scented with some herb that he found pleasant and as her fingers tightened on his arm in the darkness he cursed his own lack of self-control as he found himself attracted to her. Perhaps the rumours that persisted about women and witchcraft were true, he thought. The women who surrounded the king certainly seemed to know how to make him do their bidding.

Having seen the lady safely to her door with her bulging purse, James trudged back through the quiet streets. He was not happy in the service of the king, but there was little he could do to change it.

Lord Stanley returned home to a late supper with a face even more solemn than usual on the day that parliament heard the charges against George, Duke of Clarence. Anne was hungry as they sat down to eat yet uneasy about what news her father-in-law had brought. Lord Stanley nodded to the priest to say grace and after the butler had brought the wine and the dishes had been set on the table, the Countess of Richmond broke the tense silence by asking what verdict had been given.

"The parliament found him guilty," replied Lord Stanley, "and a sentence of execution was pronounced by your cousin the Duke of Buckingham." For a moment a shocked hush held them all in its grasp as no one put spoon to mouth or reached to carve from the meat. "By law there can be no other outcome," he added.

"When will he be put to death?" asked the countess after a moment, putting down her knife beside her platter and dabbing her lips with her napkin.

"I do not know," said Lord Stanley. "That is for the king to decide."

"And how? Surely not by hanging? A public beheading?"

"I would suppose so. Though I doubt it will be popular."

Anne pushed her food aside untasted. "Did no one speak on his behalf?" she asked. Lord Stanley regarded her for a moment.

"He was accused by no one but the king and only Clarence spoke in his own defence. He remained defiant and made many accusations against the king: that he was born a bastard and that he, George, was the rightful heir; that the king had had his wife and child poisoned and had tried to poison him. His railing was bitter. There was nothing that could have been said in his defence. It had all been said earlier. Once Clarence was arrested and accused, the process could not be stopped." He paused and she was surprised when his expression softened slightly; she had never seen any kindness in his face before. "The Duke of Gloucester has done everything within his power to save him," he told her. "But in the end Clarence damned himself. All that is left is to pray for his soul."

There was an uneasy atmosphere in the city as they waited to see what would ensue. Each day Anne expected to hear that it had been done and she dreaded Lord Stanley coming back from court with the news.

"The king's mother has also pleaded in vain for the life of her son," he told them at the beginning of February. "But the Speaker of the Commons has come to the upper house and made a fresh request that the matter be brought to a conclusion. The king cannot put off the execution much longer, though he has agreed to their mother's request that it should be done privately within the Tower."

On the eighteenth day of February it was announced that George, Duke of Clarence was dead. Lord Stanley said he had been given drugged wine and then drowned in his bath, but the talk on the streets was that he had been drowned in a butt of malmsey. Anne prayed fervently for his soul, and for Richard.

"Gloucester is to return to Middleham immediately," said Lord Stanley.

"Can we go back to Hornby now?" Anne asked her husband quietly.

"Yes," he said. "As soon as there is any sign of a thaw we will leave."

Hornby stood overlooking the Wenning as if nothing had changed and Anne was glad to be home after the journey along the snow covered roads. Her fingers had become numbed from holding the reins and the tingling in them as she had warmed them at the fire when they stopped for the night had been almost unbearable. When she reached Hornby and took off her gloves the ends of two fingers were stark white and she was alarmed until the blood seeped painfully back into them. She was still rubbing them together as she went up the steps to the blue chamber. She was weary and wanted to lie down and sleep for a while before suppertime.

But even now, whenever she closed her eyes all she could see was Anne Neville placing her hand on Richard's arm and smiling at him.

Anne kept to her chamber for days after they arrived back at Hornby. She asked for her meals to be brought up to her. She couldn't face anyone and was unable to control her tears. She even wept at the letter from Richard saying that he would send the children to visit her during June. She knew that she ought to arrange bedchambers for them but couldn't summon the energy, thinking always that she would attend to it later.

Then she woke early one morning and the strength of the sun enticed her to put on her cloak and outdoor shoes and walk down the Steep to the river. She noticed that there were tiny buds on the trees and her mood lifted a little as she stared at the hills to the east, clear against the blue sky. She thought of Richard on the other side of them. He had loved her. He had told her so, and the countess herself said that he had spoken of her warmly. Would she have preferred never to have loved and been loved, she asked herself as she bent to pick up a small rock and threw it into the water where it rebounded with a splash. "I still love Richard, Duke of Gloucester," she told the rooks as they circled above her. They cawed to one another and ignored her, but words spoken out loud can never be denied.

Anne climbed back up the hill and went to look for Edward. She had hardly seen him since they came back from court and she felt a little guilty. He too must feel lonely, she thought, as she opened the door that led to the spiral staircase of the tower chamber. Slowly she went upwards, round and round, to find him. She would go to discover what his work was about, she decided. She would try to show some interest and talk to him about his ideas and discoveries. She owed him that much at least.

As she neared the top she heard muffled voices and then her husband laughed. At least she thought it must be her husband, though she realised that she had never heard him laugh before. She pushed open the door. The trestle table was laden with flasks and bottles of all shapes and sizes. Some were filled with liquids – clear or red or yellow – and there were bowls filled with powders, and leaves and herbs strewn across the work surface. She heard the voices again and realised that they were coming from the smaller adjoining chamber. Curiously she walked across and looked in at the door. Her husband was lying on the small pallet bed that he had brought up for the nights when he was working late and didn't want to disturb the household. His clothes were half pulled off and beneath him, crying out in pleasure as he moved rhythmically against her, was Lucy Payne. Anne stepped back, holding her breath, and crept down the stairs.

PART THREE

1482 ~ 1485

Chapter Eleven
September 1482 ~ June 1483

The sound of the approaching army brought Anne to the window of the solar in the octagonal tower. She watched as the men and horses came down the road from Melling and milled around in the market place before being dismissed to their homes. She smiled at the sight of Edward, under the banner of the eagle's claw, as he turned his horse towards the castle gate; she didn't need her sister's better eyesight to recognise him, though it was not so much for his return that she was grateful as for the news he might bring.

The September evening sun was still warm as she made her way out into the courtyard to greet her husband. News of the victory against the Scots had already come by messenger but she was eager to hear the details, especially as it had been Richard's campaign. But she waited as Lucy ran forward to greet him. The couple embraced and kissed and Edward lifted up little Ned, their three year old son, and set him high on his shoulders as the laughing boy clasped his hands around his father's head. He should have been in bed but they had allowed him to stay up for the homecoming. Anne smiled at the sight of them. Lucy was expecting a second child and although she was still officially Anne's maidservant she lived as a lady within Hornby Castle and was a companion to Anne who adored her little son and spoilt him more than was good for him.

"I'm relieved to see you uninjured," Anne told Edward after pressing her lips to his unshaven cheek. "How far have you come today?"

"From Middleham," he told her, obviously tired after the long ride. "And your children are well," he reassured her.

"And it is all settled with the Scots?"

"Yes. The Scots asked for peace and the Duke of Gloucester has negotiated favourable terms. Berwick belongs to England once more and the king's daughter Cecily will marry the Scottish heir."

"And were you very brave, my love?" Lucy asked him as he stood, clad in his burnished steel armour, tall and sunkissed in the castle courtyard.

"I was indeed," he told her and Anne smiled up at the man who had grown into a soldier and commander who fought alongside his father and brother in the Stanley army. "The truth is," he confessed to Anne, "that we were left to lay siege to the castle at Berwick whilst the duke and his army took Edinburgh. He told my father that as he knew how good he was at laying sieges he would entrust the task to him. It was in fact a little boring, and nothing much happened until Gloucester returned and the castle fell to us."

"And my uncle?"

"Sir Robert is safe and well and honoured for his bravery with a banneret."

"And the Duke of Gloucester?" she asked, relieved that the fighting was over.

Her mind was never quiet when he was at war.

"He is jubilant, as he always is when he wins. You know what he is like," smiled Edward showing no jealousy. "He sends you his regards," he added as an afterthought, but for Anne it was the most important thing he said. "Oh – and this." Edward reached up into a bag that was slung across the back of his saddle and produced what looked like a dried up twig. "It is Scottish heather," he said as she took it from him. "I think it may be dead for lack of water though."

"No," said Anne as she held the token that had been in Richard's hands; a token that he had plucked for her in the midst of his busy campaign. "It will soon revive," she said as she went to the kitchen to find a jar and some water.

Richard was one of the great lords of the north now. King Edward never travelled so far and rumour had it that he had fallen into such licentiousness that he only concerned himself with feasting and women these days. But Richard stayed loyal to his brother and would hear no word against him. He stayed loyal to his wife too, though he and the duchess had been blessed with no more children and Edward of Middleham remained prone to the falling sickness.

Her own children, John and Katherine, thrived in Yorkshire however, and when she did see them Anne always marvelled at how tall and how clever they had become. John was ten years old now and could read and write in English, French and Latin. He was becoming skilled as a horseman and with weapons, and she couldn't conceal her pride in him. Katherine was eight and quite a lady. She rode fearlessly and had a little merlin hawk, which she took out hunting with her father. Her sewing was as good as Anne's and her letters full of news; John's remained more dutiful. She wished that she could see them more often, but Richard had been kind and kept his word that she should not lose them altogether and they made frequent visits to her at Hornby.

Kate enjoyed music and Edward encouraged her to practise on his clavichord. John too seemed to enjoy her husband's company and was always keen to accompany him to the top of the tower and watch his scientific experiments with awe. Edward told her that the boy asked such questions as he found it almost impossible to answer and Anne wondered what John told his father of his visits. She prayed that he would not talk about Edward Stanley's atheism for fear that Richard, whose faith was strong, would think it too bad an influence on his son and forbid him to come again.

Now Edward went to wash whilst Anne bid the servants bring the supper. They ate in the great hall by candlelight and little Ned fell asleep with his tousled head on the table. His father picked him up and went with Lucy to put him in his bed. As she watched them go, Anne felt a pang of sorrow for the days when she and Richard had watched over their children's prayers and kissed them goodnight in the nursery at Pontefract.

"Will you stay at home for a while?" Anne asked Edward later as they sat around the fire, sipping their wine.

"For as long as I can," he said, smiling at Lucy whose hand he was holding. "But we are summoned to London for Christmas."

Anne glanced at Lucy's swelling body. Her child was due in January and she would not be able to accompany them.

"Must we go?" she asked.

"Yes, my father is determined to gather all the family together at Stanley House, and there is also to be a parliament in January, which will honour the Duke of Gloucester for his success in Scotland."

"A parliament? It must be... what... five years since the last one?"

"That's why my father thinks we should all be there. It will be an important event."

Anne looked at Lucy again. She knew what it was like to be left alone with a child and a baby, but the lure of seeing Richard, albeit from a distance was very strong. Besides, even though her husband was a grown man he still bent to the will of his father.

"Do not fret about me. I have my mother," said Lucy. Anne nodded. After all, Hornby was Lucy's home and there was no finer midwife than Mistress Payne.

"We will not stay any longer than we must," Edward promised her.

Anne kissed them both goodnight before they went up the stairs together; she had given up the blue chamber to them long ago. By the time she had ensured that the servants had locked all the doors and covered the fires it was very late when she went to her own bed. It was the one where she had first known Richard and as she lay down each night to sleep she took some comfort from the memory.

As they arrived at Stanley House it looked warm and welcoming after the inns along the way. Anne was glad to see it, although she prayed that Sir William would be keeping Christmas in his own castle. But as soon as she walked in through the door she saw that none of her favourite saints had blessed her.

"My lady!" he exclaimed and strode across the hall to grasp her hand and press it to his moist mouth. "How delighted I am to see you!"

"Be assured that the feelings are not mutual," she muttered pulling her hand away from his overbearing grasp.

He laughed down at her and chucked her under the chin as if she were a small child. "Anne, you know that you like me really and that you cannot go on resisting me forever," he whispered. "Why don't you slip away from that husband of yours and come to my chamber tonight?"

"And what would your wife say to that, sir?" He roared with laughter as if she had made some huge joke, his head thrown back and his teeth on full display.

"My wife will say whatever I tell her to say, and do whatever I tell her to do – including keeping to her own chamber. But it is immensely tedious. I crave a woman with a little spirit," he replied.

"You disgust me, sir," said Anne with as much dignity as she could summon whilst glancing round to see if Edward had come inside yet.

"You deceive yourself," he told her. "You will be mine, I assure you."

Anne did not reply. She knew that no matter what she said he would insist that she did not mean it and that in truth she liked him. He seemed to have persuaded himself that his delusion was true.

"I must go and see that the servants unpack my gowns properly," she said and escaped upstairs.

Lord Stanley and the Countess of Richmond had already arrived from Lathom and with them had come Lord Stanley's eldest son George and his new wife Joan le Strange. She was a pretty girl with copper coloured eyebrows and Anne wondered if the rest of her hair, hidden under an elaborate hennin, was of the same hue. She had brought George both a fortune and the title Lord Strange of Knockin; her mother was a sister to the queen and she regarded Anne with disdain as if she were a poor relation.

Anne and Edward were given an even smaller bedchamber than usual, at the back of the house. It had only one narrow bed and Anne suspected that Lord Stanley had arranged it to punish them.

"Is there space for us to share that bed?" said Edward doubtfully when they retired on the first night of their stay. "I would not like to offend you."

"I am not so easily offended," Anne told him and after he had studied the hard, cold floor for a moment he settled beside her.

"I hope Lucy is well," he said.

"She has her mother to care for her. Try not to worry," said Anne touching his shoulder. His body was warm in the bed and she longed for it to be Richard beside her. It had been so long since she had experienced that special intimacy and her body yearned inside and out for his touch. Edward gave a slight sigh as he pulled the covers around him against the cold and Anne suspected that he lay awake as long as she did into the distant, dark hours of the night, listening to the chimes of the city bells; both of them wishing to be with someone else.

Sir William was waiting next morning when she went down to breakfast and came to sit beside her.

"Did you sleep well?"

"Yes, thank you."

"Your husband didn't keep you awake then?" Anne didn't reply but poured some ale, her hand shaking slightly. "You did not come to my chamber after he was asleep."

"Indeed I did not, sir. And if you were waiting for me then your expectations were very foolish."

"Oh Anne! You know how to drive a man mad with your dalliance," he complained. She reached for her knife to slice some cheese, but Sir William's jewelled blade flashed in his hand as he cut some for her and placed it on her platter. "You know that I will do anything for you. Whatever you want... just ask."

"Sir, I would ask you to desist from pestering me."

"Anything but that," he replied and Anne stared at the cheese, all appetite ruined because he had touched it. It was going to be the most unpleasant Christmastide, she thought.

On Christmas Day there was a thin covering of snow on the ground. After mass in the chapel they went to court at Westminster Palace for the feasting. The trumpet blasts across the icy air announced the coming banquet and although

Anne was wrapped in vair-lined mantle, she found that she was shivering as the heat from the braziers scarcely seemed to warm the thick-walled chamber. There was a multitude in there and she stood to one side, glad that Edward had grown tall enough to act as a shield from the crowd, and watched the comings and goings of people looking for the other people they wished to claw by the sleeve and ask favours from. Anne gazed around until she saw Uncle Robert coming towards her. His livery collar, with its alternate suns and roses and white boar pendant, glinted in the watery sunlight that seeped in through a high window. With a brief acknowledgment of her husband he put a hand on her arm.

"The duke craves a word with you," he said and she went with him, heart pounding, to a quiet alcove where she saw Richard waiting, half pulling and replacing his small dagger from its sheath as he often did when he was distracted.

"Your Grace," she said as she curtseyed, wondering again what it was about this man that set all her senses throbbing. He took her cold hand in his and kissed it; his mouth was warm and she longed to feel it against hers. "The children?" she asked, hopefully.

"At Middleham, my lady."

"Your wife?"

"Across the chamber." He vaguely indicated the other side of the hall.

"I've heard glowing reports of your exploits against the Scots," she said.

He smiled. "It was gratifying. I enjoyed it. But how do you fare?" She watched as he looked her over, assessing her well-being.

"I am well."

"And your husband treats you kindly?"

"He does. Although I have not broken my vow to keep from his bed," she reassured him.

"And he agrees?" asked Richard.

"He is in love with a girl at Hornby Castle, a maidservant of mine. They have a son and expect another child any day now."

"And it is not too difficult for you?" he asked. "If you wish to seek the ease of a convent I would still arrange it..."

"No, Richard. I am content as I am."

"But not happy?"

"How can I be happy unless I am with you?" she asked him and saw a frown flit across his face as he glanced in the direction of his wife.

"God does not always send us the life we desire," he said. "But you would tell me if you were in need of anything, or if your husband was unkind?"

"I would. But he is a good man and I have grown fond of him."

"He gave a good account of himself in Scotland," said Richard. "I was pleased to have him in my army."

"How long will you stay in London?" she asked him.

"Not long. There are too many affairs in the north which deserve my attention... and I will not be sorry to leave. I do not like what I see here," he told her. "My brother has grown dissolute under the influence of the queen and her adherents. My Lord Hastings and Dorset embroil the king in their adulterous pastimes. They seem more interested in the pleasures of the flesh than the perils of their immortal souls." Anne nodded. She too had heard more talk about the king's excesses, his feasting, and purging so that he could feast some more, and his appetite for women. She didn't have to see Richard's tight-lipped expression to know that he disapproved.

"At least the Stanleys are not so riotous," she said. "Though Sir William would have me for his mistress if he could persuade me."

Richard stared hard at her. "Does he pursue you?" he asked. She nodded. "But you will not comply?"

"Of course not!"

"Anne." He laid his hand on her shoulder. It was comforting and familiar. "You would ask me if you needed my protection? You must promise me that."

"I know that I can come to you," she told him as his hand dropped to his side and his attention strayed to someone behind her.

"Mistress Stanley."

"Your Grace." Anne curtseyed to the Duchess of Gloucester as she joined them. She smiled at Anne in a friendly way and they spent a few moments talking about the children as she stood with her hand resting in the crook of Richard's arm, as a reminder that she was his wife. Yet Anne could not dislike her and after a while they excused themselves and her uncle, who had been waiting nearby, escorted her back to her husband.

The celebration was opulent, and the guests praised the king, saying that he had kept a Christmas that outdid anything seen in former years. There were lutes and viols and horns for the dancing and after a little persuasion by Edward she agreed to join in. Then they sat on the benches around the walls and watched as the king's players performed Vice Titivillus, the agony of mankind besieged by the world, the flesh and the devil. Perhaps too serious a subject, wondered Anne, though one which seemed not to concern the king at all as he lolled on his throne in his new clothes, cut with full sleeves in the latest fashion, surrounded by his daughters who reminded her of angels with their blonde hair and white Christmas gowns. But Richard looked more serious and Anne knew that he was worried for his brother's welfare.

Parliament met on the twentieth day of January 1483.

"Gloucester was welcomed in as a hero," Lord Stanley told them, looking as if he had swallowed a bad posset. "He has been granted the palatinate of Cumberland and the Scots Marches."

"So now he rules most of the north," remarked the Countess of Richmond with a frown.

"Not all the north," Lord Stanley told her. "I still have enough lands throughout Lancashire, and Percy retains power in Northumberland."

But Anne thought he sounded worried at the growth of Richard's wealth and power. Lord Stanley prided himself on his own influence in the north and it was clear that this latest development had unsettled him.

At last James Harrington caught a glimpse of the high grey walls of Middleham Castle as he reached the summit of the hill. In the spring sunshine the moors were golden yellow with flowering broom and, if he had not been so intent on delivering his message to the Duke of Gloucester with all due haste, he might have paused to enjoy the angular hills. Instead he spurred on the eager dark bay that he had exchanged for his own tired mount at the castle stables at Skipton. He was keen to reach Middleham, yet dreaded the words that he must speak to the duke.

King Edward had been in good spirits at Eastertide and had taken a party of friends to row boats on the river. The morning had been warm and promising, but a cold wind had blown up after dinner time and although some of his party had tried to dissuade Edward from such an outing in the inclement weather, his mind was set and they went anyway. But torrential rain had poured down whilst they were in the middle of the river and although James and others had taken the king's oars and brought him quickly to shore his clothing had been soaked through and the following morning he had woken shivering and burning with the fever of a severe chill.

He had insisted on rising and dressing as usual but was so obviously ill that he was persuaded back to his bed and his physicians summoned. He had been prescribed herbal drinks and a bloodletting to lower the fever and balance his humours and at first had seemed to be recovered. But then had come the coughing fits that had shaken the whole of his body, dry at first and later with green sputum that he spat into the bowl beside his pillow. His strong voice was reduced to a croaking whisper as he struggled for his breath, and his physicians could only confer in the corner of his bedchamber in increasing alarm as whispers of poisoning haunted the corridors and ante-chambers of the palace. When it had seemed beyond doubt that he was dying, the king had sent for his lawyers to add a codicil to his will that appointed his brother, Richard, Duke of Gloucester, as Lord Protector of the kingdom.

Edward had rendered up his spirit to his Creator that same night and arrangements were begun for masses for his soul before his burial at Windsor. James had stood guard outside the chamber door as the deceased king's councillors had met with the queen to arrange the day on which her son, King Edward V, should come from Wales for his coronation. It seemed that the decision had been difficult and James had paced with irritation as the raised voices from within argued to and fro about the numbers of men who should escort him on the journey. At length the angry voice of Lord Hastings was raised above the others and James had heard him tell the assembly that he would go himself to fetch the king if he did not come in a timely manner and with a moderate retinue. Then the door had flung open and Lord Hastings had come out with a thunderous expression. As his eyes had lighted on James he had drawn him aside.

"You are a man who is trusted by his grace, the Duke of Gloucester," he had said. "Come to my chamber for I must send word to him about his brother's death. It seems these Woodvilles would keep him unknowing until they have taken control of the young king. They intend to disregard the late king's will. Bid the duke come in haste, and with a strong party of men," he had added as he handed James the letter and a small purse of coins to cover the expenses of his journey. "Do not delay."

Tears filled the eyes of the Duke of Gloucester as James stood in the hall at Middleham Castle and explained the circumstances of the king's death. He bid a servant find his wife and son to join him in prayers for his brother's soul.

"He died shriven and at peace, my lord," James reassured the duke, whose face looked even paler than usual.

"Will you oversee the arrangements for us to go to York?" he asked, seeming at a loss to know how to conduct such things himself. "I wish to hear a funeral mass in the Minster before we leave for London."

"Lord Hastings was anxious you should come without delay. He suggested bringing a force of men in case there were difficulties," James told him.

The duke shook his head. "A day or two will be of small matter now. I cannot go until a mass has been said for Edward's soul and I have sworn public fealty to the new king."

"Yes, my lord," said James as he watched the duke walk as if dazed towards the chapel door.

"And find my secretary," he added, turning back. "I must send letters to the queen and to my nephew at Ludlow Castle. I must ascertain when he will leave for London so that I may meet with him and escort him into the city."

A few days later the peace of Hornby Castle was disturbed by the clatter of hooves as a messenger galloped up from the main gate. Anne was teaching letters to little Ned as she had once taught John, and Lucy was rocking the new baby, Thomas, in a cradle with her foot whilst her hands were absorbed in hemming some new bed linen.

The two women glanced at one another as they heard the squire call urgently for Edward to come down from his chamber at the top of the tower.

"What now I wonder?" said Anne. "I hope it is not another Scottish invasion. Life has been too peaceful of late," she remarked. "I always did fear the calm that comes before a storm."

They waited, listening to the hurried footsteps and voices outside, until Edward came into the solar with a look of disbelief on his face.

"What has happened?" asked Anne getting up from the bench in alarm.

"The king is dead," he said and thrust the letter into her outstretched hand. "He went fishing on the river at Easter and caught a chill. They thought he might recover but he relapsed and died on the ninth day of this month." Edward stared at Anne. "It is hardly credible," he said at last. "He seemed so full of life when we were in London."

"And young Edward is barely twelve years old. That's very young to take the throne. God bless him," she said, making the sign of the cross as she thought of the boy, not much older than her own son, who had so much responsibility now heaped upon his shoulders. "Will there be a Regent?" she asked.

"The king made a new will on his deathbed and appointed the Duke of Gloucester as Lord Protector."

"That at least is pleasing," said Anne, "though I doubt that the Woodvilles will be happy."

"What makes you say that?" asked Lucy, who took little interest in the affairs at court.

"The queen's family are loose living," Anne told her. "The duke believes they led his brother astray. He will blame them for the king's death, you can be sure, and he will not be content for them to have any influence over his nephew."

The following day another messenger arrived on a horse speckled with sweat and froth. He came from Lord Stanley with a letter that summoned both Edward and Anne to London.

"Why do I have to go?" she asked as Edward read out his father's words. She wanted neither the arduous journey nor the attentions of Sir William, nor the sight of Anne Neville clinging to Richard's arm.

Edward frowned. "My father's instructions are that I am to come to London in your company. I would be grateful for your co-operation," he told her.

"Your father fears to leave me alone here at Hornby," replied Anne. "He thinks that with a new king on the throne I may assist my uncle to reclaim what is rightfully his!"

In the end she went compliantly. They wore the black of mourning and travelled at a respectful pace. The country was teeming with talk and speculation. Most of the common folk at the inns were confounded by the news of the king's death and rumours and whispers about poisoning abounded. But people seemed willing to support young Edward.

In the north there was much rejoicing that Richard would be Lord Protector but as they travelled further south the people seemed more surly when his name was mentioned, saying that they knew nothing about him and why couldn't the queen be relied upon to guide her own son.

When they reached London there seemed to be an air of shocked disbelief still hanging like a pall of smoke over the city. The workmen didn't whistle, the merchants exchanged their news in whispers and even the lions in the Tower menagerie seemed to have stopped roaring out of respect for the dead king.

Lord Stanley seemed troubled when they arrived at Stanley House. He dismissed her and Edward almost immediately to their bedchamber, and when they were called down to supper the sight of him and the countess with his eldest son, sitting near the fire, told her that there had been a long discussion that she and her husband had not been party to.

It was becoming increasingly clear to Anne that not everyone was content with the prospect of the Duke of Gloucester taking charge. Rumour was that the queen was furious and had not even written to Richard to tell him of his brother's death and it had been Lord Hastings who had eventually sent the news north.

Robert Harrington watched as the Duke of Gloucester knelt before the high altar in the Minster at York and swore duty and due obedience to his king. Waiting his own turn to take the oath of fealty beneath the carved stone arches of the cathedral, he sensed the restlessness of his brother beside him. After they had all confirmed their loyalty, they would set out to meet the new king, who was already on his way to London from Ludlow Castle with his maternal uncle and tutor, Anthony, Earl Rivers, the queen's brother.

Kneeling, he repeated the words of the vow and as he rose he looked at Diccon. He looked saddened and Robert wished that he could put an arm around his shoulders to comfort him. Others saw a grown, resilient man yet he still saw the young boy who had idolised his eldest brother and was deeply hurt by his loss.

At length they moved from the Minster to the waiting horses. The narrow streets of York were crowded with well-wishers who had gathered to watch them ride out, but the mood was sombre. There was no cheering, only the sound of hooves on cobble stones as they filed out under the Monkgate bar. Richard had received word from his nephew that he would await him at Northampton and they rode south at a pace that became their mourning, the duke and all his retinue dressed in black.

"It seems we have arrived before His Majesty," remarked Richard as they finally entered the town of Northampton. The fore-riders had found them rooms at one of the inns and the duke bade the rest of his retinue make camp outside the walls. They had barely had time to wash their hands and settle themselves before the hearth when they heard horses and Robert followed the duke out to the courtyard thinking to greet his king. But it was the queen's brother, Earl Rivers, who rode towards them. Robert inclined his head to the earl, although his defeat at the joust following the Duke of York's wedding still rankled with him and his dislike of the man was intense. But he watched Diccon welcome him cordially enough and bid him come inside.

"Where is the king?" he asked as the innkeeper brought wine.

"His Majesty has ridden on to Stony Stratford for the night. We thought to leave accommodation for you here, my lord," explained Earl Rivers. "I would not have liked you to arrive to find no room at the inn." He smiled as took up his cup of wine.

Richard laughed. "It would not be the first time I have slept with the horses," he replied, though Robert very much doubted that he ever had and knew that before long he would have to supervise the pegging together of the duke's travelling bed once it was unloaded from the wain. "Will you eat with me?" Richard asked the earl. "Or do you intend to return to the king?"

"No. The king sends his greetings to you, but he is in the care of his half-brother Richard Grey and does not need me this night. We will ride together to join them in the morning and progress from there into the city."

"Then all seems well," said Richard, waving the earl to a seat by the fire and his knights to their duties. Robert went to discover the whereabouts of the bed and to check that the men in the camp had food enough for themselves and their horses. Diccon and Earl Rivers seemed convivial enough despite James' dour warnings and he would be glad of his own bed; he was tired and his leg was aching.

Robert stifled a yawn as he waited. The duke had been deep in conversation with Earl Rivers all evening and he was relieved when, at last, the earl begged leave to go to his bed. Richard wished him a good night and Robert watched as he swept on his cloak and ducked out under the low lintel to walk to his own chambers at a nearby inn.

They were halfway up the stairs to their own beds when they heard another group of horsemen arrive outside. Robert paused, wondering if it was God's will that he should get no rest at all that night.

"Your Grace," said his brother James, coming in from the courtyard. "The Duke of Buckingham has arrived."

Robert followed the duke back down the stairs as Buckingham came in. He was a tall, broad shouldered man with a regal bearing that betrayed his own royal blood and he made Diccon look small as he stood beside him.

"Do you have custody of the king?" asked Buckingham without any preamble.

Robert watched Buckingham's face twitch with anxiety as Richard explained the circumstances.

"Your Grace," said Buckingham, "I fear that there is a plot afoot."

The two men drew back into the parlour and Robert sighed as he realised that his bedtime was postponed once more. Buckingham called for food and wine and more logs for the fire and Richard settled himself at the table to hear what he had to say.

"Truth is that Rivers delays you here as a snare," he told him as Robert stood guard with his back to the door. "Richard Grey is instructed to ride with the king at first light and escort him into London without you. In fact, my spy tells me that it is Rivers' intention that you never reach the city at all, but meet with some accident along the way."

Richard stared at the man and Robert could see that he was weighing this new information and wondering who to believe. After a moment he beckoned to him.

"Robert, arrange for men to be posted at the door of the chamber of Earl Rivers. He is not to be allowed to leave. And post men on the road between here and Stony Stratford so that no message can be taken there. We will err on the side of caution," he said, "and I pray that tomorrow may prove you misinformed my lord Buckingham."

At last they went to their beds and Robert, on a pallet at the Duke of Gloucester's door, felt as if he had only fallen asleep moments ago when he was wakened by his brother James shaking his shoulder.

"It's dawn," he told him.

Shaking off the befuddledness of sleep, Robert recalled the previous evening and as his senses came into focus he checked that his sword still lay beside him. Talk of a plot against the duke could not be dismissed as an idle threat. For all his apparent friendliness Robert would not have been surprised if the Earl Rivers did plan to thwart them. He had the sly look of someone who would flatter you whilst thrusting an unseen dagger between your ribs.

The duke was awake and judging by the dark rings beneath his eyes had not slept well. Robert poured some ale and handed it to him as he sat on the edge of his bed dressed only in his shirt and braes.

"Send men to ensure the horses are ready. We will ride on to Stony Stratford to greet the king," he told him. "I pray that Buckingham is mistaken in his talk of plots. Rivers was congenial enough last night. I do not know who to believe." He scratched his head as he stood and reached for his clothing. "But I do not like to think of our young king in the hands of such rogues as ruined my brother's health," he said as he pulled on his hose.

The air was still chilly as they took the well-guarded road in the company of the Duke of Buckingham. The birds sang in chorus, hidden amongst the leafy trees on either side of them, but the sound did not bring any joy to Robert's heart. His eyes flitted past the branches, searching for any sign of trouble, as he wondered what the day would bring.

Coming into Stony Stratford they were confronted by the sight of a young man with reddish hair under a feathered cap. He sat astride a gleaming grey with a confusion of attendants and armed men around him, obviously prepared to leave at any moment. The boy glanced towards them and his frightened eyes dwelt for a moment on the Duke of Gloucester who flung down from his horse, pulled his hat from his head and went to kneel before him.

"Your Majesty. Please know I am profoundly grieved by the death of your father, my own brother, and that I am your loyal subject and diligent protector."

Robert watched as the Duke of Buckingham, a little more reluctantly, uncovered his head and knelt to the king. Young Edward looked from them to his own attendants as if unsure what to do and, in accordance with the duke's instructions, Robert signalled his men to step forward and surround both Thomas Vaughn and Richard Grey. The king looked alarmed at this turn of events and his anxious gaze returned to the two men kneeling on the ground before his horse.

"What do you mean to do?" he demanded.

"These men are those who brought about the demise of your father. They were the companions who ruined his health," said Richard as he got to his feet and laid a hand on the horse's rein. "They will be removed from your side. A king so young as you cannot govern a great realm with the advice of such men. I am better able to discharge the duties of government on your behalf."

"But these are the ministers my father gave me," argued the boy. "I believe that they are good and faithful and I have seen no evil in them. I have complete confidence in them and my mother the queen."

"It is not the business of women to govern kingdoms," interrupted the Duke of Buckingham. "Besides the queen and her kin have plotted against your uncle and conspired his death. It is known that they mean to deprive you of the Lord Protector conferred upon you by your late father's will. Relinquish your confidence in them and place your hope in those of noble blood."

The young king shifted nervously in his saddle and looked as if he might cry. It was clear that the men under the command of Gloucester and Buckingham far outnumbered his own escort and he had no choice but to yield. Eventually he gave a reluctant nod and Richard remounted his horse and ordered the king's escort to their own homes, on pain of death. Then the company turned and rather than entering the city of London they rode back to Northampton.

At table that evening Richard pointed to a dish of sauced chicken that had been placed beside him. "Robert, take that dish to Earl Rivers in his chamber and bid him not to be fearful. Tell him all will be well."

"Yes, my lord," he replied, but as he crossed the street to where the earl was kept under close guard he wondered if this matter could be resolved without bloodshed. Diccon was determined to rule as Lord Protector, but it seemed that the queen and her kin were equally resolved to prevent him and to keep control of the king themselves.

In the chamber he presented the dish to the earl and repeated the message.

"Take it to Richard Grey," said Rivers. "He is young and has never known imprisonment before. His need of comfort is greater than mine."

Anne was in the garden at Stanley House, watching the spring sunshine catch the ripples on the river, when she heard the raised voices and went inside to discover what was amiss. Lord Stanley glared at her as she came in and then stalked out, beckoning his elder son, Lord Strange, to accompany him.

"What's wrong?" Anne asked her husband.

"The Duke of Gloucester has had Earl Rivers arrested."

"Whatever for?"

"Plotting his death."

"Where is Richard now?" asked Anne, fearful for him.

"Still at Northampton. The queen has been trying to rally support amongst the nobles, my father included, but he is reluctant to take sides just yet."

"But he must support Richard in this," she said, although she knew that the old disagreements still rankled between them.

Next morning news came that the queen, having heard that not only Earl Rivers but her son Richard Grey and Sir Thomas Vaughn had also been arrested, had fled from the palace with her children into sanctuary at Westminster Abbey, taking with her such a large amount of furniture and treasures that a wall had been dismantled to move it all in. The whole of the city had been transformed from its shocked silence at the death of a king into a hubbub of rumour and speculation as everyone from the highest to the lowest of its citizens exchanged views on what they thought would happen next.

On the Sunday, after they had heard mass in the Stanley chapel, Anne put on a cloak borrowed from a maidservant and went with her husband to stand near the Bishopsgate to watch the entry of the king into London. Lord Stanley and the Countess of Richmond had been summoned to take the oath of fealty, but Edward and Anne had not been bidden and had decided to join the crowds gathered to watch as the mayor and aldermen, all dressed in scarlet and accompanied by hundreds of horsemen, rode out under the tall gatehouse to welcome the king.

Anne followed her husband as he forged a path through the gathered Londoners. Despite their disguises they were easily recognised as nobility and people stepped back, albeit amidst much grumbling, to allow them through. Over the sound of the ringing church bells, Anne heard a rumbling in the distance and stood on tiptoe to see what was approaching. Four carts, piled high with barrels filled with weaponry, rolled by. They all bore the Woodville coat of arms and as people around her began to mutter, she posed the same question.

"Why are there weapons in the king's procession?" she asked. Edward shook his head and Anne, worried now, craned her neck as the king's escort came into view. She was relieved to see amongst the array of fluttering flags many of murrey and blue with the emblem of the white boar.

Anne felt a ripple of pride as she caught sight of Richard. He was dressed from head to toe in black and rode alongside the young king who was dressed in blue velvet. With them she recognised the Duke of Buckingham and Uncle Robert, who didn't see her despite her frantic waving as he passed.

Even from this distance Anne could see the serious expression on Richard's face as he bade the crowd, "Behold, your prince and sovereign!" But it was nothing compared to the sulky set of the king's young face as he rode by. It should have been one of the most exciting days of his life but he looked stubborn and angry.

"These weapons you see paraded before you were taken from the Woodvilles who intended to attack the Lord Protector as he approached the city," proclaimed a crier as he passed by. There were murmurings of disbelief from the crowd, and many muttered that the weapons were most likely the ones that had been gathered to wage war on the Scots. And others remarked that if someone had intended to ambush Gloucester wouldn't they have been wearing the armour rather than having it bound up in barrels.

"I fear that things will not be easy for our new Lord Protector," said Edward as they watched the tail end of the procession turn towards St Paul's. Anne agreed. Those who were close to the queen would not be content to sit back and allow Richard to take control of the country.

Next morning Edward went out onto the streets to hear what people were saying, and when he returned he told her that most of them seemed to be of the opinion that the Duke of Gloucester had done the right thing and that he was the best person to take charge until the king was old enough to rule. Lord Stanley seemed in agreement too, although Anne never heard what was said during the clandestine meetings with the men who began to frequent Stanley House. One she recognised as Lord Hastings and others, her husband told her, were Bishop Morton and Archbishop Rotherham of York. They talked together in private with Lord Stanley, and Anne could not help but wonder where his true allegiance lay.

Lord Stanley went off to a council meeting on the tenth day of May and returned to tell them that after much discussion about finding a more suitable place for the young king to dwell than the bishop's palace at St Paul's, the Duke of Buckingham had recommended that he take up residence in the royal apartments at the Tower of London.

"And Richard of Gloucester has been officially recognised as Lord Protector of England and now holds the power to order and forbid in every matter just like any other king," he said with a stony face.

It appeared that the crisis was over, thought Anne, yet Earl Rivers, Richard Grey and Thomas Vaughn remained prisoners at different castles in the north and the queen still refused to come out of sanctuary with the king's brother and his sisters.

On Friday, the thirteenth day of the month of June 1483, Anne was working on a piece of embroidery in the solar at the back of the house when she heard a disturbance in the hall and was alarmed to see armed men under the command of Uncle Robert escorting Lord Stanley inside. His head was swathed in a bandage and the Countess of Richmond was crying hysterically at the sight of him.

"Pray be silent woman!" shouted her uncle as the countess's wailing echoed all around. "Your husband is alive, which is more than can be said for the other traitor!"

"Help me," moaned Lord Stanley as he raised a hand to his head where blood was seeping through the cloths. Seeing that the countess was too distraught to be of any practical use Anne took her father-in-law's arm and helped him to a chair by the hearth where he shivered despite it being a hot summer's day.

"Bring more logs for the fire," she told a wide-eyed servant before looking back at her uncle, whose face betrayed contempt rather than any concern for his prisoner.

"Will someone silence that woman!" he shouted as the countess's voice rose to a screeching pitch.

Anne was unsure which of the Stanleys needed her comfort more and was glad when two of the countess's women came rushing to take her by the hand and persuade her to sit down and be quiet.

"What happened?" Anne asked her uncle as she stared at his pitiless expression. "Is Richard safe?"

"Yes, but only just," he replied and Anne felt the blood drain from her as she became aware of shouting and running footsteps in the streets beyond the house. "Thankfully there are people he can trust," he continued with another look of disgust in the direction of Lord Stanley, "and a warning was given that there was a plot to kill him at the council meeting this morning."

"Kill?" whispered Anne. "Did someone try to kill him?"

"Hastings."

"Lord Hastings?" she asked in bewilderment as Lord Stanley groaned and lowered his sore head into his hands. It had only been the previous evening that the lord had eaten with them at Stanley House.

Her uncle beckoned her to one side, his armour clinking as he seated himself beside her on a bench so that only she could hear what he had to say.

"A man named William Catesby was advising Lord Hastings on some legal matter when he overheard talk of a plot against the life of our Lord Protector and came to inform us of what he knew." He paused to glare at Lord Stanley who was bleating in pain as a physician attempted to bathe his head and reassure him that it needed no stitching together. "We called the duke out of the council meeting and he decided to discover the truth. Men are supposed to leave their weapons at the door, but when we searched him Hastings had a long-bladed knife concealed within his boot – and I have no doubt that he intended to use it. It was when we rushed the chamber that Lord Stanley dived under the table for cover and broke his head," he added.

"Is Lord Stanley implicated in this plot?" asked Anne as she watched the countess, calmer now, go to her husband and kneel beside him.

"I do not know. The duke has ordered him to be kept under house arrest for the present time."

"And Lord Hastings?"

"Executed."

"Already?" asked Anne in surprise.

"The evidence of treason was indisputable. Buckingham persuaded the duke that it would be politic to take swift and decisive action to set an example and deter future conspirators. Hastings was taken out onto Tower Green and beheaded."

"God have mercy on his soul," said Anne as she made the sign of the cross. "This is a horrible thing to have happened, and it sounds as if it has caused much unrest."

"There is much rumour. But criers have been sent out to reassure people that all is well and to promote peace."

Suddenly there was angry shouting nearby and a man-at-arms came across to her uncle to say that Edward Stanley was insisting on being allowed inside. Her uncle nodded his assent and Anne saw her husband push the guards aside and stride in. His expression turned to one of relief when he saw his father.

"Were you invited?" he demanded of Robert Harrington who stood to face him.

"I am charged with the duty of ensuring Lord Stanley does not leave this house until given permission to do so by the Lord Protector. I would advise you not to make my task difficult," he said with his palm on the hilt of his sword.

"Edward. Do not make trouble," said Anne, going to lay a restraining hand on her husband's sleeve. "Let us hear what your father has to say first."

"It is probably not as bad as it looks," said Robert as Edward's glance strayed back to Lord Stanley, whose physician was now wrapping a clean binding over the injury. "Head wounds always bleed profusely."

"Especially when the head is cut off at the neck!" retorted Edward, who must have heard the criers' announcements. "I must say that I am surprised at the Lord Protector for suspecting my father of involvement in this plot."

"Well, we shall see," said Robert. "In the meantime I will post guards at your doors to ensure that no one enters or leaves."

Anne did not share her husband's conviction that his father was entirely innocent and nothing that she heard within Stanley House made her change her mind. The whisperings that ceased abruptly whenever she entered a chamber continued and at every moment she was sure that her uncle would come to take Lord Stanley to prison or to his execution. But Edward reassured her that a message had been sent secretly to Lathom and that if anything happened to their father the whole might of the Stanley army would descend on London.

"The Lord Protector has sent for men to come from York but even if they arrive we will still have them outnumbered," he told her.

"I sincerely pray that you are right in protesting your father's innocence in this," replied Anne. She did not argue with her husband, but she had witnessed the long-standing feud between Richard and the Stanleys and she suspected that Lord Stanley would not hesitate to rid himself of Richard if he could.

Robert stood beside the Lord Protector at the doorway of the Star Chamber at Westminster. The council had agreed with Richard that it was unthinkable that the coronation of the king should go ahead without the attendance of his younger brother, the Duke of York.

"The boy has not sought sanctuary of his own free will," Richard had said more than once over the past week. "He is held prisoner by his mother and it is our duty to free him." The events of the previous Friday when Hastings' plot had been uncovered had brought things to a head. Robert thought that he had rarely seen Diccon as angry as he had been when the hidden dagger had been drawn from Hastings' boot and held up for all to see. His face had been contorted with rage, but rather than shouting he had remained silent as if he could form no adequate words, and when Buckingham had suggested making a swift example of the man he had agreed that the prisoner should be taken to his death.

Robert was well aware that the duke had disliked Lord Hastings. Even when they had been in exile in the Low Countries he had made no secret of his disgust at the man's morals and the way he treated women. But Hastings had been a close friend of Edward. He had been the one who sent James to Middleham when the queen had seemed reluctant to send news of the king's death, and Robert knew that Diccon had expected him to be loyal.

Now, he was determined to wrest the king's younger brother from the queen so that he had both his nephews under his control. A large company of men stood guard along the river and in the halls of Westminster as they waited for the Archbishop of Canterbury to emerge from the abbey with the boy. If he was not successful they would be ordered to breach sanctuary and take him by force and it was a prospect that made Robert uneasy.

At last the door opened and a hush fell as the archbishop came out with his hand clasped firmly around that of a small boy whose eyes were wide with apprehension. Robert heard Diccon's murmur of relief. He stepped forward to greet his nephew, putting a hand on his shoulder and reassuring him that he was safe and was to be taken by barge to join his brother at the Tower. The boy nodded silently and glanced back at the closed door. The archbishop was explaining that he had promised the queen that her son would be returned to her after the coronation, but Robert doubted that such a thing would happen.

Later that day Anne's uncle returned to Stanley House with an armed escort and a message that the Lord Protector wished to see Lord Stanley. The Countess of Richmond bade her husband a farewell that she obviously thought could be her last before he was escorted out to the barge that would take him upriver to the Tower. But before long he returned with a self-satisfied smile to tell them that he had been restored to his seat on the council and Anne wondered how much the threat of the Stanley army had influenced the decision.

"Please can we return to Hornby after the coronation?" Anne asked her husband as he walked with her in the garden that evening, enjoying the cool of the day. He was silent for a moment and she glanced up. "What is wrong?" she asked, surprised that he had not immediately agreed to get back to his work and to see Lucy and his children again.

"I have grave doubts that the coronation of the king will take place," he told her.

"What makes you say that?" she asked.

"You have not heard?"

"I hear nothing but rumours and half whispers," she told him. "Your father and the countess keep me close confined to the house and always fall silent when they see me approaching. What do you know?" she asked. Edward beckoned her to a low grassy seat, some distance from the house.

"My father has forbidden me to speak of these matters to you because he thinks you may be a spy who carries word to the Lord Protector, but what I have to say is becoming common knowledge and I see no reason to keep it from you."

"Go on," said Anne, wondering what he meant to reveal to her.

"At the council meeting before the one when Lord Hastings was executed, it was claimed by Bishop Stillington that the late king's marriage to Elizabeth Woodville was invalid because he had previously made a contract to marry the Lady Eleanor Butler."

"And such a promise is binding," said Anne, remembering their own vows made before the Stanley chaplain when they were betrothed.

"And the rumour that Edward was not his father's child but was the son of a French archer also continues to circulate. Bishop Stillington says that these are the real reasons the late king had the Duke of Clarence executed. He says that Clarence knew the truth."

"So Clarence's assertions that he was the rightful king could have been true and his brother killed him for that reason?" asked Anne.

"It seems possible."

"If this story of a pre-contract is true, what would that mean for the king? For young Edward?" asked Anne, although she already knew the answer.

"If either story is true then he has no valid claim to the throne."

"And Richard has," said Anne as the events of the past few days began to make more sense.

Robert watched the Lord Protector shake his head as the servant came forward with the black garments stretched across his extended arms.

"Not those. Fetch the purple," he told him. "I mean to ride about the city. Many of the people here do not know me and I would like to show myself to them."

"Is that wise?" asked Robert. "With all this unrest?"

"It is the unrest I would like to quell," he replied and Robert, seeing the determined set of his lips, knew that Diccon would not be dissuaded. "Besides it is your task to ensure that I remain safe," he added with a slight raise of one eyebrow.

Their progress through London was unremarkable although Robert rode close to the duke with a hand ever ready for his sword and his eyes watchful for any trouble. He could not decide if the indifference of the people was a good or bad thing. Most were more concerned with their own affairs and, as long as the peace was kept and not too many taxes were demanded from them, they showed little interest in who ruled them. But others were more vocal and said that the Lord Protector planned to usurp the throne, and as Robert rode beside him through the streets he couldn't help but wonder what was on Diccon's mind.

He was relieved when they returned to the courtyard at Crosby House without incident and the gates were closed behind them. And when he followed the duke into the hall and saw the Duchess of Gloucester come forward to greet him with a look of relief he knew that he was not alone in his concern. The duke had men who were loyal to him and who would protect him without question, but the treachery of Hastings had left them all shaken and unsure of knowing friend from enemy.

The duchess greeted the duke formally and he kissed her hand. They had been parted since they left York, the duchess having travelled to London more slowly. The sight of them together unsettled Robert, partly because he felt a pang of jealousy on his niece's behalf and partly because his own wife had not yet arrived in London. Then Robert noticed the two young people waiting anxiously behind the duchess.

"They pleaded to come. I hope you do not mind," she said to Richard in a voice that was confident he would not be angry with her. Robert watched as young Kate met her father's eyes with a wide smile. Diccon embraced first her and then his son, John. Anne would be pleased to have the news that her children were close by, he thought.

The date for the coronation was postponed again, despite the Duke of York joining the king in the Tower, and was now set for the twenty-fifth. But before the day came, London was stunned by a sermon preached by Dr Shaa, the brother of the Lord Mayor, at St Paul's Cross. He told the gathering the story that Edward had revealed to Anne, that the old king had never been lawfully married to the queen because he was, before God, promised to another. Two days later the Duke of Buckingham made a similar speech at the Guildhall and when Lord Stanley attended a meeting of all the lords of the church and the nobility, he returned with the news that there had been agreement that Richard, Duke of Gloucester, was the legitimate heir and rightful king.

Chapter Twelve
July 1483 ~ February 1484

Robert Harrington came to the door of Stanley House with a small but well-armed escort and said that the king had sent for Anne. It was clear from the faces of both Lord Stanley and the Countess of Richmond that they were displeased by such a summons, but they did not raise any objection. Publically they were both expressing their support for King Richard so Lord Stanley nodded his agreement and his wife merely looked sour as Anne, having hurriedly fetched a cloak from her bedchamber, left with her uncle.

It wasn't far through the busy streets to Crosby Hall where Uncle Robert helped her down from the horse with a smile. "There is a surprise for you inside," he said.

Anne hurried up the steps, with her skirts grasped in her hands, anticipating a meeting with Richard but it was her daughter Katherine who ran across the high-roofed hall to greet her and hug her tightly.

"Kate!" she cried, kissing the soft dark hair that escaped around the girl's forehead. "I did not know you had come down from Yorkshire! Is John...?"

Anne glanced up and saw her son smiling broadly, having stepped forward from the shadows.

"Yes, Mother, I am here."

Anne gently put her daughter aside and stretched her arms to her firstborn who was now as tall as she was. He grimaced a little as she kissed him but held her as tightly as his sister had.

"This is a joy!" she told them. "I had not even dared to hope that you would come."

"We pleaded with the Duchess of Gloucester," said Kate with the smile of a girl used to getting her own way.

"Then I am very grateful to her," Anne told them, her heart warming once again to the woman she could never quite regard as a rival. "And I am delighted to see you both. Are you well?" she asked, though the question seemed unnecessary. John grew more like her late father every day. Although he was Richard's son his looks betrayed his Harrington lineage, unlike her small, blue-eyed daughter whom no one would ever doubt was a child of the king.

After she had hugged and kissed them again, she asked them more questions about their health and well-being and whether John was making good progress under the tutelage of the Earl of Lincoln, Richard's nephew, at Sheriff Hutton. They answered with smiles and gentle teasing at her fussing over them and Anne did not see Richard come down the stairs.

"Your Grace," she said, standing up as he approached.

"My lady." He reached for her hand and raised it to his lips. He looked older, thought Anne, as her eyes drank in every inch of him, but in a way that gave him an increased dignity. He exuded an aura of authority and confidence as he stood smiling at them and his face showed no trace of the recent crises.

"How are things at Stanley House?" he asked after they had sat down on a bench.

"Lord Stanley professes his support for you, as does the Countess of Richmond," she told him.

"But you doubt him?" asked Richard, perceptive as ever.

"I have no reason to trust him," she said. "And neither do you, even if he was not implicated in the plot against you."

"He is too wily to implicate himself."

"But you keep him in your favour?"

"I keep him where I can watch him," replied Richard. "And I am also aware of your position within his household."

"It would have been easier for you if I had gone to the convent," she said.

"Maybe so, but you know that I would never force you to do anything against your wishes."

"I know that," she replied, and his words filled her with an aching physical desire for him.

He stood up to leave. "There are many matters that need my attention," he said, "but you are welcome to spend as much time as you like with John and Kate."

"Thank you, my lord," she said as he crossed the hall to run up the stairs. The next time she saw him was at his coronation.

On the fourth day of July, King Richard and Queen Anne moved to the royal apartments in the Tower of London. As she stood on the riverside to watch the royal barge rowed past, Anne wondered about Richard's nephews. Clarence's son, the Earl of Warwick, was now under the protection of his uncle as well as Lord Edward and Lord Richard. The king had promised that he would provide for them and maintain them honourably as members of the royal family, but Anne couldn't help but feel some sympathy for the young Edward who had been raised to believe that he would, one day, be king and who had indeed, albeit unannointed, been their king for a short time. He must be watching the preparations for the coronation of his uncle with disappointment, thought Anne, as she remembered how angry the boy had looked on the day that Richard had escorted him into London. It was not his fault that his parents' marriage had not been a proper one and Anne hoped that he would be found a fitting place within the new regime.

There was a hiatus as London waited and Anne hoped that nothing would postpone this coronation. But the day dawned fine and dry and the planned celebrations went ahead with no trace of the disagreements and problems of the past few weeks.

Although they were only minor members of the Stanley family, Richard had ensured that Anne and her husband were provided with more than adequate places in Westminster Abbey and Anne could just make out her daughter

Katherine in her white gown.

The triumphant notes of the trumpets sounded a fanfare and the congregation turned to watch as the heralds entered through the west door, followed by priests, abbots and bishops with their mitres on their heads and their crosiers in their hands. Next came the earls and dukes carrying the swords, the sceptre and the orb. And, with a fathomless expression, Lord Stanley followed bearing the mace of the Lord High Constable. The Duke of Norfolk carried the king's crown, and then came Richard. He walked, bareheaded and barefoot in piety, up the carpeted aisle towards the chair of state that was placed ready for him near St Edward's shrine. He was dressed in a doublet of rich blue, over which he wore a purple velvet gown trimmed with ermine. Behind him, carrying his train, came the Duke of Buckingham.

The queen's procession followed. Queen Anne, a circlet of gold studded with jewels on her long fair hair, was also barefoot and walked under a silken canopy with a golden bell at each corner. She was escorted by the Bishops of Exeter and Norwich and the Countess of Richmond carried her train.

Following the king and queen came a seemingly endless procession of other lords and nobles of the land, including Lord Edward who was attended by his younger brother Lord Richard and various other henchmen, all finely dressed in new clothes. Anne saw John in his blue and murrey livery and she willed him to look at her as he passed by, but his serious eyes were fixed on his father and Anne wiped away a tear of pride at the sight of him.

She watched as the king and queen came to the high altar where they were anointed with holy oil. Then, as the organ continued to play soft music, they were dressed in cloth of gold and Cardinal Bourchier placed the crowns upon their heads. The bishop put St Edward's cope upon the king and Richard took the orb in his right hand and the sceptre in his left and made his vows of loyalty to his country in English before the priests sang the Te Deum. A thrill ran through Anne. How could she ever have envisaged that the comely young man she had first fallen in love with so long ago at Hornby would one day become the king of England?

Anne and Edward followed the congregation that made slow progress from the church to the banqueting hall. Following her husband through the crowds, Anne saw Isabella waving frantically to attract her attention. It was so long since she had seen her friend that Anne wanted to stop and speak with her, but she only had time to promise that she would seek her out later before she was ushered to a place further down the hall where John and Kate were already seated.

After kissing them and admiring their new clothes, the trumpets sounded and everyone got to their feet amidst a scraping of benches as the king and queen came in, dressed now in gowns of crimson velvet, to be received by the mayor who offered them hot, spiced wine and wafers. When everyone was seated once more the food was borne in but Anne was too excited to notice much of what she ate during the courses of soups, fowl, meats and custards with a splendid subtlety to accompany each one, the first of which was a decorated white boar fashioned from marchpane.

She and Kate busily compared the ladies' gowns and headdresses whilst John and Edward fell into some discussion about the symbolism of the holy oil, which Anne hoped John would have the good sense not to repeat to his father. Then there was a commotion at the door and the sound of a horse's hooves, and the guests cheered as Sir Robert Dymmock, the King's Champion, ducked his head under the lintel as he rode right into the hall on his horse. The animal danced in the midst of the tables, threatening a disaster at every stamp of its feet and swish of its tail. Sir Robert flung down a shining gauntlet on the floor and challenged anyone who disputed the king's right to the throne to step forward and fight.

There was a tense silence for a moment longer than was comfortable before an unseen person raised the cry, "King Richard! God save King Richard!" and bending from his mount the champion accepted a silver gilt bowl in his ungloved hand and drank the king's health.

Even though it was July the evening grew dark as the feasting went on and great beeswax torches were brought in to light the hall. As they burned and scented the air, it grew too late for the third course of the dinner to be served and the guests began to approach the royal dais to renew their homage and to say goodnight. Anne waited hand in hand with her daughter until it was their turn. With trembling knees she approached and knelt before the king and queen. Richard beckoned his daughter forward for a special kiss then turned his warm blue eyes on Anne. She smiled up at him, knowing that he had no need to hear her devotions, but she gave them anyway, both to him and to Queen Anne, before kissing both her children and returning to Stanley House hand in hand with her husband.

Following their coronation, the king and queen rested at Windsor for a few days before Richard and his entourage started off on a royal progress around the country. Lord Stanley was to accompany him and before he left he gave Edward leave to return to Hornby, but said that Anne must remain with the Countess of Richmond in London.

"Why must I do as your father says when I am your wife?" she demanded of Edward as soon as they were alone. "Why must I be forbidden my home?"

"Anne, please. I would stay but I am worried about Lucy."

"And you think that I am not?" she demanded. She was anxious to get away from the constraints of Stanley House and be free to run her own affairs and make her own decisions once more.

"Why do you always make difficulties?" asked Edward as she paced the bedchamber like one of the caged lions at the Tower. Anne sighed. She felt a little sorry for him. His father's influence was strong and far reaching and she knew that neither of them was a match for it, but the thought of a longer stay with the dour countess when all she wanted to do was go home appalled her.

In the end she realised that she had no choice but to do as her father-in-law bid. Edward was not willing to argue with his father on the matter, fearing that he too might be made to stay in London. Anne made him promise that he would write to her with news of Lucy as soon as he got to Hornby and she also pleaded that he would send any news he heard of the king's progress. He agreed, but she wasn't hopeful. She knew that once he was back at Hornby he would climb the steps to the tower, close the door and lose himself in his work.

The Countess of Richmond seemed even less pleased when she was told that Anne was to remain behind. She said nothing in her husband's presence, but later made it quite clear that Anne was not welcome in her private solar and that she should stay away from her except for prayers and mealtimes.

Feeling like a prisoner again, Anne sat in her chamber and gazed out over the London rooftops as unseen visitors came and went. She was well aware that Richard's place on the throne of England was not entirely secure and that there were people who still supported Lord Edward. She suspected Lord Stanley was one of them and that it was for that reason Richard had insisted he join the royal progress. Anne knew for certain that it was not because Richard enjoyed Lord Stanley's company.

Robert Harrington watched as yet another coffer was carried out and stowed on the wain. Just how much baggage did one queen need, he wondered. It would be past dinnertime before they even set off at this rate and he knew that he would be the one to take the blame if they were not at Warwick, as arranged, to meet the king.

At last everything was stowed. The horses, brushed to perfection and clad in the king's colours, stood waiting impatiently and Robert was checking the girths one last time when Queen Anne and her ladies came out. The queen had a small boy by the hand and for a moment Robert thought that it was her son. Then he remembered that young Edward had been left at Middleham because, Robert guessed, the king did not want to run the risk of exposing the child to any danger. When he looked again he saw that this solemn little boy, clinging to the queen's hand and staring around at the scene before him, was older and he presumed that he was the Duke of Clarence's son.

The queen bent and whispered something to the boy and pointed towards the waiting horses where a groom stood holding a small black pony with a long, well brushed mane and tail. The boy nodded and she gave him into the care of a squire, before glancing across at Robert.

"Everything is ready, Your Grace," he told her.

"Then we had better make haste if we are to meet up with the king," she said and, as her eyes strayed back to her nephew who was leaning forward to pat the pony's neck, Robert thought that she must be anxious to see her own son who was to meet them at Nottingham.

A few days later Anne was dozing restlessly in her bed, dreaming of Hornby, when she was woken by a knock on her door. She sat up as the images of her home were snatched from her and, twitching back the bed curtain, she saw that a maidservant had come in although she judged that the hour was still very early.

The girl put down the tray she was carrying on a coffer and gave Ann a half-hearted curtsey. "My Lady Richmond bids you attire yourself to travel," she informed her. "She has decided to leave for Lathom."

Anne swung her legs over the side of the bed and stood up. The sun was still low in the sky and she judged it was not long after dawn, which came early in the summer months. The girl was already taking Anne's gowns down from the pole ready to fold them for the journey.

"Which gown will you wear, my lady?" she asked.

"The dark one," said Anne as she poured herself some of the watered wine and wondered what had prompted this sudden decision to leave.

Men came to carry the coffers down the stairs and within the hour she was sitting opposite the countess in the Stanley carriage as the horses jerked them out of the courtyard into the quiet city streets.

The three-day journey in the humid summer weather left Anne sticky and uncomfortable as the carriage rocked from side to side, making her head ache and her stomach revolt. Then, on the morning of the fourth day, they approached the shrine of Our Lady of Evesham where the countess had expressed a desire to pray. For what, Anne was not sure, but she was looking forward to a brief respite from the heat and the travel sickness within the cool walls of the abbey.

The road was crowded with pilgrims making their way towards the shrine, some on foot and some on palfreys or donkeys. They had halted once again as they waited for yet another group to move aside for them when a groom came to say that some approaching horsemen needed to pass.

"Who is it?" demanded the countess.

"It is the Duke of Buckingham," said the groom apologetically.

"Buckingham? Tell him that I desire to speak a word with him," she said.

Anne had thought that Buckingham was with the king on his progress, and the countess also betrayed her surprise as she fidgeted with the rosary beads in her hand whilst they waited for the tall figure to dismount from his horse and approach them.

"Good day to you, cousin," he greeted the countess, kissing the hand she extended to him. "I apologise for any delay to your journey. Where are you bound?"

"To the shrine of Our Lady, and then on to Lathom," she told him. "It grows too hot for me in London and I shall feel more comfortable away from the city. Do you no longer accompany the king?" she asked him.

"No." Anne watched as the duke's mouth turned down at the corners. Buckingham looked petulant, as if he had been deprived of a favourite toy, and she wondered if he and Richard had fallen out over some matter. "I begged his leave to attend to my own affairs in the Welsh Marches," he said. "He is to continue north, to York, and has lords enough without need for me," he added with a note of jealousy.

"And did you speak to the king again concerning my son?" asked the countess, not pursuing the grudge that Buckingham appeared to be harbouring.

"I did press the matter on your behalf, my lady," he told her. "I urged the king to consider your suggestion that a marriage between Henry and one of the daughters of the late King Edward would be propitious."

"And you told him that we would ask no dowry, only that Henry be allowed

174

to come home?"

"I did, my lady."

"And what did he say?" asked the countess, searching the duke's face for any crumb of favourable news.

"He said that he would think on it."

The countess grimaced in frustration. She was desperate to have her son back in England and Anne had some sympathy, knowing what it was like to be parted from a child.

"It would be a good match," said the countess, "as well as bringing about an alliance between the houses of Lancaster and York."

"Indeed it would," agreed the duke and Anne watched as the glimmer of an idea seemed to burn in his eyes. "And what of the princes?" he asked.

"Moved to the White Tower and provided with new attendants," muttered the countess. "Even though it was promised that the younger would be returned to his mother."

"The..." Buckingham hesitated and glanced at Anne and the countess drew a finger to her lips and shook her head.

"Come to visit me at Lathom, my lord," she told him. "Bring me news from your prisoner, Bishop Morton – and see that you treat him well."

"My lady," he said, raising her hand to his lips again and nodding his head in Anne's direction before returning to the horse that was tearing at the sparse, trampled grass on the roadside.

As she watched him put a foot to his stirrup and mount the horse Anne wondered what secrets he shared with the countess, who was once again passing her beads through her fingers in silent prayer.

James Harrington walked along Petergate very early in the morning beneath the banners of welcome that had been more than enough to impress the southern lords who had ridden into the city with Richard on the feast day of St John the Baptist. The sun had shone brilliantly on the royal party as he and the civic dignitaries had greeted the king and queen and their myriad attendants and led them into the city – although James had exchanged a menacing glance with Lord Stanley. It rankled with him that the man was given such prominence. Of the Duke of Buckingham there had been no sign, and when James had enquired about his whereabouts he had been amazed to learn that the duke had gone off to his own lands. Now, as he walked towards the Minster to check that everything was in place for the day's celebration, he pondered again on Buckingham's absence. It seemed to James to be the height of disrespect. As the new Great Chamberlain and Constable of England, Buckingham should have remained at the king's side throughout his progress and he wondered what had occurred between Richard and the man who had advised him so closely during recent days.

The west door to the church stood part open and James walked up the wide, shallow steps and went in. It was dark and cool after the brightness of the summer morning outside and he stood for a moment taking in the quietness and the scent of the incense. The prie dieu where the king had knelt to lead the congregation in the Paternoster was still in place, though it would not be used today. James walked slowly towards the altar, looking around to ensure that everything had been done according to his instructions. The king and queen were bringing their son, Prince Edward, to mass before going to the nearby palace of the Archbishop where young Edward would be invested with the sword and golden rod of the Prince of Wales and Earl of Chester. James was keen that nothing should be overlooked. He was proud that Richard had entrusted him to attend to affairs in the north and he hoped that if he did the job well his responsibilities might be confirmed on a more permanent basis. Although his role as a knight of the body to the late king had been an honour, his heart lay in his northern homeland and he was happier here than he had ever been in London.

In her chamber at Lathom House, Anne heard visitors arrive just in time for dinner. At first she thought that it must be Lord Stanley and his son, returned from York, but, as she paused at the head of the stairs, her spirits sank when she heard the voice of the man she least wished to see.

"Still free from the clutches of Old Dick, I see," Sir William Stanley greeted her.

"I beg you not to speak of the king using that derogatory name," said Anne, stiffly.

Sir William laughed. "It's a fitting nickname for a man who might as well have sold his soul to the devil. For all that he rides around the country, drumming up support and delighting the townsfolk with his air of charm and his refusal of their benevolences, there are some clear-sighted folk who can see the truth."

"And what truth is that, Sir William?" she asked, annoyed with herself for being drawn into a discussion with him.

"The truth that he is no rightful king and that there is another with a better claim than his."

"You mean the Lord Edward?"

"I would if the lad were still alive." Anne stared at Sir William as he gulped down the wine brought by a servant and thrust out the cup for more. "The princes have disappeared from their chambers in the Tower," he told her.

"Maybe they have been sent to live in the household of some gentleman?" she faltered.

"Murdered, more likely," replied Sir William.

"No," said Anne, shaking her head in disbelief. "Richard would never do that!" She thought of the way he doted on his own children, the love and loyalty he had always shown his brother, and his promise to provide for the nephews who had been placed under his care and protection.

"Open your eyes, Anne, and see the man for what he is!" said Sir William. "And pray for the safety of all those who cross his path – especially those who seek to hinder his ambitions. Remember the way he had Hastings executed? His brother's closest friend. Why do you insist on taking his part? Sweet Anne..." He reached to grasp her hand. The scent of his stale sweat repulsed her and she turned her head away. She smelt his wine-wet breath before his lips dampened her cheek and she squirmed to try to free herself from his grasp. "I could give you so much more if only you would be kind to me," he told her.

"I have no intention of ever being kind to you, Sir William. Please let me alone," she told him. But his words had sown doubt in her mind. Was Richard capable of ordering the execution of his nephews? She tried to convince herself that it was all rumour and lies spread by his enemies to discredit him, but she couldn't quite shake off the memory of him admitting he had killed old King Henry. But children? His own family? Surely not.

"Your lover will not be king for long," added the countess from her chair by the hearth. "My cousin Buckingham, with all of the late Lord Hastings' men at his side, is already rallying troops. When he is successful my son will come from France and he will be crowned the true king of England. You will see. You and your bastard children who have brought such shame on the Stanleys will not seem so privileged then."

Anne did not reply. She pulled her hand from Sir William's and went back to her bedchamber where she sat on the edge of her bed for a long time, trying to make sense of what she had been told and wondering what she could do to warn Richard of the growing conspiracy against him.

Robert Harrington stepped back as the king flung down the letter in fury. His blue eyes blazed with anger and his fingers strayed to the knife at his belt.

"He says he has a malady of the stomach!" he fumed, waving a hand towards the letter from the Duke of Buckingham, whom he had ordered back to court. "I can only conclude that what my spies tell me is true and that he is promoting a rebellion." Robert watched as he shook his head in disbelief. "He had every cause to be loyal. He is the most untrue creature living," said Diccon, the anger in his eyes replaced by hurt. "But he will not succeed! I will see him and his rebels subdued! Who else has a hand in this do you think?" he asked, dropping to a chair and meeting Robert's eyes. "Dorset? I suspect that he is being well hidden by Mistress Shore, whom I was kind enough to release from her prison cell. And it would not surprise me to find that Stanley and his wife have meddled here too. I know they both hate me." He sighed. "I have only ever tried to do what I believe is right. God forgive me, but I sometimes wonder if He has deserted my cause."

"God sends difficult tasks to test the strongest," replied Robert by way of reassurance. "With prayer we will prevail. I am sure of it. His will be done," he added as he made the sign of the cross.

"I pray that you are right," said the king. "Whilst Buckingham and Dorset do the work of the devil I am sure that the common men who march with these traitors are good Christians. I think I may issue word that no commoner who has been blinded by their lies will be harmed if he lays down his arms and withdraws. It may be that we can stop this before any blood is shed."

But a few days later, they had to admit that peace could not be achieved by words alone and they were forced to march to battle in their own defence.

As Robert watched a freshening wind flutter the flags and banners of their army, heavy droplets began to fall. Before long the rain had become a torrent, driving into his face, blinding him and wetting him through to his inner padded jacket. Beneath the horses' hooves the road was a quagmire and he felt his stallion slip beneath him as they slithered downhill towards the River Severn. What sort of battle could take place in such inclement weather, he wondered.

They paused around mid-morning in the shelter of some woodland and the king sent Robert ahead with a small party of men. As they headed cautiously through the trees Robert heard the torrent of water, and when they came in sight of the river he saw that it was in spate from the rain on the hills and there was no chance of crossing. On the far bank the Welshmen who had ridden in support of Buckingham were already turning for home and the rebel army appeared to be in disarray. Robert felt relief seep through him along with the rain. There would be no battle that day, nor any other judging by the reluctance of Buckingham's men.

Back at their camp, Robert handed the reins to a squire before squelching across the wet grass to where the king was sheltering under a large oak tree. The rain was spattering on the leaves above them and he heard a distant roll of thunder across the Welsh hills.

"They are trapped on the far side of the river, my lord," he said. "The rebel troops are beginning to disperse and flee."

Diccon's wet face broke into a smile that belied the gloomy weather. "Then it seems our prayers are answered," he said. "Let the common men go unharmed," he ordered, "but bring me Buckingham – and Dorset. Send the dogs after them if necessary, although I suspect the traitor will run for home. Go to surround his house and tell the men that when he comes out they may help themselves to his goods and chattels."

It turned out that, on seeing his men desert him, Buckingham had fled to Shrewsbury and taken refuge, disguised as a labourer, in the household of Ralph Banastre who had remained loyal to him. But the thousand pounds reward that the king had offered for his capture had concentrated Banastre's mind and he had handed the fugitive over to the sheriff of Shropshire.

The sun came out as the king's army rode triumphantly into Salisbury where Buckingham, still dressed as a peasant, was brought to trial before Sir Ralph Assheton. Robert watched his handsome face take on a look of disbelief as he was found guilty of treason and sentenced to be beheaded in the market place the next day.

"Allow me to see the king, I beg you," he pleaded as fear clouded his haughty eyes. "Let me throw myself on his mercy and beg his forgiveness."

Sir Ralph raised an eyebrow and gestured to Robert. "Will you take the message to the king?" he asked.

Robert nodded and, excusing himself from the courtroom, ran up the stairs with a hand on his sword to where he knew Diccon was waiting in a private chamber. He looked up from a book as Robert entered, although the verdict had never been in doubt.

"My lord, the Duke of Buckingham pleads for an audience with you," Robert told him. A look of hesitation flickered across his face. Then he carefully closed the book and pressed his lips together as he stared into the distance.

"No," he said at last. "Tell him no. I will not see him. His execution will go ahead tomorrow."

Robert inclined his head and returned down the steps to the courtroom with the message. He was surprised that the king had ordered Buckingham to be killed on a Sunday, but suspected that it was because he knew, if he hesitated for even a day longer, he might change his mind and forgive the man. Diccon had grown fond of Buckingham and had liked and trusted him and Robert knew that made his treachery all the worse.

It was early in November 1483 when Lord Stanley came back to Lathom with his son, Lord Strange, and a large company of men. Anne watched the impassive face of the Countess of Richmond as they sat at the supper table and her husband related the events of the past weeks, and although she heard her sharp intake of breath at the news of Buckingham's execution on the Lord's Day her expression never changed.

"He begged the king for an audience after sentence was passed but he refused to see him," said Lord Stanley as he reached to cut another slice of meat from the dish of chicken at the centre of the table. "What news of your son?" he asked his wife.

"Landed at Plymouth in the midst of a storm, but put to sea again to avoid a trap." Lord Stanley nodded and Anne, suddenly overcome with an uncontrollable rage at their plotting stood up and flung her platter across the table, scattering chicken, bread, trenchers, cups and wine across the floor and walls in a trail of white and red. The Stanleys stared at her.

"You are all traitors!" she shouted at them before running from the room.

The Stanleys were summoned to attend the Christmas court and Anne knew that the Countess of Richmond and her husband would have some awkward questions to answer about their involvement in the rebellion. On their first day Lord Stanley had been summoned by the king and returned around suppertime with a concerned expression and closeted himself with his wife and son in the solar, leaving Anne alone by the hearth in the hall. Since her outburst at Lathom the Stanleys had taken extra precautions never to discuss any of their affairs within her hearing.

The next day Uncle Robert came in the middle of the morning to escort her to see John and Katherine and, rather than expressing any reluctance to allow her to go, Anne had been surprised when the Countess of Richmond had sent a servant to ask Anne to attend her in the solar.

"I would ask a favour of you," she said. "Will you intercede with the king on my behalf? I am accused of being a traitor, and if I am found guilty..." Her hand strayed to the back of her neck as if she was already imagining the touch of the executioner's axe and she swallowed uneasily. "I know we have not always been friends, but I have tried to be kind to you, and surely you would not wish to see me die?"

Anne allowed herself a moment of satisfaction to see this woman whom she hated having to beg for her help.

"The king's mind is not mine to command," she replied, but then found herself softening a little. "I will mention the matter to him," she promised. Much as she disliked the countess it would not please her to see the woman go to the block.

The children greeted her joyously and Katherine especially seemed to exude excitement as she kissed her mother. They had barely sat down and begun to exchange their news when Richard came in and Anne stood up and curtseyed to him.

"How are things at Stanley House?" he asked as she resumed her seat.

"They seem to be concerned about what will happen to the Countess of Richmond."

"So they should be! Stanley's wife is lucky she is not sent straight to Pontefract – or worse!"

"She did plot against you," said Anne. "I saw Buckingham visit her on more than one occasion and there were messengers coming and going from Lathom all the time. Even though I was mostly confined to my chamber I would have been blind not to see it. I wrote a letter to warn you but it was discovered and burnt by the countess and after that I was denied pen and ink and watched even more closely."

"I thought Harry Buckingham was my friend," said Richard. "Of all the people I might have suspected of treason he was the one who had most cause to be loyal. Why did he turn against me?" he asked, and seeing the bewildered look in his eyes Anne reached out her hand to touch his arm.

"I think he may have had ambition to take the crown himself," she said. "I doubt he would have willingly stood aside for Henry Tudor."

"Tudor's bastard blood has no claim to the throne of England!" said Richard, vehemently, "and to think that I was once willing to listen to his mother's entreaties that I allow him back from France."

"What will happen to her?" asked Anne.

"That is for parliament to decide."

"Is there evidence that she plotted against you?"

"More than enough," he replied grimly.

"The countess has begged me to intervene on her behalf and ask that you will be merciful," Anne told him.

"She fears for her head?" asked Richard, with a slight smile.

"I think she does." Anne paused. "You would not have her executed?"

"Do you not think she deserves it?" he asked. "It is the punishment for treason and she has knowingly plotted against me."

"I know," said Anne. "I do not like or trust the woman. I do not like or trust any of the Stanley family, well apart from Edward. But she is a pious and godly woman and I would not like to think..." Anne stopped as a shiver ran through her at the thought of an executioner hacking the countess's head from her body amidst her blood and screams.

Richard stood with his back to the fire. "Ruling a kingdom leaves no room for sentiment," he said. "Treason cannot go unpunished." He looked at Anne for a moment and then his face softened into a familiar smile. "I will not have her killed," he said. "Not because I feel inclined to leniency in her case, and not simply because she is a woman, but because I must strive to keep the support of her husband. Stanley is a constant thorn in my side, and even though he swears he knew nothing of the plot I do not believe him. But the man has far reaching influence, to say nothing of a large army. I cannot risk him openly turning against me. But do not repeat this to her," he warned as he sat down again. "Let the woman worry a little. Some fear may help to concentrate both their minds and even change them in my favour. I will strip her of her lands and titles and give her into the care of her husband. He can take her back to Lathom and keep her confined there where she can have no more communication with her son."

Anne nodded with relief, thinking that the hardest part of Richard's punishment would be the countess's loss of the title she loved so much; having to be called Lady Stanley rather than Countess would not please her at all.

"Anne, there is another important matter I wish to discuss with you." He glanced away from her to smile at Kate. "I think it is time that a marriage was arranged for our daughter."

"Already?" asked Anne. "She will not be eleven years old until the spring. Surely there is no rush?"

Richard frowned. "It is not just a matter of her marrying, but of her making a suitable marriage," he explained. "I have a man in mind who is not only a good Yorkist and a reliable supporter, but a man whom I know will be kind and tender towards her." Anne waited to hear what he would say, praying that he had chosen well yet knowing that his decision would be final despite any reservations that she might have. "The Earl of Huntingdon has been a widower for almost two years now and although he has a daughter he has no male heir. He will be a good husband."

"But he is your age. He is old enough to be her father!" protested Anne.

"He has been an honourable and loyal lord to me, especially during the rebellion," said Richard. "Yet he is the least wealthy of any earl and it would please me to reward him. I will give them gifts of lands and estates that will secure our daughter's future as well as his."

Anne looked at her child. "Will this make you happy?" she asked, though the excitement dancing in Kate's eyes told her all she needed to know.

"I have met him, Mama, and he is very kind."

"After the marriage Kate will live in her husband's household with the earl's daughter until she is old enough for the marriage to be consummated," said Richard. Anne nodded and reached out her arms to hug her daughter to her.

"It is just so hard to think that she is almost grown up," she said with tears in her eyes.

"I will arrange for you to meet William," said Richard gently. "Then you will be reassured that he is a good and kind man." He paused. "And now I will give you some time alone with the children," he said, though, as Anne watched him go, she wished that she could spend more time with him as well.

The marriage covenant was signed on the twenty-ninth day of February, that year being a leap year, and Katherine and William were married at the small church of St Helen in Bishopsgate on Monday the eighth day of March. Richard made them generous grants of land, including some that had belonged to Lady Stanley, which would pass to them after the death of Lord Stanley, and Anne could not suppress a rueful smile at the thought of how much it would anger the woman to know that her property would eventually belong to Kate – one of the 'bastard children' whom she had claimed had brought such shame on the Stanleys.

Chapter Thirteen
April 1484 ~ July 1485

The weather had been warm for April, especially at Hornby where the spring often came late. Anne had been in the herb garden that she and Lucy had planted, cutting back the unwanted winter growth. She was washing the earth from her hands in a bucket filled with water, scrubbing at the blackness that had crept beneath her fingernails with a small brush when she heard the messenger come. She went across the courtyard with a towel in her hands and still wearing a course apron over her gown.

"I come from Middleham, my lady," said the messenger. Anne's heart raced as she took the letter, praying that it was not bad news. The sight of her son's handwriting reassured her that he was safe, but the news he sent stunned her. Edward Prince of Wales was dead. The little son of the king and queen had died unexpectedly at Middleham whilst his parents were at Nottingham Castle.

"God have mercy on his soul," prayed Anne making the sign of the cross. "Richard," she whispered, knowing how much he had treasured his youngest child, and although her heart broke for the queen as well it was mostly for Richard that she wept as she shared his grief.

When she related the news to her husband at supper she found that he had already heard.

"People are discussing it in Lancaster," he told her, "and some are saying that it is God's judgement."

"For what?" she asked.

"They are saying that the king's heir has been taken from him in retribution for his murder of his brother's sons."

"People think it is a punishment? They are saying that he murdered Lord Edward and Lord Richard?" Anne remembered that Sir William had hinted at the same thing more than six months before.

"No one knows where the princes are. They were in the Tower, but they haven't been seen since Buckingham's rebellion, so people draw their own conclusions." He shrugged.

"Do you believe it?" she asked him. She knew that his opinion of Richard had changed since the hasty execution of Lord Hastings.

"If I were in the king's place I would not have wanted two rivals whom many think were the rightful monarch and his heir."

"You speak as if you believe they are dead."

"Well if they are alive let us see if the king produces them to countermand these rumours."

"And risk them being the focus of another rebellion?"

"The king has already risked a focus for rebellion by persuading the dowager queen and her daughters to come out of sanctuary," said Edward.

"But they are all girls. Surely no one would back a rebellion to put a queen on the throne?" asked Anne.

"A woman can soon find a husband to support her," said Edward, "and my father tells me that when Henry Tudor held court at Rennes Cathedral last Christmas he made a vow that he would marry the Lady Elizabeth."

"That is what Buckingham suggested," said Anne remembering the day that she and the countess had met him on the road to Worcester.

"There are many who would like to see Tudor on the throne with the late king's daughter as his queen," said her husband. "And although she fears the shadow of the axe, my father's wife is still in contact with her son."

"How so when she is confined at Lathom and allowed to see no one" demanded Anne.

"Even the king would not deny her the comfort of her confessor – especially when he believes she is seeking forgiveness for her misdeeds against him. Christopher Urswick is loyal to her and carries messages and letters to Henry in France." Edward suddenly fell silent and gave Anne a hard look. "I should not have told you these things. I sometimes forget my father's warnings to be circumspect in my conversations with you. I trust you will not repeat any of this to the king. I do not want to forbid you to write any letters."

"I see him so rarely it is of little consequence. He is in London for most of the time now and does not have the leisure to correspond with me," remarked Anne. She would not risk a letter to Richard, she thought, but she would send word to one of her uncles the next time they sent a messenger to her.

However, the next letter she received was from Isabella, who was in London with Uncle Robert, and she also mentioned the Lady Elizabeth.

To Anne Stanley, at Hornby:

Well-beloved, I greet you well and recommend myself to you. We are all well and I hope you remain in good health.

There is much fear here in London and the king has armed men on the streets to keep the peace as the taverns and the yards are full of people whispering and their theories grow more bizarre by the day. People are saying that the king has murdered his nephews and that he plans to divorce the queen and marry his niece the Lady Elizabeth.

Robert says the king is much angered by these rumours. Yet every day new bills appear and pamphlets too and my husband is scarcely home for trying to discover who is behind it all.

There are rumours of rebellions and invasions also, and although the king has deployed warships in the channel and tried to persuade Duke Francis to hand over Henry Tudor he has so far refused and Robert fears that the threat from Tudor and his supporters is credible. Perhaps the king should not have been so lenient with Tudor's mother, the Lady Stanley. What do you know? Are you at liberty to write, or does your husband censor your letters?

I hope at least to see you again come Christmas and until then I remember you daily in my prayers.

Written at Crosby Hall, London.

Your loving cousin, Isabella.

As Christmas 1484 approached Anne and Edward travelled south once again. On Twelfth Night they attended a banquet in Westminster Hall, and although people had said the celebrations of 1483 had been lavish they were certainly overshadowed by this, thought Anne.

At each place there was a small package but, as Anne reached to unwrap the one set before her, a trumpeter announced two pages who came in bearing gifts for the queen and the Lady Elizabeth who were seated on either side of the king at the top table. Anne watched as the two women unwrapped their presents amid much laughter and then begged leave, with ladies in attendance, to retire to an ante-chamber.

"What did they receive? I couldn't see," Anne asked her daughter.

"They are gowns," laughed Kate. "Papa sent for the finest silks and had garments fashioned in the latest style for both of them."

"That was very generous."

"He said that both should be dressed finely for this feast," she was explaining when she was interrupted by a gasp, followed by a moment's silence as the two women returned. "They could be twins!" laughed Kate. But Anne could not match her smile. She could see that the queen and her niece, with their slender figures and fair hair looked eerily similar in their matching gowns. It troubled her and she wondered if Richard had not misjudged the mood of some of the assembled guests.

"He treats his niece as if she would be a queen as well," remarked Edward beside her, echoing her own thoughts. "This will not help the rumours that he plans to replace his wife with her."

"I think he just means to be generous, and fair," said Anne.

"Then it is badly judged," said Edward. "He should have had more sense."

Anne didn't reply, but she knew that her husband was right. To dress them both the same was to invite comparison and although she knew that he had done it to show that the Lady Elizabeth was still a respected member of his family, she wished that she had had the opportunity to advise him against the rashness of it.

She turned to her own gift with a frown and undid the ribbons to find a pair of soft leather gloves.

"Do you like them?" asked Kate eagerly. "I helped Papa choose all the gifts. He knows nothing about fashion!"

"They are beautiful," said Anne. "What did he give to you?"

"I am wearing it!" she said, standing up and twirling around to show off her emerald green gown. "And my husband gave me the brooch." She bent for her mother to admire the jewels and as she did so Anne noticed the swell of her young breasts.

As Anne had foreseen, the gossip about the dresses given to the queen and her niece reignited speculation that the king intended to put away his wife and marry the Lady Elizabeth.

"And it is not helped by the queen's poor health," said Uncle Robert as they sat in the solar at Stanley House one day in the early spring. Now that Lord Stanley spent much of his time at court and Lady Stanley was still confined at Lathom, there was no one to forbid Anne receiving visitors. "There is even talk that the king is poisoning her," said her uncle.

"Oh, but that is ridiculous!" burst out Anne, incensed that anyone could think that Richard would do such a thing. "But is the queen's health no better?" she asked.

"She does not come out of her bedchamber and her ladies say she has become very thin and frail and coughs much of the time."

"And what do her physicians say?"

"They say she has a wasting disease. In fact they have advised the king to refrain from her bed, though whether it is because she is so weak or because they fear it is a contagion I do not know."

Anne nodded. She felt sympathy for both of them. "Then the outcome does not look hopeful."

"I fear not," agreed her uncle sadly.

On the sixteenth day of March 1485, the sun mysteriously faded in the middle of the day.

"It is an eclipse," explained Edward. They were standing in the courtyard at Stanley House and it had grown suddenly cold and all the birds had fallen silent as the false dusk fell across the city. "It happens when the moon on its orbit comes between the earth and the sun."

"It is a bad omen," replied Anne. Her husband shook his head at her superstitions, but barely had she spoken than the passing bell began to toll. She stared at Edward. "The queen?" she asked. Edward nodded. "God take and preserve her soul," said Anne. "And God help Richard," she whispered.

The bell continued to toll as the false night darkened the city. It seemed to be the only sound as it echoed out, over the walls and across the river to the fields beyond, as if the whole of the heavens mourned the passing of Anne Neville.

Anne watched as a bubble of light appeared on one side of the shrouded sun.

"Don't look at it," Edward told her. "There'll be many blinded by the strength of the sun's light this day. I would not like you to be one of them."

But it was not only eyes that were blinded, but minds as well. Rumours abounded that the king had murdered his wife to marry his niece and thwart the ambitions of Henry Tudor. "They speak of little else on the streets," said Edward as they sat down to supper at Stanley House on the day the queen was laid to rest in Westminster Abbey.

"How was the king?" Anne asked Lord Stanley who had attended the funeral.

"He wept, though many said his show of emotion was as well-performed as that of a player."

Anne stared at her father-in-law and saw that he had no sympathy for Richard. She placed her spoon beside the bowl and saw that her hand was shaking with emotion.

"Will he marry the Lady Elizabeth do you think?" asked Edward.

"Who knows what his mind holds?" said Lord Stanley. "The man is an enigma and I will never understand him. But Ratcliffe has promised that he will talk to him, and he is one of the few men that the king may actually listen to. Though when he will manage to say his piece heaven alone knows. The king has shut himself away in his apartments and refuses to see anyone."

Although Richard was never out of her thoughts and prayers Anne neither saw him nor had any message from him until past May Day, when Uncle Robert came and said that he wished to see her.

"A moment," said Anne, suddenly conscious of her drab gown, and she ran up to her bedchamber to change and pin a fresh clean coif around her face before allowing her uncle to hand her onto the barge that would take her to Westminster. As the oars swathed through the water of the river the sun came out for the first time in weeks and Anne hoped that it was a good sign.

She was ushered into the presence chamber where Richard sat on an elaborate chair, dressed in a rich black and gold doublet with a dark gown over the top. She sank into a deep curtsey and stayed there for a moment, her eyes on the patterns of the tiled floor, wondering what it was he wanted to say to her.

After gesturing to her to rise he stood up and came towards her. "I will speak with you in private, my lady," he said.

She bent to kiss the ring on his outstretched hand, her nostrils filling with the familiar scent of him.

"Come!" he said and offered her his arm. She placed her fingers on his cuff as she had so many years ago at Baynard's Castle, although she doubted that today he intended to take her into the garden and make love to her.

He led her to an ante-chamber whose windows looked out over the mead that spread down to the river. She heard him close the door behind them and for the first time in over ten years she was completely alone with him. As he stood beside her at the open window, their arms almost touching, she saw the faint lines around the corners of his mouth and the edges of his eyes, which held traces of his sorrows. She wanted to hold and comfort him.

"Richard?" She put her hand in his. "Richard, I am truly sorry," she told him. "I know you loved her."

He lifted her hand and held it against his chest. She could feel his heartbeat and it was as quickened as her own.

"Yes, I loved her," he replied, "but not in the same way that I love you. She was my wife and I kept myself faithful to her body. And I wept when she was taken from me. But..."

He paused and looked at her, at her face and then down at her hands and his ring which she still wore. "I have always loved you," he told her. "I think I loved you from the moment I saw you at Hornby Castle. What we had was special. It could be so again."

"Would you have me as your mistress?" she asked.

"No," he said and she pulled her hand from his in sudden disappointment. "I would have you for my wife." She stared at him as he took her hand in his again

187

and raised it to his lips. "Anne, will you marry me?"

"My marriage to Edward Stanley..."

"Is not consummated?" He raised an eyebrow in query.

"No. I have never been to his bed, and it was not a marriage to which I freely consented."

"Then an annulment can be granted."

He still held her hand firmly in his and she was fixated by his imploring eyes.

"Richard," she breathed, "are you sincere?"

"Of course I am sincere! Surely you know that I would never make a mockery of such a request as this!" She smiled at his indignant tone.

"Yes," she told him. "If you can make it possible then surely you must know that my answer is yes."

He released her hand and put his arms around her. She found herself pressed into a familiar embrace with her cheek on his shoulder and her face in the crook of his neck. He kissed her and held her tightly against him and she found that she was crying tears of joy. "My lord, I will give you more sons," she sobbed. "I will give you sons without number – strong, bold Plantagenet sons."

She felt his hand move down her back and she pulled away from him. "Not here!" she said, expecting someone to come in at any moment.

"Why not?" he asked, with a look that scandalised her. "I once loved you in a pleasure garden, why not on a riverbank?" He held out his hand. In less than a few minutes his pain and sorrow had lifted from him and he was the young man she had known, with his mischievous smile and ardent desire for her. And her years of loneliness and anguish were also swept away as she placed her hand in his and he led her to the door.

"The lady and I will walk by the river. We do not wish to be disturbed," he said to his attendants as they passed.

Outside, the sun felt warmer than the shaded rooms of the palace. Anne held Richard's arm pressed tightly against her breast as they walked towards the water, where the royal barge with its blue and red canopy was gently rising and falling on the turning tide. He handed her aboard then pulled her against him and kissed her. The taste of him was familiar and she held him as she had longed to do for so many years when he had been forbidden to her, never wanting to let go. He hesitated, his hand on her thigh pressing her against him.

"May I?" he asked.

"Yes," she breathed into his ear and he eased her down onto the cushioned seat from where she could see the leaves dancing on the trees above them.

Afterwards, he lay with his head on her lap and she fingered his hair.

"Do you mind if we keep this secret for a while?" he asked.

"Secret? Why?" she asked, hoping that his request had not been insincere after all.

"That bastard upstart, Henry Tudor, preys on my mind and I would like to rout his aspirations, and those of his supporters, before we speak openly of our marriage. The idea that I may yet marry the Lady Elizabeth still concerns them and I do not want to assuage their fears just yet." He reached up to caress her cheek. "You're disappointed," he said.

"I want to be with you. Too much time has passed already."

"I know." She pressed his hand against her cheek. His palms were smoother now and she wondered if he spent more time at his administration than in honing his skills for the battlefield. She would not be sorry if he did, although his talk was not of peace. "I do not think it will take long to subdue this last rebellion," he said, "but I would like to have my kingdom secure before I marry you."

Anne nodded as she turned his hand in hers. "I can wait a little longer," she said. "And when we are married will you take me to see Middleham?"

He hesitated and she was sorry that she had mentioned the place. "Middleham has unhappy memories for me now," he said. "But I will go to the church there and to Fountains Abbey to pray for my son's soul – though such a blameless little soul should have been taken straight to heaven."

Anne looked down at his anguished face and realised that she would never have the whole of him. There was a part of him that would forever belong to Anne Neville and their son. But how could she begrudge him that? She would not love him as she did if he were cold and heartless.

"Anne," he said, sitting up. "Would you be willing to give up Hornby? If your marriage is annulled the castle will remain as your property and I have a mind to return it to your uncle. It belongs to the Harringtons by right and, besides, I owe your uncle a reward for his discretion in a difficult matter."

"It must be a very important matter that you should plan to reward him with my inheritance," she remarked, meaning only to tease him but sensing his muscles stiffen.

"I'm sorry. I did not mean to criticise," she said.

"No, I am not displeased with you, Anne," he said. "But it is a something best known to only a few."

"You do not trust me?"

"I would trust you with my life."

She was on the brink of asking him if the matter in which her uncle had been discreet had something to do with the whereabouts of Lord Edward and Lord Richard, but she sensed that he did not want to speak about it. She knew that he would become angry if she pried too far and that when the time was right he would tell her what had happened to his nephews.

"What you have offered me is more than recompense for Hornby Castle," she told him. "In fact I would be glad to see the Harrington banner flying high from the turret once again." Though, even as she spoke, she felt sad for Edward who would have to pack up his flasks and jars and move from the chamber in the tower that he liked so much.

"We had best go in," said Richard at last. "The tide has turned and it looks like rain. Anne, be patient. I promise that I will marry you before Christmas comes," he said.

They walked back to the palace, uncaring that anyone should see them. But, as she waited for the page to find her uncle to escort her home, Anne's stomach lurched as she caught sight of the figure lurking in the ante-chamber where visitors waited for an audience with the king.

"Mistress Stanley," said Sir William. "I did not think to find you here."

Anne saw the angry jealousy that glittered in his eyes. She prayed that he had not seen her hand in hand with Richard or seen the king's farewell to her as he had kissed her lingeringly on the lips.

"I am come to speak with the king about our children," she told him.

Sir William sneered in disbelief. "You disappoint me Anne," he said. "I am twice the man that he will ever be. And one day I will prove it!"

A shiver ran through her at his words. They seemed an empty threat but she knew better than to trust the Stanleys. She repeated the incident to her uncle as they were rowed back upriver, but he dismissed her fears.

"For all his bluff Sir William has always been a loyal Yorkist. He is more trustworthy than his brother. Think no more of it. He would never do anything to harm the king."

Chapter Fourteen
August 1485

As the threat of invasion from Henry Tudor intensified, Lord Stanley begged leave from the king to attend to matters on his estates in Lancashire and Anne and Edward returned with him to Lathom. Anne wanted to ride on to Hornby, but she was forbidden.

"Perhaps it is better if you do not go," said Edward. "There is a bout of the sweating sickness taken hold. Lucy writes that she and her mother are kept busy brewing medicines to alleviate the illness and she advises us to stay away for the present."

Richard, meanwhile, had begun to plan the defence of his kingdom and a messenger came from Nottingham Castle with a letter for Lord Stanley.

"The king demands I go back to court or send Lord Strange in my place," he said as he read out its contents. "I have the feeling he does not quite trust me after all," he remarked with a sly smile at his wife.

"I will go in your place," volunteered Lord Strange. "I will say that you have succumbed to the sweating sickness. He cannot argue with that."

"I doubt he will believe it," said Lord Stanley, "but if you are willing I would appreciate it, for I am more use to our cause here than under the king's watchful eye."

"Traitors!" said Anne and they turned to stare at her, as if they had forgotten that she was there.

"You had best make sure that she writes no message to her lover," advised Lady Stanley. "And in future be more careful of your conversation in her presence."

"Go to your chamber," Lord Stanley told Anne.

"So it is I, rather than your wife, you mean to keep as a prisoner is it?" she demanded.

Edward took her arm and pulled her up from the stool. "Come upstairs," he whispered. "Leave this to me." Defenceless, she allowed him to take her up to their bedchamber. "I am sorry," he said after he had closed the door. "My father has no right to treat you like this."

"Then be a man for once and do something about it!" she challenged him.

"I will. I will suggest that it would be safer for their plans if you are allowed to return to Hornby – if you are willing to risk going?"

"Of course I am willing. Why wouldn't I be?"

"I was thinking of the sickness," he reminded her.

"Perhaps if you tell your father I may die it will encourage him to send me there!" Edward didn't reply and Anne never knew if he had suggested such a thing to Lord Stanley, but the following morning she was allowed to go north with an escort of two retainers.

"Tell my uncles where I am," said Anne as Edward kissed her hand in farewell. "And take good care of yourself," she added, reaching out to stroke his face with a sudden rush of affection. "God keep you safe!"

As she rode away Anne looked back at him and wondered if she would ever see him again. She would gladly have waited for an annulment of their marriage, for as long as it took, but she knew that Richard was impatient and she was haunted by the fear that he would use the forthcoming battle to rid himself of her husband as people said he had once rid himself of the husband of Anne Neville.

She wished that she could get a message to him, not only to tell him of Lord Stanley's betrayal, but also to ask him to have pity on Edward Stanley. But she knew that her escorts on the journey would have their orders to prevent any letters being sent, and that by the time she had written from Hornby and found some reliable messenger to ride to Nottingham it might be too late. The last news she had heard before she left Lathom was that Henry Tudor and a considerable force of his supporters had already set sail from France.

Anne's mood lifted as the flat lands of west Lancashire were left behind for the rising hills and heather strewn moorland of the north. When she caught her first glimpse of the octagonal tower of the castle against the vivid blue of the summer sky she rejoiced at coming home, thinking that if only Richard and her children could have been at her side her joy would have been without measure.

As they rode up the steep drive and into the courtyard she was surprised by the silence and the absence of Lucy running out to greet her. No advance message must have arrived, she thought, as she eased her aching body from the saddle and looked around.

A door squeaked open and Martha came out. Surprised, but delighted to see her, Anne held out her arms and Martha hugged her but said nothing.

"What is it? What are you doing here?" she asked as she saw the tears in the woman's eyes and noticed how pale and thin she had become.

"Tis the sickness, my lady. Nearly everyone in the castle is sick and I've come to help nurse them. You should not have returned, my lady. This is not a healthy place."

"Lucy?" asked Anne. "And the children?"

"The little ones are well. They're safe in the tower nursery, my lady. But Mistress Lucy is very ill."

Anne followed Martha to the chamber that Uncle James had once used as his solar. It was now turned into a makeshift infirmary, filled with pallet beds.

"Mistress Payne and Mistress Lucy said that if all the sick were kept together it would be easier to nurse them and would stop the contagion spreading. It was some idea that they'd got from Master Stanley, though I told them it was a foolish one. Look how it's ended," she said, pointing to the low bed where Mistress Payne was tending her daughter.

Lucy lay pale and drenched in sweat on the straw mattress. Her breathing sounded harsh and laboured as she struggled for breath, each coming as a gasp after the last. Mistress Payne looked up at Anne with tears running freely down her cheeks. She shook her head in despair. "I have done everything I can," she whispered, "but God will take her before the day is out."

Anne stared down at the girl who had become her friend and companion. Her loose hair was damp and clung to her scalp and she looked dead already. She stretched out her hand thinking to give her some comfort during her last moments, but Mistress Payne stopped her. "No," she said. "Enough have died already. Do not risk your own life, my lady." Anne drew back nodding. She would not risk causing Richard the grief of losing her to this illness. They had the chance of happiness now and she would not be the one to destroy it.

As predicted, Lucy died that night. Her death was the last at Hornby and, as she had been the one to nurse every other victim, it seemed that she had sacrificed her own life for those who had recovered. They buried her in the priory graveyard and Anne said prayers daily for her soul and helped to comfort Ned and little Thomas as best she could, although they did not understand that their mother would not come back to them. She wrote to Edward to tell him, searching for the right words and knowing that no mention of heaven would bring him any comfort.

The August days drew shorter and hotter, interspersed with fierce thunderstorms that shook the tower and filled the bailey with mud as the rain pounded down. No one came near the village as they still feared the sickness and Anne waited, her eyes straining to the south, watching for the messenger who would come to tell her that Henry Tudor had been defeated and that she could go to Richard to become his wife.

For a moment Robert Harrington thought he had seen a ghost. Anne's son, John, had changed of late from a child into a leggy adolescent on the brink of manhood and as he strode into the hall at Nottingham Castle he reminded Robert so intensely of his dead brother that a fresh wave of grief almost knocked him off balance. But if his features betrayed him as a Harrington the boy's determination was all his father's as he gave the king a formal nod of the head before bursting out, "Papa, let me come with you. I beg you!"

John had been excused his studies for the summer months and allowed to ride with his father as a squire, but now that battle looked imminent he had been told that he must return to the castle at Sheriff Hutton.

"No," replied the king, continuing to study the map which was spread before him on the table.

"But Papa, I will be fourteen next birthday. There are other boys of my age who are going. Why not me?"

"I have said no and you will not change my mind," remarked Richard gently as he looked up from the map to study his son with obvious affection.

"But Papa, you know that I can draw my bow well and shoot a straight arrow and my..."

"No!" Richard interrupted him, with a face as determined as that of his son. "I have ordered you to return to the castle at Sheriff Hutton. And you are not yet too old for a beating if you continue to defy me!" he added.

Robert watched as they faced one another in a contest of wills and then John appeared to crumple under his father's bright blue stare and the king moved towards his son and put an arm around his shoulders, briefly brushing his lips against the boy's dark hair as if he were still a child. "I will not lose another son," he said quietly, "and your mother would never forgive me if any harm came to you. Do as you are bid."

Robert saw the tears of frustration and disappointment glistening in John's eyes. The thought of battle was exciting at that age, he thought, when all you knew of it was the boasting and the stories of those who had returned victorious. The reality was noisy, bloody and terrifying and no place for any boy so young.

With a hostile look at his uncle, as if he thought Robert should have argued for him, John stomped out and Richard turned back to the map. "I will not lose another son," he repeated with his hands braced against the table and his eyes unfocussed on the parchment before him but seeing an altogether different scene. Then, after a moment, he placed his finger on the map. "Tomorrow we will ride to Leicester where our armies are mustering," he said. "And from there we will, with God's help, vanquish our enemies."

James Harrington watched as the horsemen began to ride out of the bailey at Nottingham Castle four abreast. Each man was well-armed with honed and polished weapons and their armour was burnished to high silver and glinted in the morning sun, dimmed only by the shine on the coats of the horses and their brilliant harness. The sight of so many men with their colourful banners held aloft to catch the breeze gladdened James' heart. The king had been insistent that they should leave with a great show of confidence, allowing no trace of fear or apprehension to spoil their display.

James knew that the king still had doubts about some men, the Stanleys in particular, but none showed on his face as he steadied his gleaming white destrier as it shifted beneath him, as eager as its rider to move off. With a simple gold circlet placed over his helm and his visor up so that the people could see his face, Richard touched his spurs to the horse's flanks and it leapt forward. James urged his own horse into the line that followed. By evening they would be in Leicester and it remained to be seen who would join them.

They knew that John Howard, the Duke of Norfolk, and his son Thomas Howard, the Earl of Surrey, were already there with their forces, but Richard had privately admitted to a concern that Henry Percy, the Earl of Northumberland, had not yet arrived even though he had sent word that he was nearby. And James had also seen how alarmed the king had been at the sight of John Sponer and John Nicholson from York who had been waiting for them at their hunting lodge when they had arrived back after a day spent hawking in the forest. Richard had stood before the blazing fire in his mud splattered clothes and had not even taken any refreshment until he had heard what they had to say. Their concern that he had not sent for troops from the city to fight on his behalf had been mirrored by his own as he had pressed his lips tightly together before remarking that as Commissioner of Array in the North it had been Percy's role to call out men from York. The king had sent John Nicholson back to York to gather men, but there was sickness in the city and how many would come and when they would arrive was still unsure.

The king's army arrived in Leicester before nightfall and James attended Richard as he saw the men settled and met with the Duke of Norfolk.

"It troubles me not to know whom I can trust," remarked Richard, who had been helped off with his armour and was now in the private chamber that had been set aside for him at the White Boar Inn. "And now that William Stanley has seemingly turned traitor by doing nothing to arrest the march of the bastard Tudor through Wales, I wonder if his brother will be more loyal."

James watched as the Duke of Norfolk listened in silence. Although he and his son had brought a numerous army he had confessed that many men had no appetite for more fighting and that despite his scouts there had been deserters and many more who had refused to ride with them at all.

"But we will easily outnumber Tudor," he reassured the king as Richard paused for a moment and looked out of the open window at a group of laughing soldiers below.

"If those we have remain true," he said with a frown.

Towards sunset the following evening an army was sighted heading south and a messenger was shown into the inn as they were sitting down to supper to say that the Earl of Northumberland would be in Leicester before darkness fully fell. Studying the slice of sky that he could see through the doorway, James thought that Percy had best hurry.

"Tell him that I will speak with him as soon as he arrives," said Richard. "I would like to hear from his own lips why he chose not to raise troops in York."

They had barely touched the dishes of the first course of the meal when Henry Percy was announced and ducked in under the low lintel clad in his armour. He bowed to Richard, but even in the guttering candlelight his expression held an arrogant disdain.

"I deny any tardiness, Your Grace," he replied when Richard challenged him. "Surely you can understand that it takes three days to march from Alnwick to York and then a further two to reach Leicester? And to do that I had to force our pace."

"Why did you not raise loyal troops at York?" demanded Richard.

"They have the sickness in York. If I had called men from there and it had spread amongst my own men my force would have been decimated. It would have been the height of folly," he argued back. "Besides, if you step outside you will see that I have brought a substantial army. The Percys are loyal to our king."

As James watched the two men eye one another he wondered to which king Percy was loyal. They had been Lancastrian supporters once and James knew that the man was jealous that Richard had appointed his nephew, the Earl of Lincoln, as the head of the Council of the North rather than himself.

Richard slammed his jewelled eating knife, blade down, into the table, but his face remained outwardly calm. "We march out from here at sunrise," he told Percy.

"But it is a Sunday. My men and horses are exhausted and need to rest." He met Richard's glare with a steady gaze. "March out if you must. I will follow in the afternoon as a rear guard," he said at last, breaking the tense silence.

"That would seem sensible," broached James, attempting to bring some reason to their debate. "Tired men and horses will be of no use to us."

After a moment Richard nodded his assent and dismissed the earl. "I still do not quite trust him," he said as he pulled the knife from the table where it had scourged the surface of the scrubbed wood. James did not reply. There was nothing to say and they all knew from past experience that allegiances changed as quickly as the tides.

They rode out early the next morning, even before the church bells had begun to call the people to mass. "And bid the men keep to the roads," Richard said as James turned to leave. "The crops are ripening in the fields ready for harvest and I will not see them destroyed beneath our feet."

Although the men from York had not come, the numbers who appeared to support the king far outweighed the enemy and, if what their spies and lookouts had reported was true, there seemed little need to wait. As noon passed and the heat of the day rendered it unsafe to touch his armour with an ungloved hand for fear of burning, James turned awkwardly in his saddle and, shielding his eyes from the sun, was relieved to see the shimmering column of Northumberland's men following in their wake as promised. The king's army appeared invincible and James prayed that Henry Tudor would flee at the very sight of them.

The sun traversed westwards ahead of them and as its shadows began to lengthen, the long line of men and horses approached the village of Sutton Cheney. Richard ordered them to make camp there and as soon as his tent was pitched and the cooks at the fires had their supper ready, he called his knights to join him to eat and discuss their tactics for the morrow. He had sent an advance party to a high knoll called Ambion Hill about a half a mile away with orders to hold and occupy it during the night against the enemy. Beyond it, in the flat valley, was the meadow where they planned to engage the enemy.

"The Duke of Norfolk will lead the vanguard. We will follow and Northumberland's men will bring up the rear," he told them. "And I have ordered them to turn their weapons on Stanley should he look like deserting us for the other side. Where is Lord Strange?" he asked.

"He is within the company," replied James. "Would you speak with him?"

"No. But guard him well," he said. "And ride to Lord Stanley for me. Ask him to confirm that he will fight on our side tomorrow and remind him that his son is my hostage."

Stanley had made his camp some distance away and James mounted a fresh horse rather than the one he had ridden all day and trotted out towards the huddle of tents where the eagle's claw banner was striking at the soft evening air. Men came forward with hands poised on their weapons as he approached but allowed the swords to slide back into their sheaths at the sight of his royal colours.

"I come with a message from the king," he told Stanley as he looked down on his old enemy from his saddle. "He bids me ask you to reassure him that you will fight for him, and reminds you that your son is in our company."

Thomas Stanley stood and stroked his meagre beard in the fading light without replying. "Lord Strange will face the axe if you betray the king," James warned him.

"I have other sons," replied Stanley with a shrug and ducked back under the flap of his tent without another word, leaving James to sit and stare after him. Angrily he turned the horse and spurred it back up the incline. He knew that Stanley was prepared to take the risk that Richard would not have the stomach to harm his son, but his answer also confirmed his fear that Stanley would not fight for them – unless he saw that they were sure to win.

When he reported the encounter to Richard he agreed. "It is no more than I expected of him," he remarked with contempt.

"And Lord Strange?" asked James.

"It will do no good to kill him," admitted Richard shaking his head, "and I would not execute him for my own amusement. Walk with me," he said to James. "Let us go and speak to the men and bid them have courage."

Wearing only his padded gambeson and bareheaded, Richard walked amongst the tents of the camp, exchanging words of encouragement and thanks with the men who were sitting in the welcome cool of the evening, giving their weapons one last polish before covering their fires and preparing themselves for sleep.

They walked as far as Ambion Hill where Richard bade the guard be watchful and where he paused for a moment to watch the twinkling fires of the camps below, not knowing for certain which ones contained his allies and which his enemies. "I suppose we should to bed," he sighed at last. "The sun will rise early, and tomorrow will be a difficult day."

James lay on a pallet near the entrance to the king's tent and saw that Richard also tossed and turned on his mattress, as if plagued by bad dreams. It was always so on the eve of a battle, reflected James, although it seemed that men were never tired in the morning, but fought with the desire for survival.

At last, they gave up any attempt to sleep as the new day faded the stars. Even before it was fully light their squires assisted them on with their armour and every man knelt in the dew-moist grass to hear the priest say mass and give them his blessing and absolution. Then the horses were brought from the lines where they had been left to graze and rest overnight and were saddled up and harnessed in their protective plate and royal colours. Once his men were gathered Richard mounted his favourite stallion, White Surrey, and standing in his stirrups he addressed them all.

"Dismiss all fear," he told them, "and ride like valiant champions. If every one of you gives but one sure stroke, then the day will be ours."

Across the valley, where the red dragon standards blew on the wind, trumpets sounded and James could see men manning the heavy French guns that the Tudor army had brought. His stomach fluttered with apprehension and excitement as he saw men bracing their bows and he knew that within minutes the battle would begin.

Suddenly there was a deafening roar as the guns were fired and under a hail of shot the gunfire was returned. Trumpets sounded the advance and as men came within bowshot of each other a volley of arrows shrieked through the air with an ear splitting whine. James saw the Earl of Oxford begin a charge down the far hillside, but this was no melee of undisciplined men. The Scots and French mercenaries had closed into a solid advancing mass, and Norfolk's men were shut out, only able to attack those on the outer edges. Beside him Richard shifted in his saddle. James saw that his eyes were not on the main arena of the battle at all, but on a small party of men who were riding around the edge of the fighting towards the line of the Stanley army.

"Tudor!" he spat above the roar. He glanced sideways at James. "He's mine!" he said.

"My lord! It is too risky!" called James as the king gathered his reins into one hand.

"I will challenge him in mortal combat, and will live or die king of England!" shouted Richard, before slamming down the visor on his helm. He took his battle axe from his squire and, after weighing it for a moment in his hand, he spurred the eager stallion towards the flat plain to their right.

Before Tudor and his men could reach the safety of the Stanley camp, the king and his knights were upon them. Richard leaned from his saddle and struck at Sir William Brandon, Tudor's standard bearer, and left him unhorsed and dead at his feet. Then, as Tudor and his men turned in horror at the unexpected attack, James saw the king unhorse Sir John Cheney, leaving him open to engage the invader. With his sword in his hand James followed Richard closely, his excitement mounting as he began to believe that they would prevail. If Tudor was killed Stanley would be sure to join their side and the enemy would be routed. He watched as Tudor urged his horse away from Richard, seeing that if he stayed he was a dead man. The king spurred his stallion on to give chase. Then he heard a muffled cry from behind and as he turned to look at what was happening he saw his brother Robert throw up his visor and shout "Diccon!" in the moment before Sir William Stanley and his army bore down on them from behind.

It was evening when Anne saw the dust rising on the road as a lone horseman galloped towards Hornby Castle. As the armour-clad rider turned to cross the bridge over the Wenning, Anne called to the nurse to watch the children and running down the winding stairs as fast as she dared she called to the guard to open the gates and raise the portcullis. It was the bay stallion she had recognised before her Uncle James.

He reined the horse in as he came under the archway to the courtyard. As Anne looked at the panting, sweating horse that stood with its nose to the ground and its flanks heaving with weariness, her mind whirled. Had Richard sent for her? Was he so impatient to see her again that he had told her uncle to spare no time to bring her? But when her uncle pulled off his helm and she met his eyes, she saw that something was very wrong.

"What...?" she began, seeing that her uncle was streaked with dirt and blood as if he had ridden straight from the battlefield. "No," she whispered as her heart raced in fear and alarm. No, she thought. If anything had happened to Richard she would have known; she would have felt it. He must be safe. He had to be safe. It wasn't the first time he had had to take refuge abroad. Twice before he had come back and been victorious. Even if the battle had been lost there would be another time, another chance. Perhaps he had sent Uncle James to bid her join him in Burgundy. She would go. She would go to him wherever he was.

"Anne," said her uncle. "I am so sorry."

"For what?" she asked. At least she thought she had spoken the words out loud. But her uncle didn't answer. He ran a filthy hand across his eyes as if he were trying to wipe away the memory of a sight he would rather forget, and when he took his hand away she saw the tears amidst the dried mud on his cheeks. She had never seen her uncle cry. She would not have thought it possible and a bitter fear crept through her. Her teeth chattered against one another as the sun sank in the west.

"We did not prevail," he said at last.

Silence hung between them for a moment until Anne managed to say, "Richard?" Her uncle was staring at the horse and Anne knew that he would have reassured her straight away if the king were safe. "No," she whispered. "No." She shook her head and all the happiness she had ever felt in her life flowed from her body like its life blood and she sank to the ground, to her knees, as if she could gather it all back and retrieve the life that Richard had promised her. "No." She had a vision of her mother on her knees not far from the very spot. She had been too young then to comprehend her mother's grief. But now she knew.

"I am sorry," repeated her uncle.

"Are you sure?" she pleaded, looking up at him, silhouetted against the setting sun, turning blood red on the horizon. The light stung at her eyes. Edward had told her not to look. He said she would be blinded. Mistress Payne had told her not to touch. She said that she might die. Now Anne wished herself both blind and dead; she wished that she did not have to feel this pain, this anguish, this life that was beating and coursing through her veins and throbbing in her head. How could she live if he was dead?

"How?" she asked. She needed to know the details. Nothing her uncle told her could make it worse.

"Let us go inside," said Uncle James. "Lower the portcullis! Close the gate!" he told the guards. "And post a lookout. Tell me at the first sight of anyone approaching. I cannot stay long," he told Anne. "Do you have a fast, fresh horse that I may take?"

Through the dark mist of grief Anne realised that there was danger. "Do they pursue you?" she asked. He nodded and pulled her towards the hall. "But you are safe here," she said. "You must rest. My husband..."

"Your husband is my enemy now. It was the Stanleys who turned on the king and killed him."

"No." But even as the word slipped from her lips Anne knew that what her uncle told her was true.

"Anne, I cannot stay here. Many were killed and many more caught and slain on the battlefield. I was fortunate to escape with my life."

"Uncle Robert?"

"Alive when I last saw him. I think he made for the coast."

"Bring food and hot water," said Anne to Martha as she led her uncle to his chair near the hearth. "We were defeated," she explained briefly. "The king is dead."

Martha made the sign of the cross. "God have mercy on his soul."

"Amen," replied her uncle as he sat with his head resting between his hands.

"Tell me what happened," said Anne.

Her uncle took the cup of wine she poured and drank down its contents in thirsty gulps before he wiped his mouth on the back of his hand. "It is better that you do not know," he said.

"Tell me!"

He hesitated and then began to speak, slowly and unemotionally, as he described what had taken place on Bosworth Field. And as he described the treachery of William Stanley Anne recalled Sir William's hostile face the last time she had spoken to him at Westminster, when he had told her that he would prove to her that he was twice the man that Richard was.

"He and his men began to surround us and I called to the king that we should get away whilst we could. But he still had his eye on Tudor. I could see he was determined to finish him there and then. He wouldn't stop, and as the enemy surrounded him he struck out again and again with his axe. He caught an arrow in his back and was thrown to the ground. He struggled to his feet but before he could defend himself William Stanley struck him down, and all Stanley's men surrounded him and they beat him down so fiercely that he couldn't rise from his knees and his helmet split and I saw the blood. I pulled my horse around to try to help him and I heard him shout 'Treason!' at Stanley, and then he saw me and I think he knew it was over. 'Go!' he shouted. 'Save yourself!' But as I hesitated, I heard him say one last word. He called 'Anne' and people say he died with the name of his wife on his lips and that it was his guilt because he had poisoned her." Her uncle paused. "He died calling for you."

Anne lowered her head and rested it on her uncle's arm and felt his hand, warm, on her shoulder. She didn't know how long they stayed like that; time passed unnoticed and she didn't look up until Martha brought in a candle and she saw that it was completely dark beyond the open door.

Night had fallen.

"Where is my son?" she asked.

"His father sent him back to Sheriff Hutton before we left Nottingham. He is safe."

"Thank God."

"Anne, I must go," said Uncle James, struggling to his feet. "I dare not stay any longer. Come with me," he said. "We can ride to Yorkshire, find John, go abroad..."

Anne shook her head.

"What will you do?"

"I will wait here for my husband. He will need me."

"Are you sure?"

"Yes," she said. "But you must go."

Her uncle nodded and Anne helped him to put on his gauntlets and his helm and she found a cloak of Edward's and a tabard with an eagle's claw that he could wear as a disguise. He reached to unpin his white boar badge, with its motto *Loyaultie Me Lie,* Loyalty Binds Me, but saw that it was gone.

"I must have lost it on the field of battle," he said.

"Stay safe," she whispered as she kissed him, her cheek cold against the metal.

A groom brought out a fresh horse and Anne saw that he was the boy whom William Stanley had slapped the day he kidnapped Izzie.

"They say that Sir William Stanley found the king's crown and set it on the head of Henry Tudor," said her uncle as he gathered the reins. "He will be rich and powerful now."

"But there is one thing he desires that he will never have," replied Anne before she watched her uncle ride off into the moonless night, praying that God would light his way and keep him from harm.

And, as the hoof beats faded, Anne climbed the steps to her bedchamber. She sat down and stroked her hand across the fur cover and the pillow where Richard had slept so long ago.

"Let Edward be wrong," she prayed aloud, as she twisted the silver ring on her finger. "It cannot be true that a life only half lived is gone forever." He must be somewhere; perhaps with Anne Neville and Edward their son; perhaps in some place she could never comprehend – or perhaps he was still here with her. She turned as she caught a glimmer across the room, but all she saw was a reflection of her candle in the glass of the window.

THE END

Author's Note

The identity of the mistress of King Richard the Third is unknown. It is a fact that he had two illegitimate children – a son John and a daughter Katherine – but there is no record of the woman who was their mother, or indeed if they had the same mother.

It has been suggested that Richard's mistress may have been Katherine Haute. This is based on the evidence that she had the same name as Richard's daughter and in 1477, he granted her 100 shillings per annum for life. She was the wife of James Haute, son of William Haute and Joan Woodville, and was a cousin of Elizabeth Woodville. She lived in East Anglia, but nothing more is known about her and the reason for her annuity is not recorded.

In this novel I suggest an alternative identity for Richard's mistress – Anne Harrington. Although this is based on speculation, there is some circumstantial evidence that she may have been the mother of his children.

Firstly, she was in the right place at the right time. Anne's father and grandfather were killed at the Battle of Wakefield, fighting alongside Richard's father, the Duke of York, who also lost his life. The Harrington lands and the castle at Hornby passed to her and her younger sister, Elizabeth. Their wardships were given to Thomas Stanley who then had the right to marry them to husbands of his choosing – men who would become owners of the Harrington lands. Considering this to be unfair, James Harrington took possession of his nieces and fortified Hornby Castle against the Stanleys who tried to take it by force by bringing a cannon named the Mile End from Bristol to blast the fortifications. But it seems that the Harringtons had the support of the king's youngest brother. A warrant issued by Richard, Duke of Gloucester on 26 March 1470 was signed 'at Hornby'. This evidence places seventeen-year-old Richard and fifteen-year-old Anne together in a castle that was under siege.

Secondly, Richard's illegitimate son was named John – which was the name of Anne's father. His daughter was named Katherine. This name does occur in the Harrington family. It is also worth noting that in the church of St Wilfrid at Melling near Hornby, there was a chapel that was originally dedicated to St Katherine. Is it possible that Anne named her daughter after a favourite saint?

Thirdly, John of Gloucester is sometimes referred to as John of Pomfret, seeming to indicate that he was born at Pontefract Castle, which is very close to the Yorkshire lands of the Harrington family at Brierley in Yorkshire.

James and Robert Harrington were both in the service of the Duke of Gloucester and were with Richard at Bosworth. Given the close connections between Richard and the Harrington family it is not impossible that Anne may also have had a close relationship with him. However, there is no evidence.

I also need to clarify the mentions of Melling in the novel. There are two different places named Melling that formed part of the Harrington lands –

Melling in Lonsdale, which was near the castle at Hornby, and Melling in Halsall, which is now a part of Merseyside and which was in the very heart of the West Lancashire holdings of the Stanley family. To avoid confusion the story refers to just one village of Melling and I've used the place that was near to Hornby. In reality, Melling in Lonsdale was part of the lands inherited by Anne Harrington, and her sister Elizabeth inherited the other Melling, near Halsall.

The history of the Wars of the Roses is complex. Many of the events are open to endless speculation and debate and although I have tried to stay as close as possible to the known facts it was never my intention to write a true history of those times. Neither was it my intention to prove that Anne Harrington was the mother of the children of King Richard, just to offer her identity as a potential candidate and to tell a story about her.

If you are interested in learning more about me, my historical research and other books that I have written, please visit my website at: www.elizabethashworth.com.